Journey to a Mountain

The Story of the Shrine of the Báb
Volume 1
1850–1921

'Every stone of that building, every stone of the road leading to it, I have with infinite tears and at tremendous cost, raised and put in position.'

'Abdu'l-Bahá

'The most joyful tidings is this, that the holy, the luminous body of the Báb . . . after having for sixty years been transferred from place to place, by reason of the ascendancy of the enemy, and from fear of the malevolent, and having known neither rest nor tranquillity has, through the mercy of the Abhá Beauty, been ceremoniously deposited, on the day of Naw-Rúz, within the sacred casket, in the exalted Shrine on Mt. Carmel . . .'

'Abdu'l-Bahá, 1909

Journey to a Mountain

The Story of the Shrine of the Báb
Volume 1
1850–1921

The Gate and the Glory, 1850–1892
The Mission of the Master, 1892–1921

Michael V. Day

GR

GEORGE RONALD
OXFORD

GEORGE RONALD, PUBLISHER
Oxford
www.grbooks.com

Reprinted 2018

A catalogue record for this book is available from the British Library

ISBN 978–0–85398– 603–4

Cover design: William McGuire and René Steiner

CONTENTS

Foreword xi
Acknowledgements xiii

THE GATE AND THE GLORY, 1850–1892
1 The Retrieval 3
2 Momentous Events 8
3 Looking for a Safe Place 10
4 The Holy Land 13
5 The Casket on the Move 15
6 The Site for the Shrine 17

THE MISSION OF THE MASTER, 1892–1921
7 Setting His Strategy 23
8 Concealment and Transfer 29
9 The Sarcophagus 38
10 The Foundation 41
11 Crisis and Construction 45
12 Enemies Step Up Attacks 50
13 The Building 59
14 Release and Aftermath 72
15 Interment of the Sacred Remains 76
16 Gatherings at the Oriental Pilgrim House 85
17 War, Tyranny and Liberation 90
18 Post-war Gatherings at the Shrine of the Báb 102
19 The Western Pilgrim House 111
20 Terraces and Lights 115
21 The Shrine Becomes the Tomb of 'Abdu'l-Bahá 120

ANNEXES

1 The Báb 135
2 The Spiritual Significance of the Shrine of the Báb 151
3 The Holy Land and Mount Carmel 157
4 The Tablet of Carmel 168
5 Tablets of Visitation 170

Bibliography 173
References 183
Index 233
About the Author 240

LIST OF ILLUSTRATIONS

Between pages 16 and 17
Tabriz: The site of the martyrdom of the Báb, and the moat
Protectors of the sacred remains: Ḥájí Á<u>kh</u>und and Mírza Músa
Shrines of Imám-Zádih Ḥasan and Imám-Zádih Ma'ṣúm
Mount Carmel, Georg David Hardegg and the Templer colony in Haifa

Between pages 32 and 33
'Abdu'l-Bahá, Who arranged the transfer of the remains of the Báb and built the Shrine
Map of the route travelled, and those involved: Mírzá Asadu'lláh <u>Kh</u>án, Mírzá Asadu'lláh-i-Iṣfáhání, and Ustád Ismá'il Úbudíyyát
A palanquin, or 'running throne', and the house where the Báb's casket was hidden in Najafabad

Between pages 48 and 49
Muḥammad Muṣṭáfa Bagdadi of Beirut; view of Mount Carmel
Acre: the House of 'Abdu'lláh Pá<u>sh</u>á where the sacred remains of the Báb were concealed
Bahá'ís of Burma with the sarcophagus; Siyyid Muṣṭáfa Rúmí
Haifa: Crate containing the sarcophagus; the area where it was stored
Ali-Kuli Khan who worked in the same room
Early photos showing the construction of the Shrine of the Báb

Between pages 64 and 65
Street in Haifa showing the uncompleted Shrine
Chart of the doors of the Shrine, and photographs of the nominees Ustád Áqá 'Alí-A<u>sh</u>raf, Ustád Áqá Bála, Ḥájí Abu'l-Ḥasan-i-Ardikání, Mírzá Abu'l-Faḍl
Cypress trees behind the Shrine, 1891 and early 1900s

Between pages 80 and 81
The garden at the Shrine, 1914, and the gardener Ismá'íl Áqá
'Abdu'l-Bahá, looking towards the Shrine from the balcony of 'Abbás-Qúlí's house
Young Bahá'ís at the Shrine, with Shoghi Effendi
The water tank above the reservoir
Bahíyyih Khánum, the Greatest Holy Leaf

Between pages 96 and 97
Meetings at the Shrine with 'Abdu'l-Bahá
The Oriental Pilgrim House and its builder, Mírzá Ja'fár Shírází Raḥmání

Between pages 112 and 113
World War I: General Edmund Allenby with his wife; Jamal Pasha
Views of the Shrine from the air, and from near the House of 'Abdu'l-Bahá
Harry Randall with 'Abbás-Qúlí, custodian of the Shrine of the Báb
Murgh Maḥallih (Abode of the Birds), the inspiration for the Terraces
Electric light at the Shrine: the lighting generator
Curtis Kelsey
Roy Wilhelm

Between pages 128 and 129
The passing and funeral of 'Abdu'l-Bahá: Dr Florian Krug, who closed His eyelids; the room where He passed away
Map of the route of the funeral procession; views of the procession to the Shrine
Sir Herbert Samuel
Shoghi Effendi, appointed as Guardian of the Bahá'í Faith by 'Abdu'l-Bahá

Between pages 144 and 145
Cabinets in the International Bahá'í Archives containing a portrait of the Báb
Dr William Cormick, who treated the Báb's injuries
Places of imprisonment and execution: Maku, Chihriq and Tabriz
The Shrine of the Báb as constructed by 'Abdu'l-Bahá

With loving dedication to my wife
Dr Chris Day
who devotedly served in the shadow of the Shrine of the Báb
under the direction of the Universal House of Justice from 2003–2006

My loving gratitude is extended to a former custodian of
the Shrine of the Báb,
Fuad Izadinia
for his expert and selfless accompaniment over the days,
months and years of this project

FOREWORD

This is the first book in a series that tells the story of the Shrine of the Báb, the golden-domed monument that graces the northern slopes of Mount Carmel in Haifa, Israel.

The Shrine is the last resting place of the Báb (1819–1850), Who proclaimed Himself to be a Messenger of God. He foretold the coming of Bahá'u'lláh (1817–1892), the Prophet-Founder of the Bahá'í Faith,[1] a religion that envisions world unity based on the principle of the oneness of humanity.

This book tells the story of the early dramatic years. Two more associated but stand-alone books will bring the story further into the 20th century and then into early years of the 21st century.

The story of the Shrine has its full share of inspiration and accomplishment but also ordeals, tragedy, heart-stopping anxiety, dreadful frustration, setbacks and long periods requiring supreme levels of patience. It culminates in the appearance today of a Shrine of sublime beauty adorned by terraced gardens of such loveliness that even the hardest of hearts can soften in their midst.

Hundreds of thousands of people, including many religious pilgrims, visit this holy place every year, their expressions of wonder and upliftment witnessed by those who serve as its custodians and guides. A recent opening of more rooms in the Shrine anticipated ever-increasing numbers of visitors. It seems clear that eventually so many people will seek the blessings of this place that entry may rarely be allowed and circumambulation may become the normal procedure of visitation.

The world has already recognized its importance through its inscription in the UNESCO World Heritage register.[2] But the Shrine of the Báb is far more than its physical presence, exquisite though it undoubtedly is. It is a centre of tranquillity and uncanny spiritual power, something often remarked upon by believers and others alike.[3] Further information about the life of the Báb and the significance of His Shrine may be found in Annexes 1 and 2.

For Bahá'ís, the holiness of this place is second only to the Shrine across the bay, that of Bahá'u'lláh Himself.

ACKNOWLEDGEMENTS

My utmost gratitude goes to the Universal House of Justice, which concluded its response to my letter submitting my plan to undertake this project with these encouraging words: 'Rest assured of the prayers of the House of Justice in the Holy Shrines that your devoted endeavours in the service of His Cause may be blessed and confirmed.'

In researching and writing this volume and those subsequent in the series, I received almost daily assistance by email for some four years from a former custodian of the Shrine of the Báb, Fuad Izadinia. He was my right-hand man. To our delight, we discovered many historical facts together. Mr Izadinia generously contributed the findings of his own research, his love for and knowledge of the Shrine, his understandings of the Bahá'í Faith, his analytical abilities, his ability to research literature in Persian, his ideas, his patience with me, his sense of humour, and his loving and cheerful encouragement. If he did not know a certain point, he would contact his brother Faruq Izadinia, who in turn generously helped me by locating and translating Persian materials.

As I was considering this project, I asked the late Dr Peter Khan, a former member of the Universal House of Justice, for his advice. I was delighted that he took time to ponder, and then gave me the benefits of his analytical thinking.

During the years I was working on the story of the Shrine, I asked many questions of Mr 'Alí Nakhjavání, a former member of the Universal House of Justice, and was astounded at the speed of his replies. I rejoiced in the loving nature of his communications and his willingness to provide me with expert answers to my often persistent and perhaps nit-picking queries. He also assisted with advice on diacriticals.

A former staff member at the Bahá'í World Centre, Andrew Blake, generously and often shared with me what he had discovered in his research into the history of the Bahá'í gardens in Haifa and showed me historical photographs of great importance.

Dr Janet Khan, an author of Bahá'í books and a former staff member at the Bahá'í World Centre, was also continually interested in my progress and spent time with me answering questions, reading the manuscript, and giving me positive feedback and valuable advice. Other former staff members also encouraged me. They included former Office of Public Information colleagues Leili Towfigh, Naysan Naraqi, Yin Thing Ming, Brian Kurzius, Edit Kalman and, as always, Douglas Moore. Rosemarie Smith provided me with a useful book. Bizhan Vahdat gently encouraged me to obtain more and more books that related to the topic. Josephine Hill has continually helped and encouraged me in this work, read the text and made useful suggestions. Samandar Milani provided me with priceless information about his relatives in Tabriz. Kathryn Hewitt Hogenson gave me valuable advice. Maryam Bell generously agreed to give me advice at the early stage of this project.

As I researched in the United States Bahá'í National Archives, the chief archivist Roger Dahl displayed patience and cooperation as he located materials, and later sent me the key photographs I requested. I also extend thanks to his colleague, Lewis Walker, and to Richard Doering of *The American Bahá'í*. Kenneth E. Bowers graciously encouraged me in my work. Staff at the Bahá'í World Centre diligently sent photographs, illustrations and research materials that have contributed to this work.

I also acknowledge my gratitude to the authors of so many wonderful Bahá'í books, and particularly to the historians, many of whom have passed away. I was continually in awe of their work, and was moved to pray for them.

Dr Duane Troxell, Brent Poirier and the late Joseph Roy Sheppherd provided me with great photographs. New Zealanders Steve Cooney and Geoffrey Gore gave me advice. The late Ron Price generously lent me the text of an exquisite poem by Roger White. Michael and Farideh Knopf gave me a most useful book, as did Patrick Cavanagh. Gary Corson, a learned Bahá'í to whom I owe a deep debt of gratitude, assisted with high levels of encouragement and by reading and commenting on the draft. I was very pleased that William McGuire happily agreed to employ his undoubted talents as a graphic artist to enhance some of the historical images, and to produce two beautiful maps. Denny Allen generously consented to allow publication of two of his beautiful photographs published in the exquisite book *Bahá'í Pilgrimage*. Brendan McNamara kindly provided photographs of Dr William Cormick, and Vicky Uffindell, Dr Cormick's great-granddaughter, gave permission to print them. Khosro Vahdat gave me some useful information. Peter Lange, who manages the Templer archives, was quick to help.

Spontaneously, Dr Marjorie Tidman offered to edit my work long before I had completed it, reminded me of her offer just at the right time, and then worked day and night to meet a very tight deadline and carried out the first skillful and wise edit of the manuscripts of all three volumes. I am profoundly grateful to her.

Erica Leith, my first contact at George Ronald, provided welcome reassurance that there was interest in the project, and her colleague Wendi Momen contributed to discussions on the book. The editor of this book, May Hofman, appears to me to be a knowledgeable Bahá'í historian in her own right. She has an eagle eye for possible errors. May impressed me with her skills and good humour, and astonished me with her restraint, interfering little with my manner of expression, suggesting changes only when necessary, one of the most valuable gifts an editor can bestow upon a writer. I take full responsibility for any mistakes that may have slipped through the net which has been cast many times over the text.

My colleagues serving in the Office of External Affairs of the Australian Bahá'í Community, particularly Natalie Mobini and Venus Khalessi, were supportive and patient with me over the years as I spent breaks in meetings looking for more information about the Shrine. Karl du Fresne, Chris Lawe Davies, Keith McDonald, Ruhy Soraya, Richard Rawlings and Lee Tate were constant in their valued friendship. For their support, I also thank Sitarih Alai, Harry Bhaskara, Karen Barnett, Sabour Bradley, Edward and Noel Broomhall, Patricia Ferrier, Christine James and Jimmy Seow.

My son George, a former Bahá'í World Centre staff member, helped me with computer problems, my son Tom also advised me about the actual purchase of the computer, my sister Anna was always extremely encouraging, and my cousin, Bill Day, was most enthusiastic. I thank my late parents, Noel and Win Day, for my upbringing and spiritual education.

In the Pilgrim House in 1980, Hand of the Cause of God Mr

'Alí-Akbar Furútan advised me to be eternally grateful to my wife, Chris, for introducing me to the Bahá'í Faith and telling me so much about it. I am continuously grateful to her for that, and in addition for providing the financial resources and personal support vital for me to devote myself to this long and thrilling project on a topic of such holiness.

The Gate and the Glory
1850–1892

1

THE RETRIEVAL

The news could hardly have been worse. The Báb was dead.

Sulaymán Khán heard the shocking details as he arrived in the Persian city of Tabriz in July 1850. He had come from the capital, Tehran, on a mission to somehow save the Promised One, the great prophetic figure Who had announced He was a divine messenger and the forerunner of one even greater.

But Sulaymán Khán was two agonizing days too late.[1]

It had been just a few days earlier in Tehran, 630 kilometres away, that he had learned that the Prime Minister,[2] incited by the Muslim clergy, had ordered the execution of the Báb, Who had been attracting tens of thousands of followers throughout Persia. The Báb had angered the religious establishment, and they now wanted to eradicate Him and His Faith.

Bahá'u'lláh, a prominent follower of the Báb and the future founder of the Bahá'í Faith, also heard about the execution order, and instructed Sulaymán Khán to hurry to Tabriz to attempt a rescue. A devoted 'Bábí' – a follower of the Báb – Sulaymán Khán was a native of the city so would have more chance than most to extricate Him.

Sulaymán Khán, being a wealthy man, was able to travel on a fast horse and ensure that his Bábí companions could as well.[3] But when they arrived in Tabriz, Sulaymán Khán heard that at noon two days before, 9 July 1850,[4] a firing squad had executed the Báb, aged 30, and His younger disciple, Mírzá Muḥammad-'Alí-i-Zunúzí, known as Anís (meaning 'companion'), in a courtyard square of a military barracks near the citadel.[5]

He learned how the two had been suspended on the wall of the barracks and had faced the firing squad.

The first attempt to execute the men had failed. When the smoke cleared from the volley of bullets, the Báb was nowhere to be seen by the soldiers or the thousands of townsfolk who had been watching the event. Soon He was located back in His cell, where He was completing a previously interrupted conversation with His secretary. He was taken back and suspended with Anís yet again.

Colonel Sám Khán, an Armenian[6] who was the commander of the original firing squad, the Bahaduran Christian regiment of Urumiyyih,[7] refused to participate in the next attempt at execution, so another regiment was brought in. Commanded by the colonel of the body-guard, Áqá Ján-i-Khamsih,[8] these soldiers shot and killed the Báb.[9] Anís died too, his head cradled on the chest of his master.

Chaos then erupted as a giant whirlwind of dust arrived without warning, blocking the sun for the rest of the day and creating a swirling turmoil in the city.

Sulaymán Khán learned that the remains of the Báb and Anís, entwined together, had yet to be recovered. They had been flung onto the edge of a moat on the outskirts of the city.[10] Sulaymán Khán had to summon up the strength not only to deal with his immense grief but to carry out a rescue of the sacred remains. But how could he do that? Ten sentinels per rotating shift were at the moat with one clear order – to stop any recovery mission. Two followers of the Báb, pretending to be insane, placed themselves nearby and kept the sacred remains in sight.[11]

On 10 July, the sentinels had allowed the Russian consul in Tabriz to approach with an artist who, somewhat like a modern-day photographer, recorded the scene by sketching the remains. The drawing has been lost to history but one who saw it at the time wrote: 'No bullet had struck His forehead, His cheeks or His lips. I gazed upon a smile which seemed to be still lingering upon His countenance. His body, however, had been severely mutilated. I could recognize the arms and head of His companion, who seemed to be holding Him in his embrace.'[12]

Sulaymán Khán was the son of a respected official,[13] so he had good personal contacts in the city. He went quickly to the home of the mayor of Tabriz, Midhí Khán, who was a Sufi and not a Bábí, but was a long-time friend and well-known for his religious tolerance.[14]

Carried away by his emotions and the urgency of the task, Sulaymán Khán told the mayor he was going to try to recover the bodies in a surprise attack on the guards, even though that would put his life in peril. The mayor was sympathetic to the aims of the recovery mission but cautioned him to wait. He put forward a better plan. He arranged for one of his servants, an intimidating hulk of a man called Ḥájí Alláh-Yár to lead the recovery mission.[15] At midnight on 11 July, Alláh-Yár and some of his men led Sulaymán Khán to the moat.[16] Two other believers from the village of Milan were also in that group, Ḥusayn-i- Mílání and Ḥájí Muḥammad-Táqí Mílání.[17] When the sentinels saw Alláh-Yár and his armed associates, they realized whom they were up against and did not challenge them.[18]

Sulaymán Khán reverently gathered the remains of the Báb and Anís, placed them in a cloak, and hurried away.[19]

The guards later claimed that wild animals had devoured the bodies of the Báb and His disciple. That was the perfect line to deliver to the fanatical clergy, who had begun preaching from the pulpits that according to tradition, the body of the Promised One would be preserved from beasts of prey, yet this claimant's body had been taken by animals.

With their precious cargo, Sulaymán Khán and Ḥusayn-i-Mílání hurried on the same night to a silk factory owned by a follower of the Báb, Ḥájí Aḥmad Mílání.[20] There they wrapped the remains in a shroud, and hid the bundle under bales of silk.[21]

The next day, the men built a wooden casket, and Sulaymán Khán reverently placed the sacred remains into it. He then placed a flower on the Báb's body, closed the lid and concealed the casket in a wall. It was later removed to 'a place of safety'.[22]

That silk factory was the first of many places where, over a period of 59 years, those sacred relics would be secretly housed until, with inspired strategy and after moments of heart-stopping anxiety, the great day of culmination and achievement arrived when they were interred in the heart of Mount Carmel on the shores of the Mediterranean Sea.

Sulaymán Khán sent a rider to travel quickly to Tehran to report to Bahá'u'lláh that the remains were safely in the custody of the Bábís. Bahá'u'lláh told his brother, Mírzá Músá,[23] to send a courier to Tabriz with the instruction to deliver the casket to the capital.[24]

Sulaymán Khán and the others wrapped the casket in cotton and prepared for the journey. They would go by horseback, travelling during the cool of the night along the rocky pathways through the hills and mountains.

There were two worries. The first was about highway robbers, who preyed on travellers along the route and who tried to avoid being spotted by police and other guards whose job it was to keep them at bay.

The second was that the casket might be discovered at the customs houses which the authorities had established on the highway to obtain revenue and to stop smuggling. If the authorities had any inkling that the travellers were carrying a casket containing the bodies of the Báb and His disciple, they would surely quickly confiscate and destroy it. More likely than not, the couriers would be executed.

Fortunately, one of the believers in Tabriz, Ḥasan Áqá Tafríshí, was the deputy-director of the provincial customs office in Tabriz[25] and he knew how to avoid raising the suspicion of officials en route and how to guard against robbery. He accompanied Sulaymán Khán, who with the courier sent from Tehran, posed as importers of goods from Europe.[26] The ruse worked perfectly. After travelling on horseback in nightly forced rides[27] for about 300 kilometres, the men arrived safely with their sacred cargo at Zanjan, a town some 330 kilometres from Tehran. They spent the night there before resuming their journey. The whole journey, including likely rest stops, would probably have taken a week.[28]

When they arrived in the capital, Bahá'u'lláh was not there, having been ordered out of the city by the suspicious Prime Minister.[29] His brother, Mírzá Músá, was deputizing for him. The men concealed the casket for a short time in a building in the extensive precincts of the Shrine of Imám-Zádih Ḥasan in the city, later removing it briefly to Sulaymán Khán's home in the Sar-Chashmih quarter.[30] Those involved in this transfer and the next were Sulaymán Khán, Mírzá Músá, and Mírzá Aḥmad.[31]

On His return to the capital Bahá'u'lláh directed that the casket be removed and concealed in another Muslim Shrine, that of Imám-Zádih Ma'ṣúm to the west of Tehran. There was no permanent population in the immediate vicinity of this Shrine because it was in the middle of a cemetery. Its buildings were made of mud and straw bricks.[32] The men put the casket in an abandoned building in the northern corner of the Shrine precinct, built a wall in front of it and repaired the surrounding walls to improve security.

According to Nabíl, who produced the original chronicle of these events, the decision of Bahá'u'lláh to arrange the transfer of the sacred remains to Tehran was prompted by a wish of the Báb. That wish was included in a Tablet of Visitation once revealed by the Báb for that Shrine in Rey,[33] a Tablet which He urged his followers to chant whenever they visited. It addresses the saint buried there, but then refers to Himself. 'Well it is with you to have found your resting place in Rey under the shadow of My Beloved. Would that I might be entombed within the precincts of that holy ground.'[34]

2

MOMENTOUS EVENTS

The casket was to remain in the Shrine of Imám-Zádih Ma'ṣúm for the next 17 years, a period of momentous significance in the history of the Bahá'í Faith.

After the execution of the Báb the persecution of His followers was horrific. 'Abdu'l-Bahá[1] described what happened: 'Fire fell upon the households of the Bábís, and each one of them, in whatever hamlet he might be, was, on the slightest suspicion arising, put to the sword.'[2]

It became even worse. In 1852 persecution of the followers of the Báb exploded throughout the land following a hopelessly inept assassination attempt upon the Shah by two crazed Bábís. Urged on by the clergy, the mob put to death anybody remotely suspected of being a Bábí. Thousands upon thousands were killed. Sulaymán Khán was arrested, but as an influential person he had his case reviewed by the Shah, who decreed that his life would be spared if he recanted his faith. If not, he was to be executed in any way he himself chose.[3]

In a demonstration of his fidelity to the Báb, Sulaymán Khán refused to recant. He then announced how he wanted to die. The executioner did as he asked. He ordered his men to insert nine candles in Sulaymán Khán's flesh. Then he lit them. Sulaymán Khán marched through the town to the place of execution, 'erect as an arrow, his eyes glowing with stoic fortitude'.[4] He addressed the crowd with these words: 'Glorified be the Báb, who can kindle such devotion in the breasts of His lovers, and can endow them with a power greater than the might of kings!'[5]

As he arrived at the place of execution, Sulaymán Khán, the man whose name will be associated forever with the Shrine of the Báb, prostrated himself in the direction of the Shrine of Imám-Zádih Ḥasan, where the casket of the Báb had once been housed. The gallows only partially did its intended work. Still flickering with life, his tongue still praising the Báb, Sulaymán Khán was sawn in two. Each half of his body was gruesomely suspended on the side of the gate of the city.

Also to die for his faith that day was Ḥusayn-i-Mílání, one of the other men who had assisted in the recovery of the remains of the Báb two years earlier. Mírzá Aḥmad, who had helped in transferring the sacred remains to two locations, was another to perish in the pogroms of that year.

Meanwhile, the authorities arrested Bahá'u'lláh and cast him into an underground prison, a dank former reservoir known as Síyáh-Chál ('the Black Pit'). A servant of Sulaymán Khán's was sent into the prison in a bid to have him identify Bahá'u'lláh as one of those who had associated with his master. That servant steadfastly refused to do so, thereby helping save the life of Bahá'u'lláh.

It was in that underground prison that Bahá'u'lláh received the revelation that gave birth to the Bahá'í Faith,[6] a religion that was to promise a new age of peace and prosperity in a united world.

After four months there He was released and exiled with His family to Baghdad in what is now Iraq but was then part of the Ottoman Empire centred in Istanbul. It was in Baghdad, on 21 April 1863, that Bahá'u'lláh publicly announced He was the Promised One of whom the Báb had spoken.

Magnetic in his spirituality, eloquent in his utterances and majestic in his manner, Bahá'u'lláh won the heartfelt allegiance of the Bábí community. The scripture He gave them was not only uplifting and powerful spiritually but was exquisite literature in its own right. He wore the robes and conical 'taj', the headdress of the Persian nobleman He was, and His long black hair and beard gave Him an imposing and dignified appearance.

3

LOOKING FOR A SAFE PLACE

After Bahá'u'lláh's announcement in 1863, the Ottoman authorities, largely through the instigation of the Persian ambassador, exiled Him via Istanbul to Edirne (Adrianople) in the far west of what is now modern-day Turkey. From there, in 1867, Bahá'u'lláh issued written instructions to two trusted believers, Ḥájí Á<u>kh</u>und[1] and Jamál-i-Burújirdí,[2] for the immediate and secret removal of the casket from its hiding place.[3]

But there was a problem. Although the Bahá'ís knew the general location of the casket they were short on specifics. Two of those who knew, Sulaymán Khán and Mirza Aḥmad, had been killed more than a decade earlier. The third, Bahá'u'lláh's brother, Mírzá Músá, knew the whereabouts but the person he told[4] could not find the exact spot. However, an elderly Bahá'í eventually found the place of concealment, its location having earlier been confided to him.[5]

That problem being solved, Ḥájí Á<u>kh</u>und and Jamál-i-Burújirdí had to adopt a strategy to fulfil the directive of Bahá'u'lláh to conceal the sacred remains in a safe place. First, they sent their wives on a scouting mission for a new place to conceal the casket. The spot they were thinking about was a village near Tehran in which stood a major shrine, that of 'Abdu'l-Aẓím. The women were able to disguise their activities as a pilgrimage.

After their wives had left on their mission, the men went in the middle of the night to the Shrine of Imám-Zádih Ma'ṣúm[6] where the Báb's remains had been concealed in 1850. They opened up the wall and removed the casket, possibly persuading the custodian to look the other way.

The timing was immaculate, because shortly afterwards there was extensive reconstruction work at the shrine that definitely would have uncovered the hiding place.

Disguising the casket as luggage of pilgrims, the men took it by mule to where their wives had gone – the suburb of Sháh 'Abdu'l-Aẓím[7] – and discussed what to do next. The women said there was no suitable hiding place in the shrine so the men decided to keep travelling to see what they could find. In addition to the casket containing the sacred remains, the men had with them a silk shroud and an extra casket they had made from plane-tree timber.

On the road to the village of Chashmih-'Alí they spotted a dilapidated mosque, Masjid Mashá'u'lláh, a place not often visited. They waited there until dark. Then they decided to open the casket to check that everything was intact before they placed it into the new casket.

For two men who believed that what they saw were the sacred remains of a Prophet of God, the impact could have been nothing but overwhelming. On top of the shrouded remains was what was left of the flower that had been placed on the body of the Báb 17 years before by the long-dead Bábí hero, Sulaymán Khán.[8]

The men encased the original wrapped remains in the new silk shroud, and returned them to the original casket, which in turn they placed into the new one. They then put the precious container in one of the smaller rooms in the compound, finding a suitable spot under an arched wall. They covered up the spot and built a new wall in front of it, using the bricks from a nearby collapsed wall and mortar they had previously obtained from a local Bábí.

As soon as they had finished their secret mission, they left for a village nearby to spend the night. What they didn't know was that others had been watching.[9]

Something prompted the men to return to the hiding place the next day, just to check that all was well. Jamál had a faster mule and arrived only to find that somebody had dismantled the wall and broken into the casket.

When Ḥájí Ákhund arrived, he found his friend extremely distressed. But when they checked, they found that the weight of the casket had not changed and the remains were clearly intact. Obviously, the grave robbers had been looking for valuables[10] and when none were to be found, left the casket in its place.

Jamál's distress was transformed into exhilaration. The two then decided they had to get out of the area quickly and head back to the city. They rode towards the city gates, one holding on to the casket that was placed in front of him on his mule. Their anxiety returned. What if the gatekeepers wanted to inspect the load? That was a real possibility. Questions would be asked. The casket, and their very lives, would be in peril.

As the men were devising a plan, a thunderstorm hit. It proved a godsend. People coming from the direction of the Shrine of 'Abdu'l-Aẓím rushed for the city gates to avoid the driving wind and rain. Ḥájí Á<u>kh</u>und and Jamál used the crowd as a cover to push past the gatekeepers into the city.

With enormous relief, they found their way to the house of a Bábí, Ḥasan Vazir, who had recently passed away. Judging it a relatively safe place for their purposes, the men concealed the casket in the basement. Ḥájí Á<u>kh</u>und quickly rented the house and moved in with one purpose in mind, to protect his sacred trust.

4

THE HOLY LAND

On 12 August 1868, after a decade spent in exile in Adrianople, Bahá'u'lláh and His family and other followers – by then known as Bahá'ís – were sent further into exile. They went by land to Gallipoli where they embarked on a steamer of the Austrian Lloyd company and sailed to the northern Egyptian coastal city of Alexandria. There they changed to another steamer, and in the morning of 31 August 1868 arrived off Haifa, a coastal town in the northern region of the Holy Land, which was part of the Ottoman Empire.[1]

Bahá'u'lláh disembarked into a smaller boat and was taken to the landing stage in Haifa where all the prisoners were counted and handed over to government officials.[2] Not far away, on the slope of Mount Carmel, was the spot that, 41 years later, was to become the last resting place of His forerunner, the Báb.

Bahá'u'lláh spent a few hours in Haifa. Later He described the spiritual significance of that visit: 'Verily His Temple was established upon the Mountain of God at the beginning of His arrival; to this testify whatever has been written in the Books of the Messengers. Verily both sea and land were privileged by His footsteps and seeing Him and inhaling the scent of His luminous robe.'[3]

A sailboat then took Bahá'u'lláh and His party across the bay to the dreaded city of Acre, where they were installed as prisoners of the Empire.

Two months later, on 30 October 1868, Christians from Württemberg in southern Germany arrived in Haifa where they were soon to build a settlement at the foot of Mount Carmel. Known as the Templers,[4] they were to open seven colonies in the Holy Land, trying to live a Christian life.

Their basic mission was 'the return of the people to the code of ethics of the Mosaic law' which would pave the way for the coming of the

Messiah. Because the Jews had rejected Christ, the Templers felt they themselves were now the 'chosen people' who were to develop Jerusalem and the Holy Land and who would create the conditions for the return of Jesus.[5]

The Templers were to play an intriguing role as side players in the dramatic project to build the Shrine of the Báb. Their arrival in Haifa had not been in their original plans. They had originally wanted to come to the Holy Land via the southern sea gate of Jaffa, the gateway to the Holy City of Jerusalem. But as they set off for the Holy Land via Istanbul, they took the advice of a Christian missionary and decided to avoid the potentially rough seas off Jaffa and to dock in the more placid waters of the beautiful bay of Haifa.

The next year their leader, Georg David Hardegg, spent days walking on Mount Carmel praying for divine guidance. He felt inspired to build a settlement in the land to the west of the walled town of Haifa and there construct a road from the sea to a spot at the foot of Mount Carmel and directly below the site of the future Shrine of the Báb. Once built, it was called Karmelstrasse (Carmel Street) and now, slightly realigned, it is known as Ben Gurion Avenue.

In later years, the Templers established warm relations with 'Abdu'l-Bahá, and He certainly regarded Hardegg as a friend. Hardegg would go to Acre to see 'Abdu'l-Bahá but the authorities would not permit a meeting with somebody still officially regarded as a prisoner. 'Abdu'l-Bahá poignantly recalled that Hardegg would 'stand in the street opposite the house in which I lived, looking for me, and when he saw me, he smiled and I nodded back with a smile'.[6] However, they managed a face-to-face meeting at another time, and Hardegg wrote a positive assessment of 'Abdu'l-Bahá.

Hardegg wrote to Bahá'u'lláh asking about His spiritual claim and received a reply. Due in part to a serious mistranslation of Bahá'u'lláh's words, Hardegg could not understand the meaning of the communication, known as the Tablet of Hirtik (or Tablet of Hardegg).[7] In that Tablet, Bahá'u'lláh clearly stated that there was no difference in spiritual station between Jesus Christ and Himself. Had Hardegg understood and accepted that claim, he might have concluded that the Templers' mission had been accomplished.

5

THE CASKET ON THE MOVE

Meanwhile, back in Persia, Ḥájí Á<u>kh</u>und tried but failed to keep secret the fact that the casket was in the house of Ḥasan-i-Vazir. He was unsuccessful in dissuading increasing numbers of believers, whose emotion overcame their good sense, from coming to the house to pray at the threshold of the room where they understood the casket was buried.

Some Bábís even offered to buy the house and turn it into a permanent shrine of the Báb, an act that would have inevitably alerted the clergy and the authorities, and led to disaster.

Finally Ḥájí Á<u>kh</u>und wrote to Bahá'u'lláh in Acre, asking for guidance. In reply, Bahá'u'lláh sent his trustee, Ḥájí <u>Sh</u>áh Muḥammad-i-Man<u>sh</u>ádí,[1] to Tehran with instructions to Ḥájí Á<u>kh</u>und to secretly hand over the casket from where it had been stored for 14 months since 1867. Ḥájí Á<u>kh</u>und was instructed not to ask where it was going.

In an act which testifies to his devotion and obedience, and in line with a well-thought-out security strategy, Ḥájí Á<u>kh</u>und did not even look to see in which direction the casket was carried. In 1868 Man<u>sh</u>ádí and another believer then followed instructions from Bahá'u'lláh to conceal the casket in the precincts of the Shrine of Imám-Zádih Zayd, near Tehran.

A role played by Mullá Ṣádiq-i-Muqaddas of Khurasan in the secret changing of the hiding place of the sacred remains is unclear, probably due to the extreme care needed to keep matters confidential at the time. Mullá Ṣádiq travelled to Tehran at the request of Bahá'u'lláh to do this, probably in either 1867 or 1868. He may have been the one to have helped Man<u>sh</u>ádí.[2]

Man<u>sh</u>ádí and the other believer managed to bury the casket beneath the floor of the inner sanctuary. It was to stay there for some 17 years.

In 1884,[3] Mírzá Asadu'lláh-i-Iṣfáhání, a brother-in-law of 'Abdu'l-Bahá,[4] began to play what would become a significant role in the protection of the casket. It began when it was clearly time to move the casket on.

Mírzá Asadu'lláh located the casket with the use of a chart forwarded to him by Bahá'u'lláh. The removal of the casket without detection by guards or any others in the vicinity required him to exercise wisdom, caution and courage. He initially took the casket to his own house in Tehran.

The casket went to several other localities, but only the last two have been identified.[5] In 1891,[6] accompanied by his wife, Mírzá Asadu'lláh arrived at the first of those two places, the Tehran house of another Bahá'í, Mírzá Ḥusayn-'Alíy-i-Iṣfahání, who had been surnamed Núr by Bahá'u'lláh.[7] Mírzá Asadu'lláh told Núr that he and his wife were going to Acre and they wanted to leave with him certain objects that were contained in a box. They asked him to take great care in protecting the box. Núr readily agreed.

The next day the couple returned and put a wooden box in a room. They asked that the door be locked and that nobody be allowed to enter. They took away the key and the following day came back, bringing with them an iron container. They used their key to unlock the door and went inside, where they closed the curtains and remained for four hours. As they were coming out of the room, Núr looked in and saw the container was locked, sealed and placed in the centre of the room. A powerful aroma of attar of roses and musk wafted up from the box, perfuming the air.

The three then installed the container in a large built-in alcove in the room. Later, a young Bahá'í who was a builder came and brick-walled the front of the alcove. Mírzá Asadu'lláh and his wife then left.

Núr stood guard in the room throughout the nights that followed, often sleeping there. He believed the contents to be precious Scripture,[8] the Writings of the Báb and Bahá'u'lláh. They were rare and precious items that could bring down dire punishment should the authorities discover them.

© Bahá'í World Centre

The site of the martyrdom of the Báb:
the Barracks Square in Tabriz in the winter of a later year

© Bahá'í World Centre

The moat, photographed in much later years, from where the sacred remains of the Báb were recovered. In 1964 when the Bahá'í author Guy Murchie visited, the area that was once the moat was in a granary or warehouse for storing wheat and barley

Ḥájí Á<u>kh</u>und (1842–1910) was one of those who protected the sacred remains of the Báb. Also known as 'Alí-Akbar-i-<u>Sh</u>ahmírzádí, he was buried in the Shrine of Imám-Zádih Ma'ṣúm, once the resting place of the Báb. Bahá'u'lláh appointed him a Hand of the Cause of God

Mírzá Músá, a brother of Bahá'u'lláh, helped conceal and transfer the Báb's casket. He is also known as Mírzá Áqáy-i-Kalím

The Shrine of Imám-Zádih Ḥasan where the sacred remains of the Báb were concealed for a short time after their arrival in Tehran

Part of the Shrine of Imám-Zádih Ma'ṣúm where the casket of the Báb was concealed for 17 years

The Tablet of Carmel, the foundational scripture for the Shrine of the Báb, was revealed near this spot as drawn in the mid-19th century depicting the Mount Carmel escarpment looking towards the Stella Maris monastery. From Laurence Oliphant, Haifa, or Life in the Holy Land, 1882–1885

Georg David Hardegg, a Templer leader, who after praying for guidance on Mount Carmel established a settlement directly below the future site of the Shrine of the Báb. He received a Tablet from Bahá'u'lláh

The German Templer Colony in Haifa with houses lining the avenue leading from the sea to the base of Mount Carmel, engraving by J. Schumacher, 1877

6

THE SITE FOR THE SHRINE

While the casket was concealed in Persia, significant events linked to the future Shrine of the Báb took place in the Holy Land. Bahá'u'lláh was at last permitted some freedom of movement. He had gained a reputation for saintliness among officials and the populace alike in Acre, and His living conditions were eased through the diplomacy of His son and representative 'Abdu'l-Bahá, who had won over most officials with his charisma, warm personality and useful advice on a range of problems.

The local people too were enamoured with 'Abdu'l-Bahá. They witnessed His daily, early morning charitable assistance to the homeless, the desperately poor, and the wretchedly ill. His hands were often left bleeding as the hungry clawed for the handouts of food.

Under the newly relaxed restrictions from 1877, Bahá'u'lláh was able to move about, and this enabled Him to advance plans for the Shrine of the Báb. He first laid spiritual foundations by his presence on Mount Carmel and by revealing special scripture relating to the mountain and the Shrine.

In August 1883, on the second[1] of His four visits to Haifa, Bahá'u'lláh stayed at a hotel in the German colony. As on his first visit in 1868, He referred to Mount Carmel as the Mountain of God:

> For a few days the Mountain of God became the seat of the Temple[2] and this is the Station which had been mentioned in the past Books. The voice of the Spirit [Jesus Christ] had been raised in this place and all the other Prophets have told of this Station. This is the mountain of God.[3]

Seven years later, when He arrived on His third visit beginning on 1 April 1890, He stayed in His tent on vacant land near the Community

Hall of the Templers.[4] Later He moved into the adjacent Oliphant House, also close to Mount Carmel.

On His fourth and last visit to Haifa, starting on 27 June 1891, Bahá'u'lláh stayed in Beit Abyad, a house belonging to Elyas Abyad in the German colony.[5] He later moved to vacant land at the corner of Hagefen Street and Morad Keramin Lane, at the very base of Mount Carmel, and visited the house next door.[6]

His view was not of the verdant slopes, pines, oaks and olive trees that had existed there in the era before the Ottomans arrived in the 16th century. The mountain face had long since been largely denuded. What He saw on the lower slopes, amid the big boulders embedded in the stony ground, were the garden terraces of the diligent German Templers, who had planted olive and fig trees, grape vines and vegetable gardens. Further up, He could see a steep slope of gravel, rocks and giant boulders pockmarked with holes, crevices and caves. Wildflowers and a few trees provided the only colour.

One day during that three-month visit, Bahá'u'lláh, then aged 73, went up the slope accompanied by Abdu'l-Bahá, 47, and arrived at a circle of some 15 young cypress trees which had been planted by the Templer Wilhelm Deiss.[7]

With its panoramic view, fresh air and stands of cypresses, this spot on the mountain was a favourite place of Bahá'u'lláh, Who had become enchanted with it on previous visits, often speaking with admiration of its beauty and cleanliness.[8]

It reminded Him too of a mountain retreat outside Tehran called 'Abode of the Birds' (Murgh Maḥallih) in Shimiran, which was on the lower slopes descending from Elburz where the wealthy had their summer residences. 'Abdu'l-Bahá said that in 1849, when He was only five years old, His Father chose this somewhat isolated place to talk to groups of up to 150 people, teaching them spiritual truths.[9]

On that warm June day in 1891, Bahá'u'lláh sat on a chair in the middle of the circle of trees, which were only as thick as a finger and cast no significant shade. Bahá'u'lláh faced east and 'Abdu'l-Bahá, seated on another chair one metre way from his father, faced west. Ḥusayn Iqbál, who was present on that occasion, recorded for posterity his memory of the event.[10]

Bahá'u'lláh issued instructions to 'Abdu'l-Bahá to arrange the transfer of the remains of the Báb from their place of concealment in Persia to the Holy Land. He stood and pointed to an expanse of rock and stones a little further down the slope, below a natural terrace, and directed 'Abdu'l-Bahá to purchase it and to inter the sacred remains of the Báb in a shrine there.[11]

It was also on that visit, but in another spot further along the slope, that Bahá'u'lláh revealed the Tablet of Carmel,[12] the foundational scripture for the spiritual and administrative centre of the Bahá'í Faith that was to be established on Mount Carmel. At the heart of that centre would be the Shrine of the Báb.

Bahá'u'lláh revealed the Tablet after He had visited the Cave of the prophet Elijah, a holy one 'Whose return the Báb Himself symbolises', as Shoghi Effendi later wrote.[13] He then ascended the mountain from that western point of the mountain and arrived near the Christian Carmelite monastery, at that time inhabited mostly by French monks, a place established in the belief that Christ, returning in the glory of the Father, would sanctify it by His presence.[14]

It was close to that monastery, with His voice so loud it was heard by the monks, that Bahá'u'lláh recited the Tablet, which was simultaneously recorded by His amanuensis whom He had called to take dictation.[15]

Through the revelation of this Tablet, writes Adib Taherzadeh, the 'forces released by Bahá'u'lláh for the implementation of the mighty enterprise involving the transfer of the remains of the Báb and the building of His Shrine became effective'. He suggests that a 'simple and enlightened approach' to studying the Tablet of Carmel is to consider it as a way of expressing God's plan in the language of imagery. The style of the Tablet is that of a dialogue between Bahá'u'lláh and Mount Carmel, similar to previous Tablets where he addressed other locations.[16]

In that Tablet Bahá'u'lláh spoke of the 'City of God', a reference later authoritatively interpreted by Shoghi Effendi to refer to the Shrine of the Báb.[17] The Tablet also speaks about circumambulating the Shrine, a practice that continues on special occasions today.

> Hasten forth and circumambulate the City of God that hath descended from heaven, the celestial Kaaba round which have circled in adoration the favoured of God, the pure in heart, and the company of the most exalted angels.[18]

The term 'throne' can also be taken as referring to the Shrine[19] in this excerpt in which Bahá'u'lláh expresses his love for Mount Carmel:

> Rejoice, for God hath in this Day established upon thee His throne, hath made thee the dawning-place of His signs and the dayspring of the evidences of His Revelation.
>
> Well is it with him that circleth around thee, that proclaimeth the revelation of thy glory, and recounteth that which the bounty of the Lord thy God hath showered upon thee. Seize thou the Chalice of Immortality in the name of thy Lord, the All-Glorious, and give thanks unto Him, inasmuch as He, in token of His mercy unto thee, hath turned thy sorrow into gladness, and transmuted thy grief into blissful joy. He, verily, loveth the spot which hath been made the seat of His throne, which His footsteps have trodden, which hath been honoured by His presence, from which He raised His call, and upon which He shed His tears.[20]

The description 'Ark of God' in the Tablet: 'Ere long will God sail His Ark upon Thee . . .'[21] refers to the world administrative centre of the Faith. The Tablet of Carmel ordained the establishment of both the City and the Ark on that holy mountain.[22]

Less than a year later, on 29 May 1892, Bahá'u'lláh passed away in an upstairs room in His home, the Mansion of Bahjí just outside Acre. The news was telegraphed to the Ottoman Sultan.

The Bahá'í community was heartbroken, However, they had to rally themselves for the funeral of the One they regarded as a Prophet of God. His remains were taken to an adjacent smaller house and interred in a vault under the floor of a small room, which is now, as the Shrine of Bahá'u'lláh, the holiest place on earth for Bahá'ís.

Nine days after his death, members of Bahá'u'lláh's family as well as other Bahá'ís gathered to hear the reading of His last Will and Testament.[23] It clearly identified 'Abdu'l-Bahá as His successor and head of the Bahá'í Faith.

The Mission of the Master
1892–1921

7

SETTING HIS STRATEGY

Immediately after the reading of Bahá'u'lláh's Will, 'Abdu'l-Bahá took on the full responsibility for the security of the Báb's casket and the daunting task of fulfilling Bahá'u'lláh's directive to bring it to the Holy Land and then inter it in a purpose-built shrine on Mount Carmel.

It was clearly going to be an extremely difficult mission. It would be made all the more challenging by new conflicts which immediately arose among His relatives.

'Abdu'l-Bahá was the eldest son of Bahá'u'lláh and his first wife, Navváb. Like other prominent men of the day, Bahá'u'lláh had followed the Islamic tradition of having more than one spouse. He had three, all of whom He had married under the Islamic code prior to the promulgation of the Bahá'í law of monogamy.[1] The three sons of His second wife[2] were angered at seeing their half-brother appointed to a role in which He was entitled to receive the tithes of the Bahá'í community and other donations. They wanted the money to fund a luxurious lifestyle for themselves, whereas 'Abdu'l-Bahá used it to assist the Bahá'í community and the poor. With His role as head of the Faith also came the respect and power His half-brothers craved. They were to become implacable enemies of 'Abdu'l-Bahá and to play obstructive roles in His mission to build the Shrine of the Báb. They also incited other relatives to rebel.

Now 48 years old, 'Abdu'l-Bahá possessed the personal qualities needed to carry out what He saw as His sacred mission. Known as 'the Master', He had been the chief administrator of the Bahá'í community and representative of Bahá'u'lláh since his mid-20s, successfully dealing with obstructive bureaucrats, ruthless military officers and treacherous family members. His enemies were well aware that nobody could intimidate or dominate Him. He was his own man, possessed of obvious integrity, an uncanny spiritual charisma, an unmatched intellect and a lively sense of humour. Physically, he was also impressive. He was an excellent swimmer[3] and a superb horseman. Of moderate height, He was strongly built and gave the impression of being tall by the way He carried himself. His eyes, unusual for most Persians, were blue-grey and were set in a face adorned by a trimmed black beard and moustache, both of which later turned snowy white. He always dressed impeccably yet simply, typically in a long cloak and a white turban.

His wife, Munírih Khánum, recalling how he was when they were first married, described him in this way: 'You have known Him in recent years, but then in the youth of His beauty and manly vigour, with His unfailing love, His kindness, His cheerfulness, His sense of humour, His untiring consideration for everybody, He was marvellous, without equal, surely in all the earth!'[4]

'Abdu'l-Bahá's ability to deal with officials was eased by His fluency in Arabic, Persian and Turkish. Visitors were enthralled as they witnessed His ability to dictate instructions, spiritual insights and correspondence to secretaries in the three tongues in one session, switching between languages and topics.[5] His knowledge of history, philosophy and current events was profound, attracting to His presence scholars, political leaders, military commanders and seekers of religious truth. There are many examples of how He helped those in need, daily attending to the poor. His grandson, Shoghi Effendi, described such activity on one afternoon in 1919 when the Master was 75 years old:

> He went and visited the poor and the lonely, gave money to the poor, and walked up long distances in some of the rocky places on the slopes of Mount Carmel in order to administer to the indigent and the helpless. When he returned home it was dark, and tired and fatigued, he sat enwrapped in his cloak in the corner of His sofa and asked for a cup of tea.[6]

Shoghi Effendi gives another inspiring example:

> Streets, nay rather lanes which I myself had not traversed for seven or eight years; places which I had never gazed at before were visited by the Beloved who walked continuously long distances and ascended steps and tiring staircases only to lay some coins in the palm of an indigent or leave with a sorrowing heart [a] few words of comfort.[7]

'Abdu'l-Bahá's own life had been far from easy. He had overcome tuberculosis, frostbite and severe dysentery. He had suffered the devastating loss of four of His eight children,[8] witnessed His younger brother die in a gruesome accident, and seen His beloved parents pass away. Yet He was at once joyful and dignified, purposeful and persistent. His grandson, Shoghi Effendi, who knew Him better than most, referred to His 'inexhaustible energy, marvellous serenity and unshakeable confidence'.[9] All that strength of character would be called upon in the perilous years ahead.

His strategy to fulfil the mission given Him by his Father with regard to the sacred remains of the Báb had four components. The first was to supervise the protection of the casket within Persia. The second was to purchase the land for the Shrine at the exact spot designated by Bahá'u'lláh. The third was to arrange the safe transfer of the casket to the Holy Land. The fourth was to build a Shrine and inter the sacred remains there.

'Abdu'l-Bahá had to implement that plan in a political environment that could hardly have been more unstable, more noxious, more adverse to His intentions. The Ottoman Empire, founded in the 13th century and centred in Istanbul, was in its dying days. Its ruthless, dictatorial Sultan, 'Abdu'l-Hamid II, who also presided as the head, or caliph,[10] of Islam, crushed any overt or suspected insurrection or seditious movements and was merciless to anybody even faintly suspected of rebelling.

As a prisoner of the empire, 'Abdu'l-Bahá was confined in the walled, polluted city of Acre some 23 kilometres from Mount Carmel. He was watched by spies, betrayed by people seeking personal advancement, and was under restrictions as to where He could go and what He could do. The challenge to successfully complete the tasks required to complete His assignment would have daunted most ordinary people. 'Abdu'l-Bahá was to prove He was far from ordinary.

He was tested quickly. In 1891–2, a new outbreak of persecution of Bahá'ís in Persia erupted and posed a potential threat to the security of the casket.[11] Because mobs were targeting Bahá'í homes for pillage and plunder, there were worries about the security of the house where the casket had been hidden since 1890, the home of Áqá Ḥusayn-'Alí (Núr) and his family.[12]

Núr adopted a further plan to ensure that the iron container[13] with the casket inside would not be discovered in the event of an attack on his home. He and some of his family removed part of a thick wall in the house. Holding the container vertically, they placed it in the cavity. Then they built a wall in front of that space, plastered it and used a fire to dry it so that by morning it looked the same as other parts of the room. Núr later wrote to Mírzá Asadu'lláh-i-Iṣfáhání, telling him of his continual worry that thugs would invade his house. He asked him to come back and get the container, the contents of which he did not know.

Mírzá Asadu'lláh, well aware of exactly what was in the container, replied that he would tell 'Abdu'l-Bahá about the situation, and if its removal was wanted then he would come and get it.

'Abdu'l-Bahá gave His approval for the casket to be moved. In 1894 Núr extracted the container from its hiding place and returned it to Mírzá Asadu'lláh, who took it to another house, the home of Áqá Muḥammad-Karím 'Aṭṭar, where it remained concealed from 1895 until 1898.

Six months after the removal of the container from his house, Núr received a letter from Mírzá Asadu'lláh informing him that the trust he had been guarding all those years had been 'none other than the sanctified remains' of the Báb, and that his house would one day be a place of pilgrimage to be visited by millions. It was breathtaking news for such a devout believer. The information shared from that letter prompted the local Bahá'ís to gather and pray near where the casket had once been. In accordance with a wish of 'Abdu'l-Bahá, a photograph was taken of the room and sent to the Holy Land.[14]

Meanwhile, 'Abdu'l-Bahá had to overcome the many obstacles in the way of obtaining the site chosen by Bahá'u'lláh for the Shrine midway up the northern slope of Mount Carmel. To the local authorities it would have seemed strange that a prisoner in Acre would want to buy land there. It was the mid-1890s and He was still technically a prisoner in Acre, quite a distance from the site.

The land on the lower slopes of Mount Carmel was used mostly for market gardens and grapevines by German Templers who had bought the land piece by piece from their Arab neighbours, some of whom were also Christians. Why would 'Abdu'l-Bahá want to build there? For security reasons, He could not explain that it was for a tomb for the sacred remains of the Báb. Only a description as a meeting place might suffice.

What made the task even more difficult was that during the lifetime of Bahá'u'lláh, 'Abdu'l-Bahá's treacherous siblings had jumped the gun and gone to see the owner of the site to try to buy it. It had been an attempt to ingratiate themselves with their Father and, at the same time, a bid to discredit 'Abdu'l-Bahá.

At that time, the owner had refused to sell, and so the men returned to Bahjí, where they said to Bahá'u'lláh that they had investigated and found the land was not for sale. Chastising them for their unauthorized actions, Bahá'u'lláh told one of 'Abdu'l-Bahá's half-brothers, Badí'u'lláh, who had been involved in the failed attempt: 'This is none of your business, it is for Áqá (the Master) to accomplish.'[15]

Now, in 1896, four years after Bahá'u'lláh had passed away, 'Abdu'l-Bahá decided it was time to make a move but He adopted a better strategy than the one that had been used by His unsuccessful siblings a few years earlier. Instead of conducting the negotiation himself, He kept Himself at arm's length by engaging the services of a German businessman in Haifa[16] who was a member of the Templer community and so one likely to be able to ascertain the attitude of the owner to the idea of selling and the price that might be agreed upon.

The businessman approached the owner with an offer but soon came back bearing bad news. He could not close the deal because Muḥammad-'Alí, the half-brother of 'Abdu'l-Bahá, was causing problems between him and the potential seller.

When the owner, Elias Modavvar, finally agreed to sell, that same treacherous half-brother and his associates urged him to hang on to the land because, they said, it soon would be worth ten times its current value. They also incited other people to falsely claim to the authorities that they owned the land, a lie that took another six months to expose. The owner had previously asked the enormous sum of 1,000 Turkish pounds for the land, but it was eventually obtained in 1896 for 'a reasonable price'.[17]

It was not until at least 1908 and probably a few years later that 'Abdu'l-Bahá obtained the land behind the Shrine site, then owned by Wilhelm Deiss, one of the early Templer settlers. It was occupied by a vineyard and the circle of cypress trees, which Deiss had planted.[18]

The story of the purchase was told by Deiss's daughter, Maria, many years later. She said 'Abdu'l-Bahá visited Deiss at his home in 79 Albany Street, Haifa, almost daily. He would take a rest there, sitting on a stool next to the well and talking with her father before continuing His walk. Every now and then, 'Abdu'l-Bahá would ask him if wanted to sell his land but Mr Deiss always said no. Eventually, however, the vineyard became infected and all the produce lost. It was then that her father agreed to sell the land to 'Abdu'l-Bahá, and to become his gardener too.[19]

'Abdu'l-Bahá commented that although the price was high, at 2,000 tumans, if He had not been able to buy this land which had been trodden by the holy footsteps of Bahá'u'lláh and where He had sat and received the friends,[20] it would no doubt have been used for construction, which would have caused additional problems.[21]

8

CONCEALMENT AND TRANSFER

In 1898, the third part of the strategy – the transfer of the sacred remains – was set in motion.

It was a little short of seven months before the first Western Bahá'í pilgrims arrived in Acre in December 1898, that 'Abdu'l-Bahá ordered the casket be brought from Persia to the Holy Land. In late spring 1898 He entrusted the mission to Mírzá Asadu'lláh-i-Iṣfáhání, who was on pilgrimage in the Holy Land,[1] sending him to Persia with 'some others'. As the Master wrote in a Tablet after the event, they carried the sacred remains with 'utmost reverence and humility' on a 'running throne'[2] from Persia to Beirut.[3]

Using a 'running throne' was a special method used in the Middle East to transport a prominent person, a greatly revered item, or valuables. This would involve the use of a larger container with handles at each end. Some would hold the handles at the rear, others at the front. They would proceed on foot, as with a sedan chair or palanquin. This was the way the Jews carried the 'Ark of the Covenant', which was said to contain the Shekhinah, 'the divine presence of God'.[4] A link with the Jewish Ark of the Covenant becomes clear through a Tablet by the Master who interprets a Quranic verse that alludes to the Jewish Shekhinah as also referring to the casket and sacred remains of the Báb.[5] Thus, for Bahá'ís, what was historically called the Ark of the Covenant was carried from Persia to the Holy Land in a running throne and is now interred in the Shrine of the Báb.

Although the Tablet by 'Abdu'l-Bahá confirms that a running throne was used, the secrecy involved in the mission has meant that certain details have yet to be yielded up. But from the facts so far uncovered it is clear that the transfer of the casket ranks among the most dramatic, perilous and ultimately thrilling episodes in the history of the Bahá'í Faith.

The journey began after Mírzá Asadu'lláh had returned to Persia from the Holy Land and had recovered the casket from its hiding place in Tehran. He then set off with the assistance of other believers, including a 'capable and devoted' Bahá'í named Ḥusayn Rúḥí, who was the son of Ḥájí 'Alí-'Askar, a distinguished Bahá'í who had attained the presence of the Báb. Like his father, Ḥusayn Rúḥí had been in prison in Acre with Bahá'u'lláh.[6]

The men took the casket 150 kilometres south to Qom, a city holy to Shi'ah Islam.[7] Walking from Persia to the holy shrines in Iraq had long been a custom, so seeing men carrying a running throne would not have seemed to others to be particularly unusual. The group would have ensured their personal safety, and the security of their sacred cargo, by being part of a caravan, in which the wealthy rode horses, others were on donkeys, and still others walked. Mules were commonly used for transporting loads and so could have carried the possessions of Mírzá Asadu'lláh and his colleagues.

The road south encountered some hills and desert areas but was wider and far less rocky than the one Sulaymán Khán had taken with the casket nearly 50 years previously from Tabriz to Tehran. It was a popular route for Muslim pilgrims heading for pilgrimage in Mecca or to Karbila in Iraq, as well as for others heading just for Qom itself or the beautiful cities of Isfahan and Shiraz further south. There were stops along the way in caravanserai where there would be a mosque and ablution facilities and sometimes, to the delight of travellers, an oasis. Mírzá Asadu'lláh's companions did not know the actual contents of their cargo, thinking that it was a box of the Báb's sacred Writings.[8]

In Qom, they stored the casket for three days in the house of Áqá 'Abdu'l-Razzaq Tabrízí.[9] There is a short account of what happened there, written by a Bahá'í of that city, 'Ustád Ismá'íl Úbudíyyát:

> I had the privilege of carrying the coffin containing the remains of the blessed Báb two times. The first time was when the coffin was brought to Qom by the person responsible for it [Mírzá Asadu'lláh], who placing it on my shoulder, asked me to take it into the house. And a few days later, the same person handed me the same coffin and asked me to carry it out of the house. Later on I understood that the coffin contained the remains of the blessed Báb.[10]

After Qom, Mírzá Asadu'lláh and his companions headed off with the precious cargo towards the great city of Isfahan, about 315 kilometres south. On the way they passed through Kashan, Natanz, Tar and Tarq.[11]

Then they arrived in that city, the former capital of Persia, a place where the Báb had once stayed under the protection of the Governor, Manúchihr Khán. It was now the home of an influential and trusted Bahá'í, a brother-in-law of Mírzá Asadu'lláh and with the same name. Mírzá Asadu'lláh Khán was the Vizier, the chief minister of the provincial governor, Ẓillu's-Sulṭán, a son of the Shah. Mírzá Asadu'lláh-i-Iṣfáhání conveyed to him the instructions 'Abdu'l-Bahá had given him. The Vizier naturally greatly admired and honoured 'Abdu'l-Bahá, and years before had walked as a pilgrim to Acre to see Him,[12] so he was happy to provide assistance by hiding the casket in the upper section of the residence he shared with his wife, Mírzá Asadu'lláh-i-Iṣfáhání's sister, who was respected as a Bahá'í of great 'servitude, steadfastness and love'.[13]

Given the Vizier's rank, his home in the suburb of Shahshanan would have been used for official occasions to entertain high-ranking government and religious officials and so be decorated accordingly. The residence would likely have had windows of coloured glass in the external walls; internal walls decorated with carved wood; glass and ceramic art works on display; silk carpets and tapestries covering divans and other pieces of furniture; entrance ways inlaid with semi-precious stones; the facades adorned with ceramics in floral designs, and with Quranic verses inscribed on them. In such a grand mansion, the sacred remains of the Báb found a temporary resting place in the heart of Persia, in a city that had family links to 'Abdu'l-Bahá Himself.

Soon, instructions from the Master reached Mírzá Asadu'lláh-i-Iṣfáhání to move the casket on to the Holy Land. The Vizier summoned his trustworthy 25-year-old nephew, Mírzá 'Aṭá'u'lláh Núrbakhsh, and told him in confidence that Mírzá Asadu'lláh-i-Iṣfáhání had some Tablets and Holy Writings that had to be taken to 'Abdu'l-Bahá and had asked for a trusted person to be his confidant. The Vizier told Mírzá 'Aṭá'u'lláh that he had been selected to assist in this mission. He called upon him to be obedient, not to ask questions, and not speak to anybody about the matter.[14]

The casket was placed in a running throne, and three days after the young man had received the instructions from the Vizier, he and 'many servants' joined the party led by Mírzá Asadu'lláh-i-Iṣfáhání and set out on the 1,000-kilometre journey from Isfahan to Baghdad.[15] They would probably have been in a caravan of horses and mules with howdahs,[16] escorted by a guard in front who scouted for potential trouble and one in the rear for a similar reason.

Some 30 kilometres to the west of Isfahan, they stopped over for three days in the town of Najafabad, where they stayed in the house of a Bahá'í called Ḥájí Báqir.[17] Mírzá Asadu'lláh placed the casket in one of the rooms of the house, saying that it contained writings and Tablets, and not revealing to Ḥájí Báqir, or to the Bahá'ís who came to visit, that the trunk carried the sacred remains of the Báb. He told 'Aṭá'u'lláh that if he (Mírzá Asadu'lláh) had to leave the box alone for any reason, 'Aṭá'u'lláh was responsible for looking after all the luggage, including the box.[18]

About two years later, on 27 November 1900 (after the casket had arrived safely in the Holy Land), Zaynu'l-Muqarrabín,[19] who came from Najafabad and who was an amanuensis to 'Abdu'l-Bahá, wrote to Ḥájí Báqir on the Master's behalf requesting that, with due wisdom, Ḥájí Báqir should prepare the room where the casket had been as a place of pilgrimage for men and women to enter and to read the prayers and verses of God, asking Him for His bounties.

Then, in a letter dated 27 March 1901, the Master in His own handwriting told Ḥájí Baqír that the room where Mírzá Asadu'lláh had left the sacred trust should be reserved as a place of prayer, a place to ask for the necessities of life. A candle should be lit there every night. The Master told him that he should never forget the special divine favour conferred upon him, and then said that the location of all other pilgrimage places in Najafabad (of the previous religious era) were only guesses and based on hearsay, but this place of his was real and he should value it.[20]

The journey to the border, more than 500 kilometres away, went northwest from Najafabad via Arak to Hamadan for a very brief stay, and then moving on to Kermanshah (now also known as Bakhtaran), the city near the departure point for Iraq. It probably took about two to three weeks.

In Kermanshah, Mírzá Asadu'lláh decided the group should pause and rest, staying in a house for two to three days. In later years, while referring to that house, the Master described the constant danger posed

'Abdu'l-Bahá.
In obedience to the directions of Bahá'u'lláh, He arranged the transfer of the casket of the Báb from Persia to the Holy Land, built the Shrine of the Báb at the spot indicated by His Father, and interred the sacred remains there. Photograph by Underwood & Underwood, New York City, 11 April 1912, from the album of George Latimer

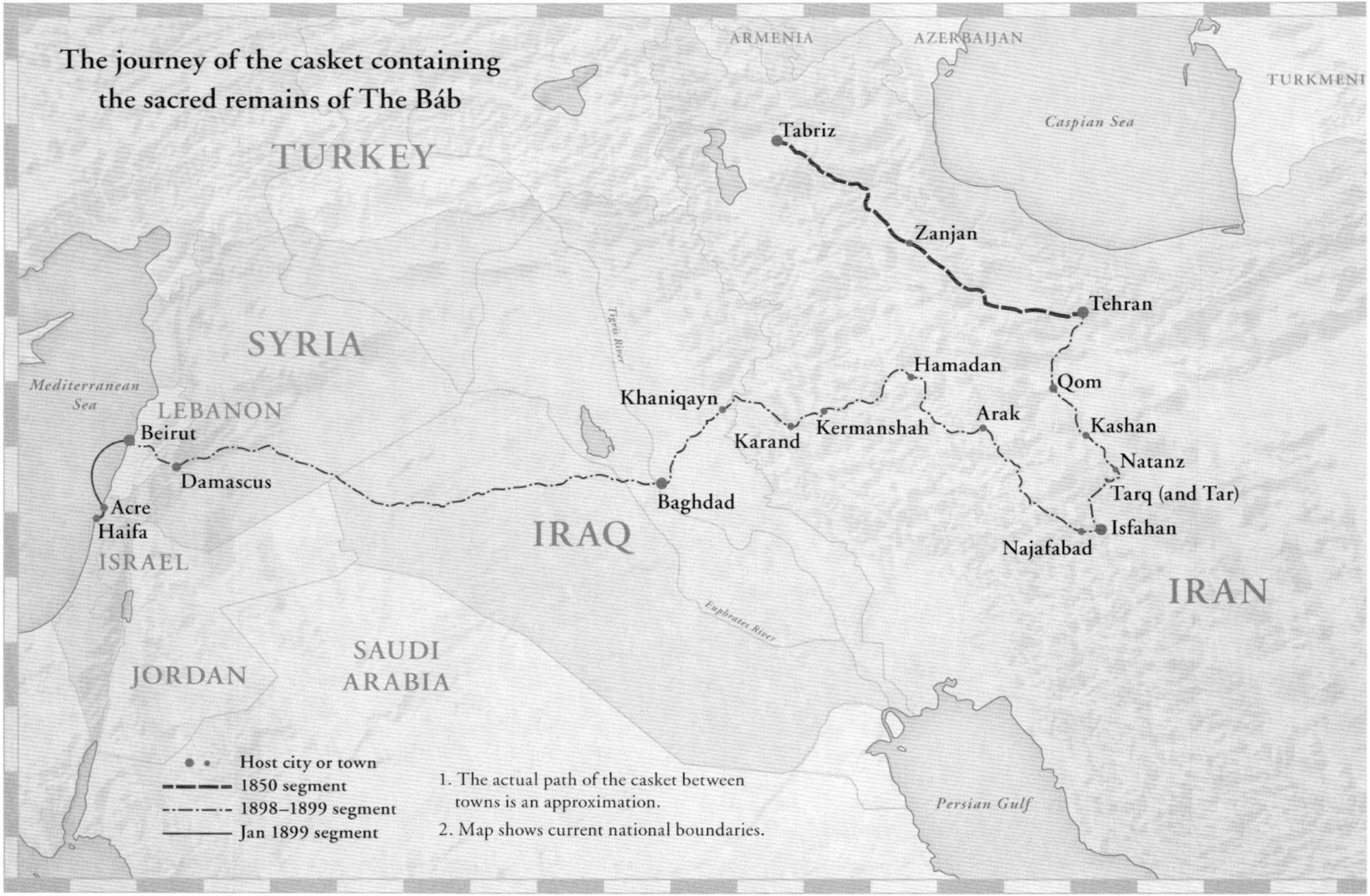

The route the casket of the Báb travelled in 1850, and in 1898–99

Mírzá Asadu'lláh Khán, the Vizier, chief minister of the provincial governor of Isfahan. A staunch Bahá'í, he concealed the casket of the Báb and helped with arrangements to take it out of Persia

Mírzá Asadu'lláh-i-Iṣfáhání. As directed by 'Abdu'l-Bahá, he was the leader of those who carried the casket of the Báb from Persia to the Holy Land

Ustád Ismá'íl Úbudíyyát carried the casket of the Báb in Qom and Haifa

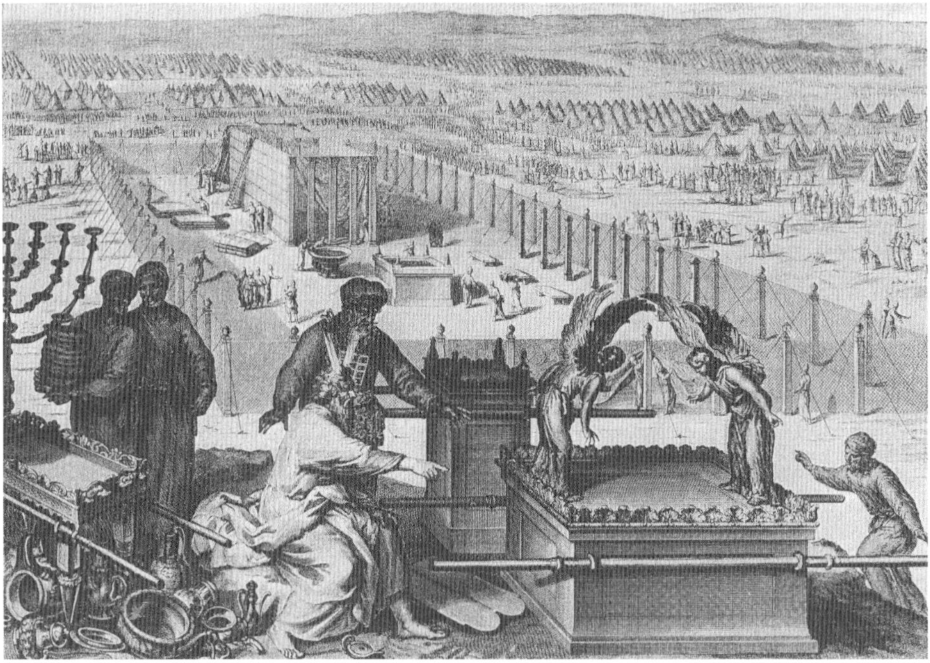

The Jewish Ark of the Covenant travelled in a palanquin, a box carried on two horizontal poles as depicted here. This method for carrying sacred objects, holy books and important people was also used in Persia and other parts of the Middle East and Asia. In 1898, eight men carried the casket of the Báb in a palanquin-style 'running throne' from Persia to Beirut

Part of the residence in Najafabad where the Báb's casket was stored briefly

at that time to the sacred remains by the enemies of the Faith, saying that the enemies were vigilant, and if the casket had fallen into their hands they would have burned it.[21]

The border stations were often filthy, dangerous and uncomfortable, not places anybody would want to stay for long. Crossing was difficult to negotiate for ordinary travellers with any kind of cargo. The police there were notorious bribe-seekers who had the practice of sending spies to roam among the groups waiting to go through the border to find out details about valuable cargo. That knowledge would help them extract payments from those wanting to transport their goods with as little trouble as possible and with no delay. However, Mírzá Asadu'lláh had with him a government decree,[22] and it required that officials along the way should treat this group of travellers with respect, an order that prevented customs officers from inspecting the holy cargo.

The group crossed the border without incident. Accompanying them were probably pilgrims heading to the sacred sites in Iraq, some with horses carrying corpses to be buried near the holy places there. Ahead of them lay the route along passes through the Zagros mountains, the same mountainous path to Baghdad as Bahá'u'lláh had travelled during his historic journey of exile 45 years earlier when He went via the village of Karand (now called Kerend-e-Gharb or Eslemebad-e-Gharb) near the border and on to Khaniqayn (now Khanaqin) before heading south-west to Baghdad.[23] That journey in the midst of winter and with families with young children took Bahá'u'lláh's party three months, but Mírzá Asadu'lláh and his group, travelling in a more benign season, probably arrived at their destination after about three weeks.

In Baghdad a photograph was taken of Mírzá Asadu'lláh and seven other travellers and was sent to the Vizier with a message to say that the 'Throne of God is being carried by eight'.[24] One of those was Ḥusayn-i-Vakil, who had guarded the casket in Baghdad.[25] After visiting the shrines of that city, 'Aṭá'u'lláh Núrbakhsh and the servants returned to Persia.

Instructions then came from 'Abdu'l-Bahá to move the casket on to Beirut. Mírzá Asadu'lláh had with him a request from the Persian government to the governor of Baghdad that the travellers be shown respect. That document protected them from inspection by customs officers.[26]

Mírzá Asadu'lláh and the seven others joined a camel caravan[27] as they carried the running throne over the vast desert to Damascus, 850 kilometres away. It is recorded that the group gave the casket the glory and splendour it ought to have, so that means it was carried in a running throne.[28]

The journey would have been difficult, blisteringly hot in the day and bitterly cold at night, and with the ever-present danger of robbery by highwaymen. Such caravans were usually led by men on mules to watch out for danger. Men walked at the front, in the middle and at the rear of the caravan. Some wore shoes of coarse woven cotton while others preferred to go barefoot. The sand along the way was irritatingly fine. At night they wore treated sheepskins to keep themselves warm. They would usually start about 2.30 a.m. to avoid journeying in the heat of the day. Then they would stop and, using the inflammable desert bush, make a fire to boil the water they carried in animal skins. After tea and a meal, usually of dry bread and cheese, they would move on. When they arrived at a remote village they would stay in a caravanserai, a two-storey inn for travellers with a courtyard in the middle. More substantial food was available there, such as chicken or mutton, but a stop in such a place had its own challenges, including the threat of theft.[29]

After Damascus, the men travelled with the casket to the coastal city of Beirut. There they concealed it in the home of Mírzá Muḥammad Muṣṭafá, later named by Shoghi Effendi as one of the 19 Apostles of Bahá'u'lláh and described by him as a 'brave and vigilant custodian and bearer of the remains of the Báb'.[30] Long before, Bahá'u'lláh had instructed Muḥammad Muṣṭafá to live in Beirut, where he often helped Bahá'ís travelling to Acre. His loyalty was unquestioned. The crowning act of his service was surely guarding the sacred remains of the Báb and being one of those who escorted them to Acre from Beirut.

He had three sons, one of whom, Dr Zia Bagdadi, became widely known and loved.[31] Fortunately, the story of what he remembered from his youth has been recorded:

> Zia was born in Beirut, where he attended the American University. The memory of Beirut was particularly dear to him because it was there that the body of that great martyr, El Báb, was kept in their home for some time before it was delivered to 'Abdu'l-Bahá in Akka by an escort of Bahá'ís . . . Dr Zia told me that he remembered a

> large, long box in his home which, as a child, he was never permitted to touch, and not until long years afterward did he learn that it held the Sacred Remains of El Báb and His martyred companion, rather than Sacred books.[32]

As a young boy, he may have perceived the box as being large and long, but others have not described it as such.

Despite efforts to maintain utmost secrecy, the news of the impending arrival of Mírzá Asadu'lláh and his colleagues had somehow leaked to disloyal family members in Acre, 110 kilometres to the south. They were determined to take possession of the casket. Motivated by their greed for money, they saw an advantage in anything that would tear down 'Abdu'l-Bahá as head of the Bahá'í community. They thought that seizing leadership would give them the opportunity to get their hands on the donations that the Master carefully and economically used, not on Himself and His family, but on the poor and destitute of whatever faith, on dependent relatives of Bahá'í martyrs and on projects such as purchasing land in preparation for the building of the Shrine of the Báb.

The story of what happened next is related in the memoirs[33] of Dr Bagdadi. He said that those Covenant-breakers had previously told thieves and highwaymen that 'Abdu'l-Bahá was bringing a box full of treasures from Persia and that it would reach Beirut, and when those antagonistic relatives heard of the arrival of the box, they reported that fact to the Ottoman authorities. One way or another they wanted to get hold of it.

> They even bribed the telegraph clerks in 'Akká to report to them all the communications sent from and to 'Abdu'l-Bahá.[34] However, 'Abdu'l-Bahá was aware of this formidable blockade set by the enemies of the Faith
>
> The government was watching the sea and the thieves lay on the land watching the road between Beirut and Acre.
>
> On the other hand, 'Abdu'l-Bahá kept the wires busy. First he wired to Mustafa Bagdadi (father of the author [i.e. Dr. Bagdadi]) to come by land. Horses and mules were prepared and just at the moment of starting from Beirut, a second wire came, saying to come by sea.[35]

> There were [a] few days to wait for one of the regular boats, when suddenly the small Turkish boat as from a clear sky made to port and announced that she was leaving the next day directly for 'Akká and would carry passengers.
>
> So Mustafa Bagdadi and the rest decided at once and sailed. While at mid-sea, a third wire was sent from 'Abdu'l-Bahá to Beirut, saying to postpone coming. The boat was already nearing 'Akká.
>
> The enemies on land and sea, believing that no one was leaving from Beirut and not knowing that the boat 'The Bounty of God' was nearing 'Akká, went to sleep for a while. The little boat made port very quietly and all landed safely.

As rendered in Persian, the name of the unscheduled steamship that had suddenly appeared could be translated as the letters J-U-L-Y (pronounced Julie).[36] The group had seemed thwarted at first because they had just missed the scheduled ship, but now they could board the unscheduled vessel and conceal the casket among different boxes of merchandise.[37]

The next problem was getting the casket past the customs officers whose job it was to examine cargo arriving by sea at Acre. Fate intervened. On the day of the arrival of the boat carrying the casket, 31 January 1899,[38] the death occurred of a prominent figure in Acre, one Shaykh Muqarrábí, and so businesses, the market and government offices, including customs, closed for the day out of respect.[39] This was very fortuitous for 'Abdu'l-Bahá. The cargo from the vessel was carried to the customs office but all the inspectors were absent, leaving only one security guard, who told the Bahá'í involved, Núri'd-Din Zayn, that he could take his cargo and leave because there was nobody to check it. The guard was given a tip and the precious cargo was taken away.

The casket went first to the house of Mírzá Asadu'lláh and a few days later was moved to 'Abdu'l-Bahá's house near the sea wall of the ancient city.[40]

After decades of extreme anxiety, careful planning, long periods of inactivity, and providential happenings, the sacred remains of the martyred Prophet were at last safe and reasonably secure in the Holy Land.[41]

'Abdu'l-Bahá did not inform many people about that triumph but He was heard to remark: 'If I were to tell you what happy tidings I bear, old men would dance in joy alone in their rooms!'[42] Later He wrote:

'You can imagine how spiritually uplifting an act it was!'[43]

After the secret arrival of the casket at 'Abdu'l-Bahá's house, the Master stored the casket in the room of His utterly trustworthy sister, Bahíyyih Khánum, known by her spiritual title of the Greatest Holy Leaf which designates her descent from Bahá'u'lláh.

Mr 'Alí Nakhjavání, who grew up in the Holy Land, has related how his aunt, Zeenat Bagdadi, told him she often wondered why it was that the Greatest Holy Leaf would sit in in utter silence for hours on end on the *mandar* – the bench running along the side of the room. He writes:

> My aunt described my mother [Fatimih Khánum] sitting at the feet of the Greatest Holy Leaf, also remaining silent and motionless, hour after hour. She said it was only later that she understood that it was because the remains of the Báb were in that room . . . it is as though we were asked to live and sleep in the Shrine of the Báb.
>
> Obviously, we can well imagine that the Greatest Holy Leaf lived in reverence, turning her heart to the Báb, realising the sacred trust she had to protect . . . in that room.[44]

'Abdu'l-Bahá would soon adopt a strategy that would protect the casket from potential threats in that prison city, which was inhabited by unfaithful relatives as well as by capricious and sometimes hostile authorities.

9

THE SARCOPHAGUS

'Abdu'l-Bahá had another complicated task to carry out – obtaining an appropriate sarcophagus for the remains of the Báb. It could be no ordinary container for a coffin containing the sacred remains of the Manifestation of God.

He decided to ask the Bahá'ís of Burma to be responsible for its construction, sending letters outlining His requirements to a great exponent of the Faith, Siyyid Muṣṭafá Rúmí, who was living in Burma.[1] Included in the extensive correspondence was a plan of the required item.[2]

'Abdu'l-Bahá asked for a one-piece sarcophagus to be made of the finest marble.[3] He wanted it to be 'unique and of brilliant lustre'.[4] He also ordered a hardwood coffin of the best Indian wood and of the right size to fit inside the sarcophagus.

The heavy cost of £700 for the sarcophagus was contributed by the Bahá'ís of Rangoon, in particular Ḥájí Siyyid Mihdí of Shiraz, his son Siyyid Ismá'íl, and Siyyid Muṣṭafá Rúmí. It appears it was made in Rangoon, and could well have been made from materials obtained by the Bahá'ís of Mandalay from near that city.[5]

There were many difficulties in its construction. When finished it measured about 2.5 metres long, 1.25 metre wide, and one metre deep, and to survive the sea voyage to Haifa without cracking it had to be between 8 and 10 centimetres thick.

'Abdu'l-Bahá wanted the sarcophagus to be decorated with gilded calligraphy on the sides saying 'Yá Bahá'u'l-Abhá' (meaning in English 'O Glory of the All-Glorious') and 'Yá 'Alí'u'l-A'lá' ('O Exalted of the Most Exalted Ones'), and so he directed the gifted calligraphist Mishkín-Qalam, who was visiting Burma, to inscribe the invocations into the marble.[6]

A photograph of the sarcophagus before it left Burma shows it on display under an ornate banner which has the date in the British

Empire style, 22–5–98 (22 May 1898).[7] The photo shows Mishkín-Qalam's inscriptions in three adjacent panel-like spaces on one side, and these were probably repeated on the other side. There appear to be three inscriptions on the lid but cannot be read. They are likely to be 'Yá 'Alí'u'l-A'lá'. The sarcophagus had a rounded convex lid, and a base with arches between what appears to be some seven supports or legs. The lid and sides had ornate borders.

'Abdu'l-Bahá received a sample of the marble sent by Siyyid Muṣṭafá Rúmí, and as he looked at it against the sunlight, He said: 'Observe how you can see the sun's rays through this stone. It is the finest piece of stone excavated from the mine and purposed for this sacred sarcophagus. In quality, it truly is peerless in the entire world.'[8]

The prelude to the journey of the sarcophagus and coffin to Haifa began with due ceremony. The Burmese Bahá'ís loaded them into two carts. Two hundred believers chanted as they pulled them towards the port – they did not want horses to pull the carts.[9] Another report of the journey said they were carried 'almost two farsakh [12 km] on the shoulders of the believers of Rangoon to the port to be shipped'.[10]

Details of the sea journey to Haifa are sketchy but 'Abdu'l-Bahá later spoke cryptically of great difficulties.[11] The ship carrying the precious cargo sailed via Bombay and arrived off Haifa at night in 1899. A Bahá'í whose father played a part in the unloading of the cargo described what happened: 'By the order of 'Abdu'l-Bahá, a few friends [went out in] light winds to receive it . . . My father got to the ship and as soon as his eyes met the sarcophagus, he bent over it and started to cry and say prayers.'[12]

An amenable customs official was told the cargo was for 'Abdu'l-Bahá and that it should be released upon arrival without inspection. The official complied.[13]

One of the Bahá'ís who accompanied this important cargo from Burma to Haifa was Siyyid Muṣṭafá Rúmí, whom 'Abdu'l-Bahá had first contacted about building the sarcophagus. He was graciously received by the Master.[14]

'Abdu'l-Bahá directed Hájí Mírzá Ḥasan-i-Khurásání to hire Arabs to haul the sarcophagus to the place where it would be stored. These strong men placed the crates on wooden rollers[15] and used rope to drag them from the pier, all the while chanting in unison in Arabic,'Ya Abu'l-Abbas, Anta Imamu'n-nas' (O thou father Abbas, Thou art the guide of the people).[16]

The crates were first taken to the house of Mírzá Muḥsin Afnán, a son-in-law of 'Abdu'l-Bahá, and then transferred to the guest house for Western pilgrims in Haifa.[17] One of three houses 'Abdu'l-Bahá had rented, it was called the Ḥaẓíratu'l-Quds,[18] essentially a Bahá'í meeting place, and was in the area once known in Haifa as Sahna'tul-Hanatir (Carriage Square), later called Paris Square and now known as Kiryat-Ha-Mimshala (Government Village).[19]

Ali-Kuli Khan, who as a young man acted for a time in 1900 as secretary to 'Abdu'l-Bahá, and worked in that house, said the sarcophagus was stored in the very room assigned to him for his duties, a room next to 'Abdu'l-Bahá's reception area.[20]

'Abdu'l-Bahá wrote later than none of the Bahá'ís in the Holy Land knew for what purpose these two boxes were intended, and presumed they were for the Shrine of Bahá'u'lláh.[21]

10

THE FOUNDATION

As 'Abdu'l-Bahá was preparing to start the construction of the Shrine, there was great ferment in the Holy Land. The dramatic decline of the Ottoman Empire was having a toxic effect, with suspicion, communal violence, danger and tension plaguing the towns and cities, including Acre and Haifa.

The Ottomans took measures to retain control of this colony, which was important to them not only for trade but also as a buffer zone against their enemy, the Egyptians.[1] They knew that one way to control a potentially restive population was to divide them, so they stoked the fires of hatred, especially between Muslims and Christians, worsening the disorder.

Acre was enclosed in walls, a city of narrow alleys, so it was easier for the authorities to maintain a tighter grip there than across the bay in the walled, though more open, town of Haifa, which had a population of about 9,000.[2] Many men in Haifa were armed, and they often used their weapons to settle arguments. Criminals could easily escape capture after committing murder either by fleeing the town or by bribing the authorities.[3] There was a real chance of bystanders suffering accidental injury or even being killed by gunshot. The sound of gunfire was common. Firing weapons into the air was also a way to celebrate weddings, and bullets often went astray. Even some estranged relatives of 'Abdu'l-Bahá who had abandoned the Bahá'í Faith carried guns. They associated with criminals and sometimes threatened the lives and businesses of Bahá'ís.

Through this environment strode the confident figure of 'Abdu'l-Bahá. He would not be turned back from His sacred mission to build the Shrine. He was afraid of nobody, neither tyrant nor thug. By now in his mid-50s, he remained fit and strong. He rejected the idea of a bodyguard or even a lantern carrier in the unlighted areas near where He stayed, a short distance outside the walls. Inside the city, he carried His own lamp. Often individual Bahá'ís, in particular His household staff, would worry about Him when He walked alone. They would secretly follow Him, and watch from a distance in case there was trouble.

One night it was the turn of His secretary, Yúnis Khán, to guard Him. 'Abdu'l-Bahá was returning home just after midnight when a shot rang out from a side street but, used to the sound of gunfire, Yúnis Khán paid no attention. Then the flash of a second shot sent him running towards 'Abdu'l-Bahá because he feared an assassination attempt was under way.

He had reached the intersection when a third shot was fired. He saw two men running away. He was now no more than a step behind 'Abdu'l-Bahá, who walked on without changing His pace or turning His head. His tread was firm and dignified. Never one to panic or be intimidated, He paid no attention to what had occurred. At the gate of His house He acknowledged Yúnis Khán's presence, turning to him and bidding him goodbye.[4]

There were other attempts on His life. Two estranged Bahá'ís attempted to kill Him. One twice placed poison in a jug of His water but it was discovered in time. Another carried a dagger hidden under his clothes with the intention of assassinating Him. 'Abdu'l-Bahá 'forgave one and turned a blind eye to the other'.[5]

At this tumultuous and perilous time, 'Abdu'l-Bahá had to decide upon the architectural design for the Shrine. He wanted it to be immensely solid so that it would last for centuries.

He found His starting point locally. Shortly after their arrival in Haifa in 1868, the German Templers had built sturdy structures, using local stone for their own buildings and for those of others outside their community.[6] 'Abdu'l-Bahá was strategic and economical. It made sense for Him to adapt an existing design for His special purpose. He had contact with Templer engineers – they had an unsuccessful attempt at building the initial cistern for the Shrine – so it is probable He also consulted with them on the design for the building, given that they had built structures similar to the one that eventuated. He was on good personal terms with the Templers, so if he had required the services of a Templer architect, he could have easily contacted one. However, architectural plans for the Shrine have yet to be located.

The Shrine building had many exterior features that were included in some Templer structures – for example, the porthole windows, the buttresses and the course of bricks encircling the oblong structure near the roof. Arched windows as in the Shrine appear in other Templer buildings such as railway stations that were built by the Templer Josef Wennagel (1878–1949). Similar-looking buildings included the Gemeindehaus (community hall) in Haifa, the first Templer building in the Holy Land.[7] A building in 'Bethlehem in Galilee', a village near Nazareth, has the same kind of buttresses and, although the arches of its lower windows are Gothic rather than the Eastern style in the Shrine, they bear other similarities to those seen in the Shrine, and the stone decoration around the window facades is almost identical.[8]

Any design collaboration with the Templers did not extend to its interior design, which was totally different from the inside of their buildings. All the rooms of the Shrine have eastern-style arched ceilings, making the building in its entirety a unique fusion of East and West.

To build the Shrine 'Abdu'l-Bahá needed skilled stonemasons. Two such artisans arrived as pilgrims. They met with 'Abdu'l-Bahá and soon received permission from Him to remain in the Holy Land after their pilgrimage so they could work on the Shrine project.[9] These master-masons, Ustád Áqá 'Alí-Ashraf and Ustád Áqá Bálá,[10] were Turkish-speaking Bahá'ís whose native town was Baku in what is now Azerbaijan, and they were active members of the Faith there. Sons of Mullá Abú-Ṭálib, a prominent and wealthy Bahá'í whom they had accompanied on pilgrimage, the brothers became the two principal masons in the construction of the building and also donated a substantial amount of their considerable wealth for the project.[11]

The Master permitted Mullá Abú-Ṭálib, a devoted and generous believer and one of the first Bahá'ís of Baku, to live for the rest of his life downstairs in the Eastern Pilgrim House. His legacy lives on elsewhere in the Holy Land too because he left the large garden he owned next to the Riḍván Garden to his son 'Alí-Ashraf, who later donated it to the Faith. It is known as the Ashraf Garden.[12]

Another Bahá'í from Baku, a Persian by the name of Ustád 'Abdu'l-Karím, had accompanied the other two pilgrims to Haifa, and he also worked on the construction of the Shrine, making valuable contributions through his dedication, expert knowledge and experience in building.[13]

In early 1899, 'Abdu'l-Bahá, accompanied by a prominent Lebanese Bahá'í, Ibráhím Khayru'lláh, drove to the site of the future Shrine and, with His own hands, laid the foundation stone.[14] Formerly a Christian, Khayru'lláh had successfully taught the Bahá'í Faith in the United States; he had accompanied the first Western pilgrims to Acre and was on pilgrimage at the time but why he was given the honour of witnessing the laying of the foundation stone is as yet unknown. The location of the stone – when it was laid, and where it is now – is also unknown.

During the early days of construction, the three houses 'Abdu'l-Bahá had rented to the west of the walls of Haifa proved useful to Him as a base. He was able to come along the beach from Acre without entering the town itself and would stay a few days every week without causing too much attention to His activities.[15]

Shortly after the laying of the foundation stone, the workers established the construction site on the spot identified by Bahá'u'lláh eight years earlier. With the basic digging tools then available, it was a labour-intensive job to cut into the mountain to build a flat surface. The next job was to excavate the central area of the site to make a vault that would be below the ground floor level of the Shrine. That involved work on an ancient underground cistern, a big cavity that had been transformed by the ancient Nabatian inhabitants out of a pre-existing cave.

The builders extended that cavity to become the vault to house the sacred remains of the Báb. To the east of the central cavity they built an open section, later used as a route to transport the sarcophagus into the vault. In front of the northern wall of that vault there was a corridor, created by rocks to the west and the foundations of the wall to the east, a space that was to play a special role in the future. The vault was made deep, about three to four metres, and its walls were made of blocks of stone or fine bricks. The rock floor was probably levelled with lime-stucco. Building designs of that time for such a vault included an arched roof.[16]

After the builders completed the vault, they constructed the foundations of the building.[17] The stone foundations to the west rested on the solid rocks of the mountain with a strong lime grout in between the rocks. To the east, because of the nature of the slope, the foundations went deeper.

11

CRISIS AND CONSTRUCTION

Just as good progress on the construction was being made, work came to an abrupt halt. The British Vice-Consul in Haifa, James Monahan, summed up what he saw:

> About the beginning of October [1900] the work of building was stopped when half-finished, and it seems probable that the Turkish government stopped it. However, it is said that it will now soon be resumed. The visit of the Vali (Governor) may perhaps not have been unconnected with this matter.[1]

What had happened, in fact, was that the Haifa authorities had stepped in and told 'Abdu'l-Bahá that He needed a building permit.[2] The deputy governor of Haifa, known as the Qá'im-Maqám, had ruled that the building was in an unsuitable position, too far from the town. Acting on that finding, the head of the Land Registry ordered construction to be stopped forthwith.

There was no religious motivation for the decision. The authorities did not know the real purpose of the building. Representatives of foreign governments in the area did not realize the intended use of the structure either – Monahan referred to the building as 'a large house on Mount Carmel for an unknown purpose'.[3]

'Abdu'l-Bahá himself would have mentioned just one of its purposes – to contain rooms for 'meetings and services',[4] again using the term for a Bahá'í centre, a Ḥaẓíratu'l- Quds. It was starting to become clear that 'Abdu'l-Bahá was moving some of his activities to Haifa, so building a meeting place did not seem as unusual as it would have been had He begun construction when He bought the site four years earlier.

The real objection to the plans was that the local officials wanted to protect their own positions, that well-recognized common tendency in many bureaucracies. A likely influence on their decision originated in the devious machinations of the enemies among the Master's relatives and their associates, who were falsely alleging that 'Abdu'l-Bahá had bought vast parcels of land overlooking Haifa, Acre and the sea on behalf of neighbouring governments. They had told the authorities that representatives of those governments travelled to and from Haifa in disguise to further their conspiracy. They had claimed that the properties were being used to build large warehouses to store arms and ammunition.[5] Taking all these allegations into account, the deputy governor would not want to be seen as acquiescing in a building project if there was even a remote chance that some of the charges might turn out to be true.

The Governor, based in Acre, was not quite as worried. When the case went to him, he appointed his own architect, Ṣálih Effendi, and a Haifa official to study the situation.[6] Their report was favourable to 'Abdu'l-Bahá, pointing out that there were no political or strategic grounds to stop the project. The proposed building would have only six rooms, and it was not totally isolated. There was a monastery nearby and in the vicinity of the site there were buildings owned by the Templers.

Even that wasn't good enough for the buck-passing deputy governor of Haifa, the Qá'im-Maqám, who somehow rejected the report and refused to issue the building permit, saying it needed the consent of the Sultan in far-off Istanbul.

'Abdu'l-Bahá knew that any application sent to the imperial capital would raise suspicions in the mind of the Sultan, and could lead to a prohibition on any building work on the site. He went in person to see the Qá'im-Maqám to see if He could influence him to change his mind. That official said he had no personal enmity to 'Abdu'l-Bahá but admitted he was afraid to take on the responsibility of agreeing to the permit. There was a dramatic conclusion to this episode, as Abdu'l-Bahá later described:

> We left his office together. I thought if I accompanied him to his house it might be fruitful. We arrived at his door but I noticed that it was useless. He climbed the first stair, then the second stair and as he was putting his foot on the third stair he just collapsed and died. I called out, 'Qá'im-Maqám, Qá'im-Maqám'. No use, he was dead![7]

That unexpected and dramatic death removed the bureaucratic barrier to the construction of the Shrine. But there was another hurdle.

For the building work to take place and to safeguard uninterrupted access in the future, 'Abdu'l-Bahá could not rely on the existing narrow, rocky track to the site because it was too difficult to negotiate for camels and mules which were carting in heavy stone and other materials.

'Abdu'l-Bahá wanted a level access path down from above the site[8] so, sometime between mid-1900 and August 1901, He arranged for negotiations for the appropriate strip of land. Usually it would have been a routine transaction to buy such an access path, but not this time. 'Abdu'l-Bahá's antagonistic brothers stepped in.

The results of their meddling were swift. 'Abdu'l-Bahá's secretary, Youness Afroukhteh (Yúnis Khán) tells the story. Induced by these Covenant-breakers, the landowners began to create trouble, and

> encouraged others to lay claim of ownership to a part of that ownerless wilderness and block all possible access routes to the incoming traffic hauling construction materials to the building site. All these activities gradually increased the value of the land on the slope. As soon as the edifice began to take form, the Covenant-breakers spread far and wide the rumour that the structure actually concealed an ammunition dump.[9]

'Abdu'l-Bahá then offered a very good price, many times its real value, but the owner refused to sell because the antagonistic brothers had persuaded the owner to demand a price far higher than 'Abdu'l-Bahá was prepared to pay. He Himself takes up the narrative.

> As much as we tried to buy the land involved, the owner declined to sell. The enemies of the Faith provoked him. After two months he agreed. Then he reneged. Again he agreed. Again he reneged. A third time he agreed and a third time he reneged. He said we should return to him the trees. We accepted. He asked for a fence between the properties. We accepted and told him we would build the wall. He asked for a mediator. Ṣádiq Páshá was named and he agreed.
>
> We arranged for a meeting at Ṣádiq Páshá's house. The owner did not show up. Ṣádiq Páshá went to fetch him; still he would not come and Ṣádiq Páshá returned alone.[10]

There seemed no obvious solution. 'Abdu'l-Bahá said: 'One night I was so hemmed in by my anxieties that I had no other recourse than to recite and repeat over and over again a prayer of the Báb which I had in my possession, the recital of which greatly calmed me.' He later spoke of what eventuated. 'The next morning the owner of the plot himself came to Me, apologized and begged Me to purchase his property.'[11]

Yúnis Khán described what happened in detail. 'Abdu'l-Bahá told the owner he had no further need of the land. The owner replied that it was not his fault, and that 'Abdu'l-Bahá's brother had deceived him by telling him he would double any offer made for the land.

'In any case,' 'Abdu'l-Bahá is reported to have said, 'he pleaded and I refused until he threw himself at my feet and begged me to take the property at no cost; then I sent him to Áqá Riḍá and instructed him to pay the landowner a sum of money and complete the purchase.'[12]

That may have been a general summary of a more detailed situation. Other accounts say that when 'Abdu'l-Bahá woke up late in the morning, his assistant, Ustád Muḥammad-'Alí, told Him that the nephew of the German Consul and the dragoman (aide and interpreter) of the Consul had been waiting to see Him since early that morning.[13] These men told Him that a German woman was prepared to sell Him as much land near the site as He needed. 'Abdu'l-Bahá went to the land transfer office and saw that the documents for an unconditional purchase were already signed and sealed by the Consul, who was the lawyer for the woman.

The dragoman explained that, hearing of His difficulties, they had come to be of service. 'Abdu'l-Bahá asked that an access path to the building site be built on the land and an access wall erected alongside it, stating that He would pay all the expenses. German engineers later did as He requested.

It was the stressful circumstances surrounding the purchase of that vital access route that prompted a now famous heartfelt lament by 'Abdu'l-Bahá in connection with the project to build the Shrine: 'Every stone of that building, every stone of the road leading to it, I have with infinite tears and at tremendous cost, raised and put in position.'[14]

Sometime after the purchase, Phoebe Hearst, an American Bahá'í, donated £500 for the upgrade of the access road that some called for a while 'Hearstway'.[15] 'Abdu'l-Bahá accepted the donation because of Mrs Hearst's sincere motive but in return, He sent her a ring with a

Muḥammad Muṣṭáfa Bagdadi of Beirut, described by Shoghi Effendi as a 'brave and vigilant custodian and bearer of the remains of the Báb'

The insert of this photograph of Mount Carmel shows a close up view of the foundations of the Shrine of the Báb and, behind them, the circle of cypress trees

The two windows at right on the upper floor of the house of 'Abdu'lláh Pá<u>sh</u>á in Acre are of the room where the sacred remains of the Báb were concealed. The room on the roof was built for 'Abdu'l-Bahá

© Denny Allen

A modern-day photograph of the room of Bahíyyih <u>Kh</u>ánum where the casket of the Báb was concealed from 1899 to 1900

Bahá'ís of Burma with the sarcophagus they built for the sacred remains of the Báb

Siyyid Muṣṭáfa Rúmí, an organizer and financier of the construction of the sarcophagus for the casket of the Báb. Martyred in Burma in 1945, he was posthumously named a Hand of the Cause of God

A crate containing the sarcophagus for the casket of the Báb in a house in Haifa some time before 1909. The smaller crate probably contained its lid. The identity of the Bahá'ís has yet to be established

Ali-Kuli Khan, a secretary of 'Abdu'l-Bahá, who worked in the room where the sarcophagus was stored

The circle on this 1918 photograph shows the likely area in Haifa where the casket of the Báb was concealed from 1900 to 1909 in a house rented by 'Abdu'l-Bahá in Sahna'tul-Hanatir (Carriage Square), later called Paris Square and now known as Kiryat-Ha-Mimshala (Government Village)

This Templer building in 'Bethlehem in Galilee', a village near Nazareth, bears some architectural similarities to the Shrine of the Báb

This pathway to the Shrine was for a while called 'Hearstway' after the donor for its upgrade, Phoebe Hearst. She later received from 'Abdu'l-Bahá a ring worth more than the donation

Construction under way of the Shrine of the Báb. Rudimentary terraces are in place.
Photograph by Edward Getsinger

A rudimentary stairway leads to the Shrine under construction.
Photograph by Edward Getsinger

The rear of the Shrine under construction

Behind Edward Getsinger, a Bahá'í pilgrim from the United States, is the construction site of the Shrine where considerable progress had been made

The Shrine of the Báb about the time of the interment of the sacred remains

turquoise stone which He had obtained for a modest price but which was worth more than the donation, thereby demonstrating His integrity. He had his own source of funds in the voluntary payments made to the Head of the Faith under Bahá'í law.[16]

In his memoirs, Raḥmatu'lláh Najaf-Ábádí, the caretaker of the Shrine, wrote that there was an American lady who had offered to pay all the expenses to build the Shrine of the Báb but her offer was not accepted by 'Abdu'l-Bahá, who asked her instead to pay that money to the poor in America.[17] 'Abdu'l-Bahá is reported to have said later that the Christians had always said the propagation of Islam was due to the money of Khadijah (the wealthy wife of Prophet Muhammad), and He did not want those kind of statements made about the Faith.

Funding, nevertheless, was an ongoing problem. Relying on the timely arrival of those payments could test the patience of a saint. 'Abdu'l-Bahá would often have to wait a long time for any cash to arrive. On one occasion he just handed all the money he had received directly to the head mason, who had been waiting for it for a long time.[18]

By encouraging Bahá'ís to purchase property in the vicinity of the site, 'Abdu'l-Bahá was able to provide a buffer for the site of the Shrine. Some Bahá'ís bought parcels of land there and donated them to the Faith. However, the intrigues of His enemies continued, and later, when more land was needed to expand the gardens around the Shrine, they did their utmost to prevent Him from obtaining it.[19]

12

ENEMIES STEP UP ATTACKS

Happiness replaced stress for the Master during those initial stages of building the Shrine. When 'Abdu'l-Bahá was in Haifa directing construction activities, He displayed such an exhilaration that others were caught up in His delight, as his secretary Yúnis Khán described:

> 'Abdu'l-Bahá's description of the future of that location and that edifice was uttered with such joy and excitement that while only the foundation work was commencing and all that could be seen was a large hole in the ground, a few dirt movers, and otherwise an expanse of rough and rugged land, nevertheless one could see with the eye of imagination the immaculate, spotless cleanliness and pristine beauty of the present structure.
>
> 'Abdu'l-Bahá described in detail what portions of the work had been completed and what was planned for construction in the future. He indicated the locations of each flowerbed and the sites of various other ornamental features. The foundation of the edifice was so sound and solid that I frequently expressed my observation to 'Abdu'l-Bahá that in its strength and substance that foundation resembled the foundation of the Faith of God itself.[1]

'Abdu'l-Bahá now took another step to protect the casket containing the sacred remains of the Báb. It had been stored for more than a year in the room of His sister in His house in Acre but there were inherent dangers in keeping it there.

There would be great difficulty in continually keeping secret the existence of something special in a big house where there was a constant coming and going of many people, some of whom were enemies from within His extended family as well as their associates. Had these foes any inkling of the whereabouts of the casket, the security of the precious legacy that had been obtained, concealed and protected with extreme difficulty over the decades could well be in peril. If the capricious and vindictive Sultan, or any other enemies of the Faith, received information that indicated the possible location of the casket of the Báb, there would almost inevitably have been a raid on the house to confiscate the precious relics.[2]

'Abdu'l-Bahá decided that rather than leaving the casket where it was, He would send it to Haifa where trusted Bahá'í custodians could maintain a 24-hour watch and where fewer people were about. Accordingly, in 1900 the casket was secretly removed from the hiding place in His sister's room and taken to the other side of the bay where it was concealed in the house that 'Abdu'l-Bahá had rented in Haifa originally for Western pilgrims.[3]

The Master stored the casket in the sarcophagus, a fact revealed years later in a letter by Ali-Kuli Khan, who had worked as a translator in that room: '. . . I heard, I believe from Mohammad Ali, the Master's servant, that the box containing the Sacred Remains, which had been brought from Persia in the previous months, had been put in that empty sarcophagus. But I knew nothing of this while for many months I sat at the table near the window in that room and did my translations.'[4]

Meanwhile the construction continued at good speed. The local Arab workmen employed by the German Templers to construct similar buildings in the past were experienced and skilled in the techniques required. They were well familiar with the local stone and able to endure the summer heat. They made quick progress. The techniques of building in those days involved the builders sitting on the ground at the site where they used iron adzes to cut down to size the blocks of stone that had been transported there. They climbed up wooden scaffolding inside the structures to complete the walls and build the ceilings.[5]

In spite of 'Abdu'l-Bahá's elation at finally making a good start on the project, He was certain there would be trouble ahead. The Ottoman authorities had been closely observing the activities of the 'Bábís' (Bahá'ís) in the Middle East and the United States.[6] The Ottoman Ambassador to the United States, Ali Ferruh Bey, had investigated the 'Babi sect' in that country and had sent a report dated 11 May 1901 proposing that the Empire make use of 'Abdu'l-Bahá and His followers for political purposes, an idea that came to nothing. He expressed astonishment that there were more than a thousand 'Babis' in Chicago with a range of professionals among their ranks, and predicted that the 'sect' would gain astonishing strength in the United States. He was aware of the activities of the Master's jealous half-brothers Muḥammad-'Alí and Badí'u'lláh.

The Ambassador said that 'Abdu'l-Bahá had contacted him and asked him to allow American 'Babis' to visit him in Acre. He had promised to assist on the condition – which he said was accepted by 'Abdu'l-Bahá – that the Bábís would express loyalty to the Sultan. A group of not more than 15 people would be allowed to visit Acre, but only for a week, and furthermore, no property was to be bought around Acre using American capital. (There is no evidence confirming any such agreement by 'Abdu'l-Bahá along those lines.)

Soon 'Abdu'l-Bahá's enemies stepped up their machinations. In 1901 his cousin Majdi'd-Dín, with the backing of Muḥammad-'Alí, went to Damascus to meet with the Governor of Syria, Nazim Pasha.[7] He took with him plenty of money for bribes, much of it coming from mortgaging the Mansion of Bahá'u'lláh, a holy place for the Bahá'ís.[8]

In their attempt to seize the reins of the Bahá'í community from 'Abdu'l-Bahá, the disloyal relatives were misrepresenting the building on Mount Carmel as a fortress for rebellion against the Ottoman Empire.[9] They raised suspicions about Bahá'í gatherings in Acre by alleging that the American pilgrims were actually military advisers or spies.[10]

Alerted to their plot, 'Abdu'l-Bahá predicted that the conspirators, including ringleader Muḥammad-'Alí, would be caught up in their own web. Meanwhile, He took the precautionary step of suspending pilgrimage by Western and Eastern Bahá'ís to Acre and Haifa because their very presence, not to mention the meetings and festivities associated with them, risked heightening the suspicions aroused by the allegations.[11]

But 'Abdu'l-Bahá did not halt the work on the site. There was no point in trying to disguise the fact that a substantial building was under construction.

Upon receiving the bribed Governor's report in the Ottoman capital, Sultan 'Abdu'l-Hamíd[12] became alarmed. He issued orders that the previously relaxed restrictions on all the brothers be reimposed.[13] 'Abdu'l-Bahá was incarcerated again in Acre on 20 August 1901.[14]

As observed by the British vice-consul in Haifa, James Monahan, the Sultan's order required 'Abdu'l-Bahá and His half-brothers not to step outside Acre.[15] 'Abdu'l-Bahá was already spending most of His time living in modest circumstances there, apart from visits to supervise the work on the site, but his half-brothers were forced to come into the city from their home in the far more comfortable country mansion in Bahjí. His cousin Majdi'd-Dín was brought back from his home in Tiberias.[16] The plotting had backfired against the plotters, just as 'Abdu'l-Bahá had predicted.

The Sultan's edict seriously inconvenienced 'Abdu'l-Bahá but construction work did not stop for very long. By 31 December 1901, Monahan was reporting that although the Persian Government was requesting that the 'Babist leaders' be confined, the 'construction of the Babist house on Mount Carmel . . . which has been several times stopped by the Turkish Authorities and resumed, was again resumed and is being carried on actively.'[17]

From the time of the Sultan's order in 1901 until the completion of the Shrine, 'Abdu'l-Bahá could not visit Haifa to supervise the building work at the site. He had to direct the construction by remote control, hearing reports from his staff and issuing instructions.[18] From His prayer room on the roof of the House of 'Abdu'lláh Pá<u>sh</u>á, He could gaze in the direction of the site where the men were building the Shrine, but even if He had powerful binoculars, He would not have been able to see any detail from some eleven kilometres away. He had to rely on reports. His secretary Yúnis <u>Kh</u>án later wrote: 'The progress of the construction on the Shrine of the Báb on Mount Carmel was very slow at this time, but thank God, it never slowed to a halt.'[19]

As the construction continued, so did the machinations of 'Abdu'l-Bahá's enemies. They did not relent in using the Shrine project to play on the fears of the Ottoman rulers, continuing to allege that the building had military purposes as part of an attempt to rebel against the Ottoman Empire. The aim of this deceit was to seize control of the Bahá'í community by having 'Abdu'l-Bahá exiled – or even hanged for treason.

The Ottomans had security and religious concerns about efforts that they suspected challenged the position of the Sultan as caliph. As a Turkish researcher has noted, it was 'against the background of widespread Salafi activities in Syria that the Bahá'ís were also presented as dangerous . . .'[20]

In 1904 a new Governor of Acre, one hostile to 'Abdu'l-Bahá, took up his post. Taking advantage of the change, the supporters of

Muḥammad-'Alí used bribes to persuade some Acre residents to sign a document containing false allegations against 'Abdu'l-Bahá. They then sent the petition to Istanbul. Among the many allegations was that 'Abdu'l-Bahá had secretly raised an army of 30,000 men. Another was that He was engaged in 'the construction of a fortress and a vast ammunition depot on Mt. Carmel'.[21]

The petition prompted an intervention by Ottoman investigators, a dangerous development for the project to build the Shrine. Bahá'í historians have referred to the arrival of investigators in 1904 and 1907 to inquire into the activities of 'Abdu'l-Bahá, including the building of the structure on Mount Carmel. Recent research suggests that 1905 is perhaps a more accurate date.[22]

'Abdu'l-Bahá responded to the arrival of the commissioners by advising the Bahá'ís to temporarily leave the city. Some seventy went to Egypt. He also halted all pilgrimages. He met with the commissioners several times and told them the charges against Him were baseless. He showed them the Writings of Bahá'u'lláh to point out that He, His father's successor, would never be involved in any plot to overthrow Ottoman rule.[23]

The allegations that had been put to the authorities by the foes of 'Abdu'l-Bahá charged that He was rebelling against the government, and that He was intent on establishing His own rule and building fortifications. They also alleged that His followers, seeking support for 'Abdu'l-Bahá's so-called political ambitions, had incited revolt by hoisting a banner in Galilee as well as among the Bedouin people beyond Jordan.[24]

'Abdu'l-Bahá later wrote about the accusations He had faced when He met the Commission and showed how they linked the Shrine with insurrection:

> Among his [Muḥammad-'Ali's] slanders was that the Shrine on Mount Carmel was a fortress that I had built strong and impregnable – this when the building under construction compriseth six rooms – and that I had named it Medina the Resplendent, while I had named the Holy Tomb[25] Mecca the Glorified. Yet another was that had I established an independent sovereignty and that – God forbid! God forbid! God forbid! – I had summoned all the believers to join me in his massive wrong doing. How dire, O my Lord, is his slander!

> Yet again, he claimeth that since the Holy Shrine hath become a point visited by pilgrims from all over the world, great damage will accrue to this Government and people.[26]

When the commissioners asked him why the Americans came to Acre, 'Abdu'l-Bahá told them it was to visit the Shrine of Bahá'u'lláh and to learn of spiritual matters.[27] In a talk He gave to local Bahá'ís at the time, 'Abdu'l-Bahá demonstrated the ridiculous nature of the charges made against Him:

> How can a prisoner and an exile establish a new government? Anyone who could do that deserves to be congratulated . . . It would be a miracle for one who is a captive in the hands of the authorities to build fortifications strong enough to be capable of withstanding bombardment by powerful naval ships.[28]

He expressed surprise at the complaint about the banner, noting that government agents posted all over the country had failed to see it. As far as the ownership of land went: 'I am willing to sell them all for the small sum of one thousand liras.'[29]

The commission decided to take no action. When asked at the time how long 'Abdu'l-Bahá thought the Covenant-breakers could continue to attack him, He replied that in four years' time they would lose their power to oppose. His prediction was to prove accurate.[30]

According to Bahá'í historians, the enemies of 'Abdu'l-Bahá decided to re-open their case against Him. A new Governor was put in place and new officials were appointed, including those in charge of the telegraph and post offices. The enemies sent a new petition to Istanbul, listing various allegations. The findings of these officials could determine whether 'Abdu'l-Bahá would be sentenced to exile or death. They met with those who had supported Muḥammad-'Alí's petition.

'Abdu'l-Bahá declined an invitation to meet with these commissioners,[31] who had taken evidence from the accusers and accepted the false allegations as true. 'Abdu'l-Bahá neatly summarized the situation – the accusers had functioned as 'plaintiffs, witnesses and judge'.[32] Urged by a messenger to show the members of the Commission His usual deference, kindness and hospitality, 'Abdu'l-Bahá replied:

> I have always been the first to offer hospitality to a newly-arrived official, regardless of rank, and you yourself know well my gentle and loving nature. But this Commission has come to prove the false accusations made in these testimonials against me, and therefore if I express any greetings or welcome them, or offer hospitality and friendliness, they may mistakenly consider my motive to be fear, flattery and appeasement, whereas we are innocent of these accusations. It is not befitting for me to express such sentiments, for they should be allowed to conduct their investigation free from all influences. 'We rely on none but God.'[33]

Rumours circulated that the authorities would exile 'Abdu'l-Bahá to the remote deserts of Fezzan (Fizan), a dreaded area of southern Libya that had been controlled by the Ottomans since the 17th century. He took no notice and went ahead attending to repairs on His house, planting trees and buying and storing fuel for the winter. It was clear that He did not think He would be going anywhere.

The rumours, however, had some substance. According to an official Ottoman report on 10 June 1905:

> Ahmad Abbas [sic], who was previously exiled to 'Akká due to rendering service to the expansion and dissemination of the Bábí sect and, as was understood from the actual petitions, owing to continuing to follow the same harmful doctrine (*meslek-ii-sakim*), the Imperial rescript (*irade*) of His Highness the Caliph . . . decreed that the aforementioned and his accomplices be banished to Fizan.[34]

A shipping agent offered Him safe transport out of the Holy Land but He refused saying: 'the exalted Báb and Bahá'u'lláh, in situations far more dangerous than this, chose not to defend themselves and kept their peace and composure: so I, too, follow the path of those sanctified beings and choose to remain rather than flee. Therefore, I will not leave.'[35]

The commissioners visited the building site, where there was now a six-room building. 'Abdu'l-Bahá was not present, being confined to Acre. They noted its deep walls and strength. One of them placed his hand on a corner of the Shrine and said in Turkish: 'This is a solid fortress.'[36] They thought the fact that there were vaults under the building was very significant because it backed up the claim that 'Abdu'l-Bahá was building a fort, despite the fact that there were large buildings of a similar design in and near Haifa, and none of them were forts. Prompted by the rumours spread by the Covenant-breakers that arms were stored in the vaults, the commissioners asked workers at the site how many such basements had been built underground.[37]

In their report of 6 July 1905 the commissioners referred to the exile of 'Abdu'l-Bahá and others as 'an effective lesson' on the grounds that Babism had beliefs contrary to religion, that it was the cause of much mischief and revolts in Iran, and that its followers distributed their superstitions by publishing all sorts of books and newspapers in Egypt.[38]

Around this time, when 'Abdu'l-Bahá's safety and the Shrine project were in the balance, He revealed a poignant prayer of great literary and spiritual beauty:

> O God, my God! Thou seest me plunged in an ocean of anguish, held fast to the fires of tyranny, and weeping in the darkness of the night. Sleepless I toss and turn upon my bed, mine eyes straining to behold the morning light of faithfulness and trust. I agonize even as a fish, its inward parts afire as it leapeth about in terror upon the sand, yet I ever look for Thy bestowals to appear from every side.[39]

One dramatic afternoon, the ship carrying the members of the Commission left the port of Haifa and headed for nearby Acre. The Bahá'ís in both cities were certain they would apprehend 'Abdu'l-Bahá and haul him away as a prisoner. At sunset, as the ship approached, 'Abdu'l-Bahá was seen calmly pacing all alone at His house near the great sea wall of Acre.[40] Some Bahá'ís began to weep.

Then, to the shock and relief of those watching, the ship suddenly changed direction and went out to sea. As 'Abdu'l-Bahá later wrote:

> The Commission hath now returned to the seat of the Caliphate [Istanbul], and reports of a most frightful nature are coming in daily from that city. However, praised be God, 'Abdu'l-Bahá remained composed and unperturbed. To none do I bear ill will because of this defamation. I have made all my affairs conditioned upon His irresistible will and I am waiting indeed in perfect happiness, to

> offer my life and be prepared for whatever dire affliction may be in store.[41]

It turned out the Commission had been recalled via a secret telegram from Istanbul because of an assassination attempt on the Sultan. He had summoned them home so that they might discover the source of the conspiracy. This was an assassination attempt by Armenians on 21 July 1905 when a bomb exploded at the Friday prayer ceremony at the Yildiz Palace. The Sultan escaped unharmed.[42]

'Abdu'l-Bahá later wrote that at the moment the ship changed course, the guns of God had gone into action, removing the chains from His neck and placing them on the neck of 'Abdu'l-Hamid, the Sultan of Turkey. He also referred to the incident as the 'cannon blast of divine confirmation'.[43] Within a few years, the Sultan was deposed and made a prisoner.

Upon their return to the capital, the commissioners[44] presented their report to the Sultan. They said the building was indeed a fortress, and even upheld the other charges. But their report was put aside due to much more important events on the minds of the sovereign and his officials.

13

THE BUILDING

The Shrine, completed by 1907 when the Western pilgrims first visited it, was a flat-roofed, north-facing, rectangular stone building with a pleasant, roughly-hewn, golden-brown limestone exterior. Its frontage measured some 26 metres wide (East-West) and was 16 metres long (North-South). From the outside it had much in common with some other Templer buildings in the Haifa area. Internally, however, it was different. It had six internal rooms, two rows of three each.

Walls

The Shrine was built with two kinds of stone. For the inside course of the exterior walls, the masons used hard stone blocks, probably transported from the ruins of the Crusader castle in Atlit, about 12 kilometres south of Haifa.[1] This expensive stone, ideal for a solid building, was dense and heavy, the weight of each block ranging from 12 to 50 kilograms. A limestone grout was used in between those blocks.

The blocks of stone had been cut to a rough size before transportation to the site. Further work was done on them there. Camels, and perhaps donkeys, mules and horses, transported the stone to the site.[2] There was a road to the site from the south that avoided the route from the north, but it nevertheless remained a steep and difficult climb up the mountain and down the access path.

The masons clad the sturdy walls with an attractive yellowish limestone obtained from Mount Carmel itself[3] and cut to size at the site. Each block had different dimensions and irregular exteriors. A smooth, different stone was used for the edgings of the windows and buttresses. These and other stone blocks would have come from inland and were similar to that used by the Templers for their buildings.

The builders still used the traditional method of building the walls to more than two-thirds of the eventual height of the roof, before turning arches in from both sides. To carry out this part of the construction they stood on scaffolds and built wooden supports.[4] High up on the walls and encircling the Shrine, the builders laid a course of yellow blocks, a decorative design typical of many Templer buildings.

Roof

Once the arches were made, the builders continued the outside walls to their final height. They used a mixture of soil and stones to fill in the gaps between the curve of the arches and the wall itself.[5] That was topped with lime and later by asphalt to allow a stone roof to be built.

Buttresses

The builders incorporated buttresses as integral parts of the exterior walls to counteract any tremors or movements of the earth down below. These were vital because Mount Carmel is a honeycomb of cavities where the water moves under the surface from the top to the bottom, taking with it fine particles, producing sub-surface caves and facilitating the movement of the sub-surface rocks. The deep foundations of the Shrine, together with the buttresses, limited the danger of cracks opening in the building's walls, floor or roof. On a buttress at the northwest there remains a number written into the stone but the meaning is as yet unknown.[6]

Windows

Just above the top level of the buttresses in the facade of the front and rear of the building, the masons built five 'porthole' style windows, with the one above the central doors bigger than the others. Porthole style windows were also put in the internal walls dividing the rooms. This was to facilitate total air circulation. The facade porthole windows were framed and glassed, but the inside ones were only connecting holes with neither frame nor glass. The builders also made six windows at the front and rear using semi-circle arches. They put in similar windows on the sides.

Interior

The masons constructed arched ceilings over the two rows of three rooms. In both rows of rooms there were internal doors that connected the western and eastern rooms with the middle rooms. In later years arches replaced the doors into the original central rear room.

Doors

The inside doors were of solid wood except for their arched tops, which had a sunrise design of glass framed by wood. For the entrances to the building, the men installed glassy white double-doors made of iron sheets with decorations punched over them. The decorations on the front and back doors included a crescent moon and star symbol (a common Turkish or Islamic symbol) as well as rosettes and wreaths. The decorations on the side doors, which are slightly wider than the front and rear doors, are generally similar.

Terraces

A path of crushed white stone led from near the circle of cypress trees down along the side of the Shrine. Photographs taken by an American pilgrim show that as the Shrine walls were being completed (1900–01) there were rudimentary terraces in front of the building, and a path leading up from the slope below. It came to a stop at the terrace at the level of the Shrine.

A photograph taken in 1904 shows three terraces below the Shrine with walls made of stones. Later a massive stone wall was built to the north. Stone and rubble were tipped into the gap between the wall and the foundations of the building to make a wide terrace. The front wall had recessed sections to ensure its stability.

Reservoir

At the northwest of the Shrine, 'Abdu'l-Bahá arranged for a water reservoir (more accurately termed a cistern) to be built. It collected rainwater via downpipes from the roof of the Shrine.

Because He was imprisoned in Acre He was not able to oversee the construction, which was undertaken by German and Ottoman engineers. They left the work unfinished. This caused the north wall to collapse and wasted a lot of effort. 'Abdu'l-Bahá Himself then designed the cistern, which was built much stronger. It remains there to this day. Making a point about the size of the reservoir, 'Abdu'l-Bahá is reported to have mentioned that this was not a water reservoir but a 'sea' (it held about 340 cubic metres). He dedicated it in honour of a relative of the Báb, Mírzá Muḥammad-Báqir Afnán.[7] Its dimensions were approximately seven metres deep, seven metres long and 14 metres wide. There was (and still is) a wall with a big window-type opening which divides this cistern into two times seven metres.

The cistern was about nine metres from the Shrine and had two access points, one to the north-west on the terrace next to the retaining wall and the other a couple of metres from that point on the pathway. The workers took water from the cistern for the construction of the Shrine.

'Abdu'l-Bahá had also built a second cistern above and to the south-west of the Shrine. It remains an open question as to its purpose or how it was filled. It might have fed water to the header tank above the reservoir to the north-west.

Naming the doors

To acknowledge the contribution of the three stonemasons to the construction of the Shrine, 'Abdu'l-Bahá named the front door after Ustád Áqá 'Alí-Ashraf, and the door to what is now the eastern prayer room of the Shrine of the Báb after his brother, Ustád Áqá Bálá. The door to the eastern prayer room to what later became the Shrine of 'Abdu'l-Bahá was named after Ustád 'Abdu'l-Karím.[8]

The Master was to name the western door to the antechamber of the Shrine of the Báb after Ḥájí Amín,[9] the second trustee of the Ḥuqúq'u'lláh, the fund contributed to by Bahá'ís.[10] He had shown exemplary loyalty and enthusiasm during the last years of Bahá'u'lláh's life, served the Master right through His 29 years as Head of the Faith, and continued his work in the difficult first years of Shoghi Effendi's ministry.

Ḥájí Amín was a respected businessman who had married into a Bábí family and became a follower shortly after the Báb's martyrdom. He had seen Bahá'u'lláh in the Holy Land in the public baths – he found that by coincidence he was sitting next to Him – and had recognized Him immediately as a Manifestation of God. He then returned to Persia to sell his belongings to serve his new Faith, and became assistant to the first trustee of the Ḥuqúq'u'lláh, Ḥájí Sháh-Muḥammad-i-Manshádí, one of those entrusted by Bahá'u'lláh to safely conceal the sacred remains of the Báb, and who was martyred in 1880.[11] Ḥájí Amín then became the trustee ('Amín': trusted) of the Ḥuqúq'u'lláh. He would travel about Persia, making his living by trading and by writing for the illiterate; and he would collect letters that Bahá'ís wanted to send to Bahá'u'lláh as well as distribute Tablets from Bahá'u'lláh.

In 1891, he was imprisoned for his faith for two years in Qazvín with Ḥájí Akhund,[12] one of those who concealed the sacred remains of the Báb. He was then transferred in chains and fetters to spend a year in jail in Tehran. Ḥájí Amín said that one cent spent in the path of God was worth more than all the riches spent on personal desires. He continued as trustee during the Ministry of 'Abdu'l-Bahá, and so trusted was he that the Master indicated to the Bahá'ís of Persia that any receipt issued by Ḥájí Amín was as if it were directly from 'Abdu'l-Bahá Himself. Ḥájí Amín visited the Master in Acre and Haifa, and joined Him for a time while He was in Europe. In the course of his duties he travelled all over Persia, Turkmenistan, Turkey and elsewhere. He passed away in 1928, after being nursed in his bedridden days by his assistant Ḥájí Ghulám-Riḍá.[13] Shoghi Effendi wrote a tribute to the services of Ḥájí Amín and his high rank in the Faith. He is buried in the Bahá'í cemetery in Tehran, and his name will be forever associated with the Shrine of the Báb.

The Master named the western door of what would later be the Shrine of 'Abdu'l-Bahá after Mírzá Abu'l-Faḍl (1844–1914), one of the greatest teachers of the Faith, the most celebrated Bahá'í scholar of his times, and whom the Master described as 'peerless', 'erudite and learned' and 'a standard bearer of the oneness of the world of humanity'.[14] His books, 'Abdu'l-Bahá said, 'contain incontrovertible proofs and evidences concerned this impregnable, blessed Cause'.[15] His masterpiece is said to be *Fará'id* (Priceless Jewels), his response to a critique by a prominent cleric. He had been a prominent Islamic scholar, head of a religious college, and was introduced to the Faith by a humble blacksmith. His conversion resulted in him losing his position and being imprisoned, initially for five months and later for 22 months. Most of the Jews of Iran who became Bahá'ís learned of the Faith through his writings.

He travelled widely spreading the teachings, including to Samarqand and Bukhara, and in 1894 was in the presence of the Master for ten months before he went to Cairo, where he brought theological students into the Faith, and then travelled to France where he clarified the teachings for the local Bahá'ís. The Master sent him to the United States to counter the attempts of Khayru'lláh to divide the Bahá'í community. He lived first in Beirut and then in Alexandria. He passed away in Cairo in January 1914; a beloved American Bahá'í, Lua Getsinger (d. 1916), is buried next to him.

On 13 February 1914 at a Memorial Service for him at the Shrine of the Báb, 'the gentle, mellow voice of 'Abdul-Bahá was raised, now in a low and anon in a higher tone, chanting the Visiting Tablet'.[16] In the reception room, the Master delivered an eloquent eulogy, an excerpt of which is:

> Truly he was a worthy man! Strange, passing strange, that there was not a breath of self-desire in this person . . . In short, the hearts of all the believers of the world were attached to him. He was the brilliant lamp of the Cause, the shining light of guidance, the sparkling star of knowledge, the luminous orb of understanding and a sea tumultuous with the waves of wisdom.[17]

Shoghi Effendi named him an Apostle of Bahá'u'lláh.

According to Shoghi Effendi, the Master said that so precious is 'the Báb's holy dust' that the very earth surrounding the edifice enshrining this dust was endowed with such potency as to have inspired Him in bestowing the names of the five doors.[18] This is mentioned in the Tablet 'Abdu'l-Bahá revealed about those doors:

> He is God!
> A copy of this Tablet should be bestowed upon each of the mentioned personages and the original must be kept in the Háḍíratu'l-Quds.[19]
>
> He is God! O God and my Beloved! Praise be upon Thee for Thy greatness and thanks be unto Thee for Thy generosity. Thou grantest what Thou dost wish, Thou willest what Thou desirest, and enablest whosoever Thou inclinest in whatsoever Thou ordainest.
>
> All things are in Thy grasp and destiny resides in Thy hand. Thou bestowest honor on whomsoever Thou wishest, endowest sustenance

In the distance the walls of the Shrine are up but not completed in this photograph by Edward Getsinger

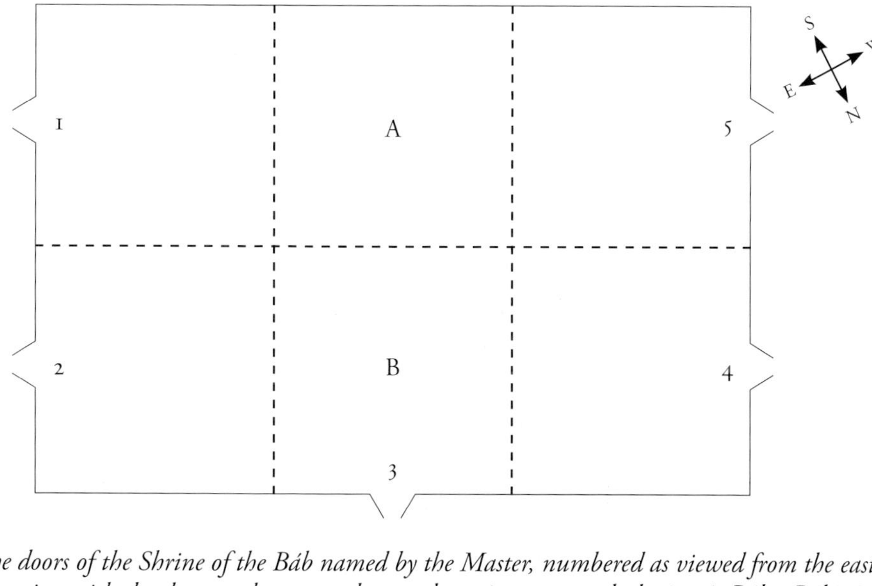

The doors of the Shrine of the Báb named by the Master, numbered as viewed from the east, starting with the then south-eastern door and moving counterclockwise. 1. Báb-i Bálá. 2. Báb-i-Karím. 3. Báb-i-Ashraf. 4. Báb-i-Fadl. 5. Báb-i-Amín. The rooms above the tombs of the Báb (A) and 'Abdu'l-Bahá (B) are also shown in the diagram

Ustád Áqá 'Alí-Ashraf, a stonemason from Baku, who worked on and donated to the building project. The front door of the Shrine is named after him

Ustád Áqá Bálá, a stonemason from Baku. Like his brother, Ashraf, he worked on and donated to the building project. The door to what was then the rear eastern room (now the central eastern room) was named after him. A photograph of their fellow stonemason, Ustád 'Abdu'l-Karím, after whom the front eastern room is named, has yet to be located

Ḥájí Abu'l-Ḥasan-i-Ardikání (Ḥájí Amín) who was the second trustee of the Ḥuqúq'u'lláh, the fund contributed to by Bahá'ís. 'Abdu'l-Bahá named what was then the rear western door, now the central western door, after him

Mírzá Abu'l-Faḍl (1844–1914), the most celebrated Bahá'í scholar of his times. 'Abdu'l-Bahá named the front western door after him

When at this circle of cypress trees in 1891 Bahá'u'lláh pointed to the site for the Shrine of the Báb, they were slim saplings and at that time owned by the one who planted them, Wilhelm Deiss, an early Templer settler

This view from the uphill side of the cypress circle was taken in the early 1900s. Note the stone surrounding and the grape vines in the foreground. It was published in Views of Acca, Haifa, Mt. Carmel, and Other Places *(Chicago, 1911)*

on anyone Thou desirest and deniest it to whom Thou willest.

All goods are in Thy hand and Thy station is benevolence. Thou art the All-Bountiful, the All-Giving, the Compassionate, and the Merciful.

A number rose in service of the Háḍíratu'l-Quds and with utmost devotion and spirit exerted much effort. Some others had spiritual attachment and profoundly desired to aid in the labour and work of that sacred Shrine.

Therefore the water-cistern is named after the illustrious Afnán of the sacred Lote-Tree, the honored Mírzá Báqir.

The first entrance on the eastern side is named the Báb-i-Bálá, and the second door on the east named the Báb-i-Karím, named after Ustád 'Abdu'l-Karím. The northern door is the Báb-i-Ashraf; and the first door on the western side is to be known as the Báb-i-Faḍl, while the second on the same side will be the Báb-i-Amín.

By these names are meant: Áqá 'Alí-Ashraf, Áqá Ustád 'Abdu'l-Karím, Áqá Bálá, the illustrious Abú'l-Faḍl and the honored Amín. These designations must endure forever. Thus the Almighty inspired Me by the earth of the point of adoration of the Supreme Concourse. 'A 'A.[20]

Early descriptions of the building

An American Bahá'í, Florence Khan, gave her impressions of the 'Tomb' as she saw it in 1906.[21] She described the edifice as 'an imposing structure . . . two stories high . . . and which will, when finished, I understand, have an added story.'

Florence praised 'Abdu'l-Bahá's achievement in building this Tomb, though Himself a captive, describing Him as the 'humblest and mightiest of the servants of Bahá'u'lláh'. She said that according to Bahá'í prophecy, ships of all nations would one day ride down in the blue Gulf of Acre,[22] and how, up gleaming flights of white marble stairs, pilgrim kings, gifts in their hands, would be climbing to the Shrine. Her daughter, the writer and historian Marzieh Gail, continues:

> One day when she was invited to drive with the ladies to Haifa Florence asked them about the nine cypress trees on the slope of Mount Carmel, where Bahá'u'lláh had walked . . . Khánum[23] pointed out

the path to her and pressed some jasmine blossoms into her hand. Florence climbed up to the 'sacred circle' and counted the trees, and listened to the stillness . . . She prayed and meditated in the gentle, fresh breeze and looked at the vineyards below the Báb's Shrine and thought of the Holy Ones, all the way back to the Prophet Elijah[24] (his cave not far away), who had trodden the paths of 'the Mountain of God'.

She thought how 'Abdu'l-Bahá, Himself a prisoner, slandered by the Covenant-breakers, therefore suspected by the aroused authorities who were His captors, had against all odds raised up the Shrine of the Bab (the location of His sacred remains, near as they were by then, still a secret to her).Under the turquoise sky the fruit trees, their emerald branches glowing with golden oranges and red pomegranates, begemmed the terrace of the Shrine.[25]

In 1907 more pilgrims arrived from the United States and visited the building, but 'Abdu'l-Bahá could not accompany them to Mount Carmel because He remained a prisoner in the grim stone city of Acre across the bay.

One of those pilgrims was Corinne True.[26] A driving force behind the building of the Bahá'í Temple in Wilmette, Illinois, Mrs True wrote of her experiences:

> At half past two we went to . . . the home of Abbas Effendi, to meet Rhooah [Ruha] Khánum who had invited us to drive with her to the Holy Tomb of the Báb on the side of Mt. Carmel.
>
> The blessed Master's carriage drove up for us and our hearts almost beat aloud to realize we were to drive in His carriage, with His beautiful daughter, to that Holy Tomb of the Báb, which every believer in the world knows about . . .
>
> A great interest existed in our hearts to see thoroughly this wonderful Tomb, and this desire had grown out of the work we had been doing for the Temple in America. After seeing its massive walls and solid masonry, we did not wonder that the Turkish Government might believe that the Master was building a great military fort.
>
> This Tomb is built to last for thousands of years, and one can quite believe it will after seeing it. There is a flower garden in front of this building and the wife of the keeper gathered a lovely bunch

of red roses and brought them as a gift to us and later she came with a handful of violets.

After Rhooah Khanum had explained the inner rooms – three in breadth, and, when complete, three in depth[27] – we came out of the building to find this keeper's dear little wife had placed four chairs in front of the building and was waiting to serve us a cup of Persian tea, and we sat in that wonderful place, looking over to Acca and down to Elijah's cave and the wide sweep of the bay, and we knew there was nowhere else on earth another such a place . . .[28]

A few months later, in April 1907, Thornton Chase, whom 'Abdu'l-Bahá had designated the 'first American believer' and who was on pilgrimage with a group of Bahá'ís from Chicago, visited the building. He described the view from the home on the lower slopes of Mount Carmel of Mírzá Asadu'lláh, the Bahá'í who, at the direction of the Master, had transferred the sacred remains within and from Persia.

The view was fine of the city below and of the Tomb of the Bab high up on the mountain side above. We could scarcely appreciate the sacredness of that historic ground, but as we looked up to the Tomb and thought of its meaning, of the wonderful lives of the Bab and of Baha'o'llah, of their sufferings and apparent defeat at the hands of oppressors, and of the victories which are now following the Word of Truth, for which they suffered, we began to realise that we had indeed entered the border of the 'Holy Land', the land that Abraham knew, where Melchizedek dwelt, where Elijah prophesied and sacrificed on Carmel unto the Lord whose fire descended upon his altar and put to shame the hosts of Baal.[29]

He described walking down from his hotel (Hotel Pross) at the top of Mount Carmel and his visit to the Shrine:

The next day [11 April 1907] we walked to the Tomb of the Bab. We went on the smooth, broad road along the ridge until we came to the top of the trail which goes almost directly down the side, the same on which we had seen donkeys loaded with wood picking their way the day before. It was very steep and all of loose, crumbling stones. The sides of the mountain are terraced and cultivated everywhere. The larger loose stones are gathered into walls; the rich reddish brown soil and smaller stones are leveled or gently sloped from the foot of one wall to the top of another, thus making steps from ten to twenty or thirty feet wide, in which are fig and olive trees, grapes and vegetables. Men and women were loosening the soil with mattocks.

After going down about 1,000 feet we came to the road and found a neat carriage way between walls leading from the main roadway to the tomb.[30] It is a square [sic.; it was oblong] of brownish yellow limestone with white iron paneled doors, simple in architecture and with little outside ornament. A considerable space was cut out from the side of the mountain and leveled around the tomb. A portion of it is a stone surface in which is the mouth of a large cistern for water. Another portion is a flower garden, beyond which is the house of the caretaker, a Persian Bahai.[31] He lives there with his wife and baby and has an Arab assistant.

When we came onto the stone platform we saw no one, but in a few minutes the Arab appeared, came over to us and said 'Acca' and 'Abbas Effendi'.[32] We smiled and nodded assent. He went to the garden and brought a flower to each of us. Then the caretaker, Rahmatu'llah,[33] came from the house with his little baby boy and greeted us. He brought out chairs and I asked him to sit with the baby for a picture . . . But the picture was never taken, for just then two Persians appeared, who had come up the trail from below. They greeted him joyfully with the 'Greatest Name',[34] embracing him, and then, as we also repeated that Name, they took us in their arms with expressions of great gladness and praises to God.

They were M. Mohammed Ali Yazdi and Hadji Mohammed Schushtari of Cairo with his seven year old boy . . .

Then the door of the tomb was opened and we were invited to enter. It is simple and beautiful, although it is not finished. It is divided into three large compartments, a center and two sides, and these into sections named after notable Babis and Bahais. The floor of the centre is slightly raised. The roof is in arches, those of the sides being at right angles to the arches of the center. We bowed in silence for a few minutes, then withdrew and bade our friends adieu, while they exclaimed again and again – 'Koosh amadeed! Koosh amadeed!' – the Persian expression for 'You are welcome!' As we left the road and began to climb the trail we looked back and saw them going into the

> little grove of ten cypress trees[35] in a circle on the hillside just above the tomb. It is said that Baha'o'llah used often to sit in that grove which commands a beautiful view of the sea and the Valley of Acca.[36]

Thornton Chase took photographs during his visit. One shows the terrace in front of the Shrine and the Shrine itself. The fenced garden is comprised of small shrubs. A photograph taken, probably by Mr Chase, of the Shrine from the north-west shows the two entrances to the cistern, one with an iron fence and a loop above, presumably to attach a rope with a bucket.[37]

Another Bahá'í who occupies an important place in the history of the Faith, Roy Wilhelm of the United States,[38] also visited the Shrine at that time. His description conveys the loving relationship between the Eastern and Western Bahá'ís:

> [We] visited the Tomb of the Báb, which is about a mile above Haifa on Mt. Carmel and which overlooks the city and the bay. The Tomb faces 'Akká, which place one can plainly see on a clear day.
>
> I preceded the others a half hour in order to make some photographs before the sun was too low. Upon reaching the Tomb I found only one room open and within were several Persians sitting about a table. They did not understand English, but by tapping my camera and making signs I made my wishes known and received permission to take some pictures.
>
> I saw upon the finger of one of them, a venerable man with flowing white beard, a ring such as is worn by many of the believers.[39] As he was close to me, I whispered in his ear in Arabic the universal Bahá'í greeting;[40] he immediately cried it aloud, and as he grasped me in his arms and kissed me on both cheeks, the tears came into his eyes. Then they all crowded round, pressing my hands, and I knew that I was among friends. In the meeting of the West with the East is fulfilled the prophecies of the books.[41]

Vision

In 1907, while 'Abdu'l-Bahá was still confined within the wall of Acre, He expressed His vision of the future of the Shrine and its surroundings, and spoke of their spiritual significance:

> All these Prophets and chosen ones . . . affirmed that the Tabernacle of the Lord would be raised on Mount Carmel, beneath which the representatives of the Most Great Peace would assemble and from whence they would bestow a New Order upon the world . . . This land is Palestine. It is a Holy Land . . . The Shrine of the Báb shall be raised in the most excellent manner.[42]

In addition, toward the close of that year, 'Abdu'l-Bahá gave the pilgrims an outline of the spiritual history of the mountain combined with a vision of the future:

> This mountain [Carmel] is where Israel's prophets passed their nights in prayers. Every step of it has been blessed by the footsteps of the prophets . . . This land will be the envy of the world, the centre of arts and sciences. 'Akká and Haifa will be connected and all the vacant lands will be cultivated.[43] All these caves that you see have been the abode of the prophets, step by step. Every atom of this soil is holy. All the prophets, while praying, longed to reach this day and give the glad tidings of the coming of the Lord. They prophesied that the Lord of Hosts would come and the tent of the Lord would be pitched on Mount Carmel . . . In all these mountains and caves the prophets of God prayed at night, shed tears, and longed to be with us in these days of the Blessed Beauty.

Then He spoke of His confinement, and issued an exhortation to the Bahá'ís:

> Since I am a prisoner and cannot move, you make a pilgrimage on My behalf. My utmost desire is to go and visit in freedom, but I cannot. You go on behalf of 'Abdu'l-Bahá and make a pilgrimage to all of the Holy Places . . . and beseech God's bounty. I cannot go. I am a prisoner. I am reincarcerated, and I have no permission to go out. The government prohibits me.[44]

It is recorded that about this time He spoke of His vision for the Shrine:

> I have seen many places; nowhere is the weather as mild as at the Shrine of the Báb. Soon this mountain will be developed; fine

buildings will be built on it. The Shrine of the Báb will be built in a most glorious way. Gardens will be made with flowers of different hues. Terraces will be built. From the bottom of the mountain to the Shrine there will be nine terraces and nine more terraces will be built from the Shrine to the top of the mountain. From the sea to the Shrine there will be one road; everything will be beautified with gardens and flowers. The pilgrims, who come by ship, will see the dome of the Shrine. Removing their crowns, the kings of the earth, as well as the queens of the world, while respectfully coming to see the Shrine of the Báb carrying bouquets of flowers, they will kneel and prostrate on the ground and offer their crowns to Him . . .[45]

And on another occasion He is reported to have said:

The future of Mount Carmel is very bright. I can see it now covered all over with a blanket of light. I can see many ships anchored at the Port of Haifa. I can see the kings of the earth with vases of flowers in their hands walking solemnly towards the Shrine of Baha'u'llah and the Bab with absolute devotion and in a state of prayer and supplication. At the time that they put a crown of thorns on His head, Christ could see the kings of the earth bowing before Him, but others could not see this.

And now I can see not only powerful lamps which will floodlight this mountain brightly, but I can also see Houses of Worship, hospitals, schools, homes for the handicapped, orphanages and all the other humanitarian institutions erected on Mount Carmel.[46]

14

RELEASE AND AFTERMATH

Some six months after 'Abdu'l-Bahá described his vision for the Shrine, the Sultan decided to study the reports of the commissioners but political events took over and he did not go any further. Bowing to the demands of the Young Turk revolutionaries, he established a constitutional government and released all political prisoners. Officials in Acre checked to see if the decree also applied to 'Abdu'l-Bahá. A positive reply was quick in coming.

In September 1908[1] when he was 64 years old, 'Abdu'l-Bahá stepped free from the clutches of the Ottomans. He had been their prisoner, under various degrees of restrictions, since He had arrived in the Holy Land 40 years previously, and for the fifteen years prior to that in the lands that are now Turkey and Iraq.

As He reviewed the past years of imprisonment, 'Abdu'l-Bahá wrote a spiritual treatise of great literary beauty, saying that that this world is more a 'workshop' than an 'art gallery',[2] more an arena of tests and trials than a place of ultimate happiness. He wrote:

> O ye my spiritual friends! For some time now the pressures have been severe, the restrictions as shackles of iron. This hapless wronged one was left single and alone, for all the ways were barred. Friends were forbidden access to me, the trusted were shut away, the foe compassed me about, the evil watchers were fierce and bold. At every instant, fresh affliction. At every breath, new anguish.
>
> Both kin and stranger on the attack; indeed, one-time lovers, faithless and unpitying, were worse than foes as they rose up to harass me. None was there to defend 'Abdu'l-Bahá, no helper, no protector, no ally, no champion. I was drowning in a shoreless sea, and ever beating upon my ears were the raven-croaking voices of the disloyal.

At every daybreak, triple darkness. At eventide, stone-hearted tyranny. And never a moment's peace, and never any balm for the spear's red wounds. From moment to moment, word would come of my exile to the Fezzan sands; from hour to hour, I was to be cast into the endless sea. Now they would say that these homeless wanderers were ruined at last; again that the cross would soon be put to use. This wasted frame of mine was to be made the target for bullet or arrow; or again, this failing body was to be cut to ribbons by the sword.

Our alien acquaintances could not contain themselves for joy, and our treacherous friends exulted. 'Praise be to God,' one would exclaim, 'Here is our dream come true.' And another, 'God be thanked, our spear-head found the heart.'

Affliction beat upon this captive like the heavy rains of spring, and the victories of the malevolent swept down in a relentless flood, and still 'Abdu'l-Bahá remained happy and serene, and relied on the grace of the All-Merciful. That pain, that anguish, was a paradise of all delights; those chains were the necklace of a king on a throne in heaven. Content with God's will, utterly resigned, my heart surrendered to whatever fate had in store, I was happy. For a boon companion, I had great joy.

Finally a time came when the friends turned inconsolable, and abandoned all hope. It was then the morning dawned, and flooded all with unending light. The towering clouds were scattered, the dismal shadows fled. In that instant the fetters fell away, the chains were lifted off the neck of this homeless one and hung round the neck of the foe. Those dire straits were changed to ease, and on the horizon of God's bounties the sun of hope rose up. All this was out of God's grace and His bestowals.

And yet, from one point of view, this wanderer was saddened and despondent. For what pain, in the time to come, could I seek comfort? At the news of what granted wish could I rejoice? There was no more tyranny, no more affliction, no tragical events, no tribulations. My only joy in this swiftly-passing world was to tread the stony path of God and to endure hard tests and all material griefs. For otherwise, this earthly life would prove barren and vain, and better would be death. The tree of being would produce no fruit; the sown field of this existence would yield no harvest. Thus it is my hope that once again some circumstance will make my cup of anguish to brim over, and that beauteous Love, that Slayer of souls, will dazzle the beholders again. Then will this heart be blissful, this soul be blessed.[3]

His special room

After His release 'Abdu'l-Bahá liked to spend days and nights up on Mount Carmel. He had a special place to stay.

Less than 50 metres to the east of the Shrine was the two-storey house of 'Abbás-Qulí of Qom, whom 'Abdu'l-Bahá had appointed custodian of the Shrine of the Báb. The first formally appointed custodian had been Yaḥyá Unsí Iṣfahání but when he became aged and was physically unable to do the job, he had to be replaced.[4] 'Abbás-Qulí had bought some land near the building and built his house there, the front door facing south, looking up the mountain. A small white room was built on the roof of this building so that 'Abdu'l-Bahá could stay as long as He liked.

How that room came about and some of what happened there became part of a pilgrim's account in later years.

> Here, in this little room the Master used to stay; often at night the friends would hear him walking about on the house-top, chanting. Here he used to receive the notables of the town and country . . . Abbas Gholi talked to us for quite a long time about the Master and the days he had spent there near the Tomb. He told about the building of that upper room. The Master had said that he would like a room there near the Tomb. He asked Abbas Gholi if he could not build him one, and the care-taker of the Tomb said, yes, where would the Master like to have it. The Master suggested that he would like to have it on the top of the house. Abbas Gholi said that the walls of the house were not strong enough to have another story built on top of them. Then the Master said that he would like to have it built in the garden, or above the Tomb. Abbas Gholi said that much excavation would be required for that. Finally the Master said, 'Never mind; do not trouble about it.' Not long after that one of the friends had built for the Master a little room on top of the stable, at the Master's house. Then the Master said to Abbas

> Gholi, 'Could you not build a house like that on the roof?', and he said 'Oh, yes.' The Master said, 'But I thought that you told me you could not build a room on top of your house!' So Abbas Gholi said, 'But a small room like that would have thin walls, and that could easily be built.' The Master smiled and said, 'Very good!', and so the room was built.[5]

In those exultant days after His release, 'Abdu'l-Bahá would host visitors there, and would stand on the northern balcony of the house, turn westward and gaze upon the Shrine He had built.[6]

Gardens

From the very start of the Shrine project, 'Abdul-Bahá paid particular attention to the beautification of the surroundings of the building.

It was at His request that the 25-year-old Raḥmatu'lláh Najaf-Ábádí came to the Holy Land in 1901 to take care of the gardens. He was a strong man, which suited his other role as a guard. He assisted 'Abbás-Qulí, and lived in the same house as him.[7] To beautify the surroundings 'Abdu'l-Bahá, with Raḥmatu'lláh's help, created a garden next to the Shrine comprised mainly of citrus trees and flowers.[8]

Among the trees were pomegranate, date palm, mulberry, orange and, possibly, carob.[9] The flowering plants included roses, Mary lilies, carnations, marigolds, verbena, violets, Chinese lilies, sapphire lupine, freesia, jessamine, anemone and zinnia.[10] Sometime after His release, in the area behind the Shrine and bordered by Mountain Road that had previously been a vineyard,'Abdu'l-Bahá also planted an orchard of peach, almond, loquat, fig, olive trees and a table-grape vine.[11]

15

INTERMENT OF THE SACRED REMAINS

Within six months of His release, 'Abdu'l-Bahá took the necessary steps of prepararation to complete the implementation of the mission given to Him by Bahá'u'lláh to inter the sacred remains of the Báb in their permanent resting place. In early March 1909, He directed that preparations be made for the interment ceremony.[1] It was necessary to ensure that in the eastern prayer room of the Shrine of the Báb there was a functioning entrance way and stairs down to the vault below the central rear room, the inner Shrine of the Báb.[2]

As we have seen in Chapter 12, some nine years earlier, the Master had removed the box containing the casket from its hiding place in the bedroom of the Greatest Holy Leaf in Acre and concealed it in a house He had rented in Haifa. He now directed that it be taken up to the site of the Shrine on Mount Carmel to be ready for the interment ceremony that would take place on 21 March.[3] The casket was inside a box which in turn was inside a bigger box, three boxes in all.[4]

In a highly secret mission, eight men carried the precious cargo up the steep slopes of the mountain.[5] One of them was Ustád Ismá'íl Úbudíyyát, the Bahá'í who, some ten years earlier, had helped carry the box containing the casket when it passed through the city of Qom on its passage to the Holy Land. In his account in later years, Ustád Ismá'íl did not say where they stored the box on Mount Carmel. However, what better place would there have been than underground in a locked vault in a building that was under the watchful eyes of the immensely strong and trustworthy Raḥmatu'lláh Najaf-Ábádí and the custodian of the Shrine, the utterly loyal and responsible Abbás-Qúlí?[6]

After they placed the box in its hiding place, the men remained for a while in the close vicinity of the Shrine. 'We planted roses in the flower beds,' Ustad Ismá'íl said:

> During the night we could not sleep because of too much happiness . . . we sang and sobbed.
>
> We were shedding tears of which each drop would take away the sadness of the last fifty years.[7] That blessed night that we were most happy and singing and praying, we took a piece of paper and wrote to 'Abdu'l-Bahá the names of all eight of us. As we saw that there are only eight, we added His name to ours too, because 'Thou art with us everywhere.'
>
> We took the path to Akka that same midnight and around dawn we reached Akka. 'Abdu'l-Bahá was outside on His terrace and was pacing back and forth and as He saw us from far.
>
> He made a gesture with His hand calling us in. As we entered He welcomed us and inquired if we did plant roses and if the flower beds are all in order, and soon He said, 'I wish you would count Us as one of you.' At this time, we took the letter and offered it to Him. He blessed us with wonderful words and revealed [a] Tablet in our honour.[8]

On the Holy Day of Naw-Rúz, 21 March 1909, a Sunday, 'Abdu'l-Bahá, His family and a few veteran Bahá'ís set out from Acre for Haifa in a horse-drawn buggy along the beach for the momentous event of the interment of the sacred remains of the Báb. Half-way along, the party stopped for lunch at a small government-built house used by a security detail at a point now known as Checkpost. An hour and a half later they arrived in Haifa.[9]

Ahead of His arrival on that special day, 'Abdu'l-Bahá had directed that the sarcophagus be removed from where it had been stored in the house that He had rented originally for western pilgrims, and then be taken up the steep slopes of Mount Carmel. Inside the sarcophagus was the empty ebony coffin made in Burma. Raḥmatu'lláh recorded in his memoirs: 'Naw-Rúz was approaching. We were informed that the beloved Master had decided to inter the remains of the Báb in its eternal abode. Some Arabs were hired to haul the sarcophagus [from the guesthouse to the Shrine] and on the way they would chant "Yá Abu'l-Abbás".'[10]

As the 20 men hauled the sarcophagus up the slopes, waiting at the Shrine for its arrival were those assigned to carry it down to the vault: Raḥmatu'lláh, Najaf-'Alí, Dadash-'Alí, Ḥusayn 'Abdu'l-Karím *gush borideh,*[11] 'Abdullah Arab, Ustád Muḥammad-'Alí Yazdí, and one other whose name Raḥmatu'lláh had forgotten when he prepared his memoirs.[12]

There was an incident after the sarcophagus arrived at the Shrine. Raḥmatu'lláh and the others suspected that 'Abdu'l-Karím *gush borideh,* the foreman of the team, appeared to have been in league with the Covenant-breakers. Their suspicions were aroused when the men saw that the treacherous cousin of 'Abdu'l-Bahá, Majdi'd-Dín, and his daughter had arrived at the Shrine building without the permission of the Master. Raḥmatu'lláh and his colleagues suspected that Majdi'd-Dín wanted to take custody of the casket, and had induced 'Abdu'l-Karím to steal it. However, when Majdi'd-Dín and his daughter saw how well it was guarded they left the scene.[13]

That afternoon, after 'Abdu'l-Bahá arrived in Haifa, He asked that the door to the vault[14] be opened. After removing His turban and shoes, He walked down the wooden stairs and entered the vault where he picked up the box containing the casket and held it to his chest, sobbing so loudly that the Bahá'ís rushed towards the vault, no doubt to see what was the matter. The Master then left, looking pale.

'Abdu'l-Bahá then directed the assembled men to follow the instructions of Ḥusayn Á<u>sh</u>chí, which were to take the sarcophagus down into the vault. Wooden stairs, about two or two and a half metres wide, wide enough for the 1.2-metre width of the casket, led down through the opening to the floor of the vault, several metres below. Wooden planks were placed on the stairs, making it a ramp, to allow the men to slide the sarcophagus down. They did so by tying a rope around the sarcophagus and easing it slowly down the ramp.

Mírzá Munír Zayn commented later: 'Abdu'l-Bahá gave the last instructions and it was slowly slid down into the under part of the Tomb. This must have been performed with the help of the Kingdom of El-Abha, for though the work presented great difficulty and was done by inexperienced men, everyone wondered at the ease with which it was done.'[15]

Once the sarcophagus reached the ground directly under the rear eastern room, it was taken through the doorway into the vault directly below the inner room of the Shrine of the Báb. The sarcophagus, with its empty wooden coffin inside, was laid south to north, as if facing the Shrine of Bahá'u'lláh.

The arrangements were now complete for the interment to take place in the evening, in the presence of Bahá'ís from the East and the West.

At the centre of this most solemn and moving of occasions was the venerable figure of 'Abdu'l-Bahá. Now aged 65, His once black hair and beard had turned silvery white and his former muscular physique was now that of one who had suffered severe physical deprivation, threats to His life, and levels of stress beyond comprehension. His presence, though, remained one of nobility and simplicity, of dignity and loving humility, of wisdom and a radiant spirituality. With Him for the ceremony were His grandson, the 12-year-old Shoghi Effendi,[16] His sister Bahíyyih Khánum and His wife Munírih Khánum.[17]

Others at the event would have included:[18] Raḥmatu'lláh Najaf-Ábádí (the caretaker of the Shrine); Mírzá Munír Zayn (a scribe); 'Abbás-Qulí (the custodian of the Shrine); Vakílu'd-Dawlih (a cousin of the Báb);[19] Ḥájí Mírzá Ḥaydar-'Alí (known as the Angel of Carmel); Edwin Scott (an American Bahá'í who lived in Paris, an artist), May Woodcock and her parents Mr and Mrs Woodcock (all pilgrims from Canada); Ustád Ismá'íl Úbudíyyát; Ḥusayn Áshchí (the cook who had served Bahá'u'lláh); and seven of the eight[20] of those who placed the sarcophagus in the vault – Najaf-'Alí, Dadash-'Alí, 'Abdullah Arab, Ustád Muḥammad-'Alí Yazdí, and one other. There were also Bahá'ís from Beirut and Egypt present.[21]

By no means could all fit in the vault, which was about 3.5 by 3.5 metres and which had in its midst the sarcophagus, measuring 2.5 metres long and 1.25 metre wide. The ladies were standing or kneeling about the entrance to the Tomb,[22] probably near the door of the vault or on the lower steps. Others would have been in that crammed space, and probably on the upper steps and above.

On that auspicious night, 'Abdu'l-Bahá entered the rear eastern room of the Shrine, the place from which the stairs descended to the corridor that led to the door of the vault. As He stood there in that dimly lit room, He removed His turban. His shining white hair fell its full length to His shoulders, merging with parts of his beard, framing his noble head. He removed his shoes, His bare feet firm on the stone floor. Then he took off his dark outer cloak and cast it aside, leaving Him standing there barefoot, bareheaded and wearing simple white garments.

Few of the others in that room had seen Him without His formal attire. It was a scene of humility, yet majesty too. But there was little time to absorb the vision in front of them because the Master could wait no longer. It had been 18 long and often agonizing years since Bahá'u'lláh had commissioned Him with the historic task of bringing the sacred remains from Persia and then interring them deep in this holy mountain.

With rising emotion, 'Abdu'l-Bahá moved down the wooden stairs and along the corridor and entered through the unlocked door into the vault.

Then, at the direction of the Master, Raḥmatu'lláh withdrew the small casket carrying the sacred remains from inside the larger box that had arrived from Persia.

What followed has been described by Shoghi Effendi, an eye-witness, in his masterly history, *God Passes By*:

> [I]n the evening, by the light of a single lamp, He ['Abdu'l-Bahá] laid within it, with His own hands – in the presence of believers from the East and from the West and in circumstances at once solemn and moving – the wooden casket containing the sacred remains of the Báb and His companion.
>
> When all was finished, and the earthly remains of the Martyr-Prophet of Shíráz were, at long last, safely deposited for their everlasting rest in the bosom of God's holy mountain, 'Abdu'l-Bahá, Who had cast aside His turban, removed His shoes and thrown off His cloak, bent low over the still open sarcophagus, His silver hair waving about His head and His face transfigured and luminous, rested His forehead on the border of the wooden casket, and sobbing aloud, wept with such a weeping that all those who were present wept with Him. That night He could not sleep, so overwhelmed was He with emotion.[23]

The ebony lid of the coffin was put in place and the sarcophagus closed forever with its marble lid. It was perhaps at this stage that 'Abdu'l-Bahá chanted the rhythmic, majestic prayer for the dead.

Lady Blomfield later spoke to eye-witnesses of that 'sacred ceremony' and wrote about their descriptions:

The garden for the Shrine of the Báb was flourishing in 1914 when this photograph was taken by US pilgrim George Latimer

Ismá'íl Áqá, the Master's gardener, who died in Haifa in 1939

© USBNA

'Abdu'l-Baha looks westwards towards the Shrine from the northern balcony of the nearby house of 'Abbás-Qúlí

Shoghi Effendi, dressed in white (seated, centre) with other young Bahá'ís on the Terrace in the front of the Shrine, which is out of sight to the left

Water tank arrangements above the reservoir at the north-west of Shrine

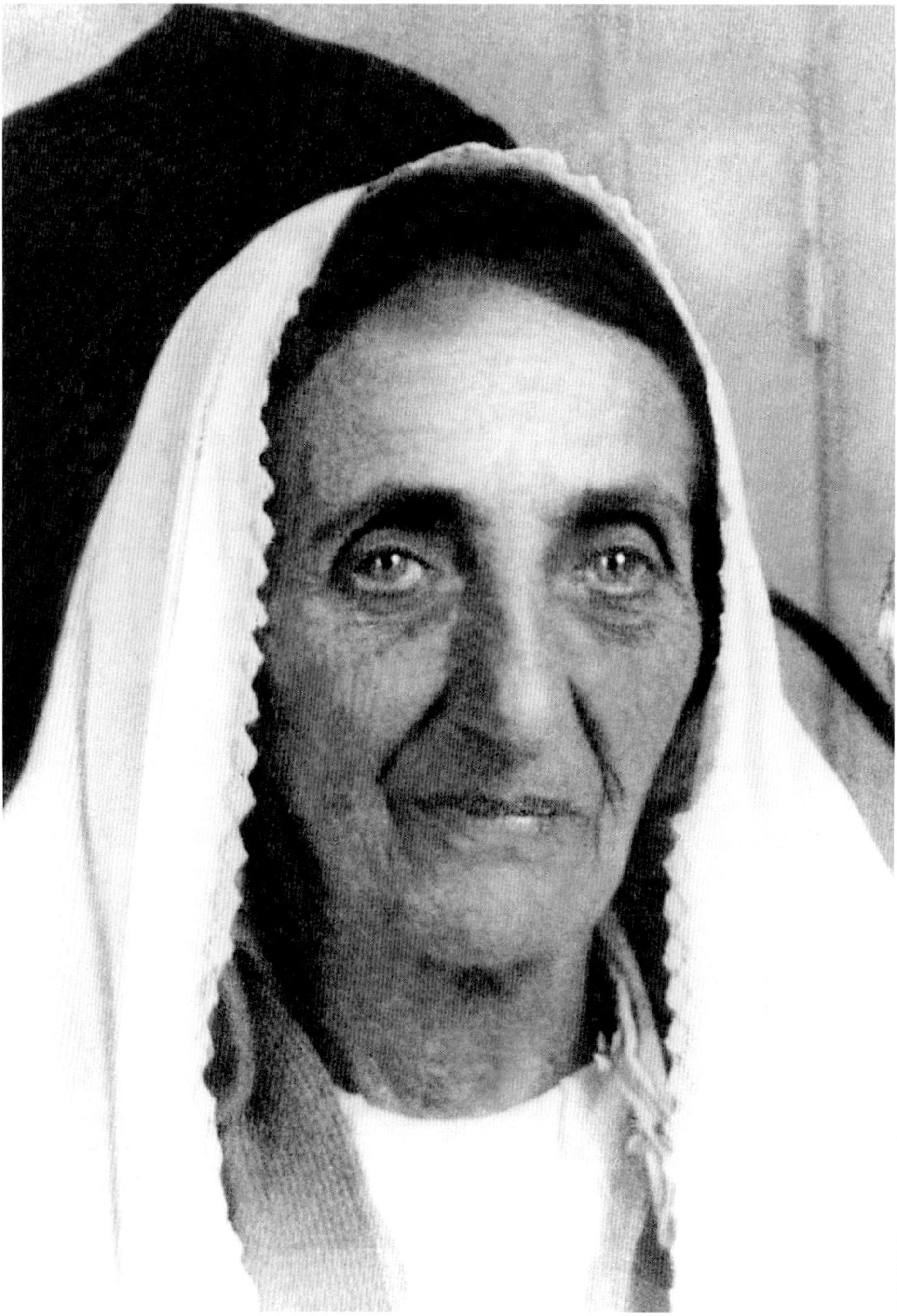

The Greatest Holy Leaf (Bahíyyih Khánum) was the Master's representative in the Holy Land when He was overseas and would take on a similar leadership role in 1922 when Shoghi Effendi went abroad

> But it is impossible to find the words with which to tell you of the event of that great day. Perhaps you may touch the spirit of it with your spirit. The Master, bare-headed, with His hair like a halo of silver, His white robe falling around Him, His feet bare, descended into the tomb. His beautiful voice rose and fell in the cadence of the funeral chant, His face all shining and glorious, as though it were lighted from within.
>
> He Himself placed the earthly body of His Holiness the Bab, with that of His beloved and faithful disciple, in the marble sarcophagus.
>
> And when He spoke to us of the meaning of that day's event – of sacrifice, of love, of steadfastness, of heroism, shown all down the ages by those Great Messengers of God – our hearts, you can imagine, were too full for any utterance. We could but feel, Oh, the blindness of humanity! How it is unworthy of those whom it tortures and martyrs. And Oh, the stupendous love which came and endured for the sake of that same humanity![24]

'Abdu'l-Bahá later wrote to the Bahá'ís of the world:

> The most joyful tidings is this, that the holy, the luminous body of the Báb . . . after having for sixty years been transferred from place to place, by reason of the ascendancy of the enemy, and from fear of the malevolent, and having known neither rest nor tranquillity has, through the mercy of the Abhá Beauty, been ceremoniously deposited, on the day of Naw-Rúz, within the sacred casket, in the exalted Shrine on Mt. Carmel . . .[25]

'Abdu'l-Bahá also announced to the eastern Bahá'ís that the whole of the remains of the Báb were interred in the sarcophagus, thereby preempting any person ever saying with any credibility that they had a relic in their possession. The following excerpt from a Tablet by the Master makes the point:

> It is possible that the covenant breakers and the hypocrites will clamour and lie afterwards and say that the Noble Temple 'the Body of the Báb' hath a different resting place or that a part of it is in another place. The friends should know these are mere vilifications, heresies, and cunning meant to cause discord. That Blessed and

> executed body of the Báb was put in its entirety to rest on Mount Carmel. However the villains will not be silent. They surely will lie and claim that they have possessed the Blessed Body, or transmitted it, or found a part of it, or that sprites have stolen it from the sincere believers! Know that all of these are lies and vilifications. The truth is what is said.[26]

Raḥmatu'lláh quoted 'Abdu'l-Bahá as saying: 'I was intending to send the outer box which contained the Holy Remains back to Iran. Then I thought it may become the source of contention among the friends, and different opinions and thoughts will arise. That is why I gave the idea up.' Raḥmatu'lláh said he had thought to take the box for himself but that 'Abdu'l-Bahá had said, 'No one has the right to take anything of these items from here,' and He later had it destroyed.[27]

There is a report that immediately after the Bahá'ís had left the vault, 'Abdu'l-Bahá indicated His own future burial place by pointing to a passageway next to the vault containing the sarcophagus of the Báb and saying 'And this should be a place for Us.'[28]

When the Master had emerged from the vault after the interment, after fulfilling the prophecy of the Prophets that the Temple of the Lord would be built by 'the Branch',[29] He turned towards Persia, and as He faced eastward said that the interment of the remains of the Báb required sacrifice, and that the Bahá'ís of Nayriz had accepted that sacrifice on that very day, eighteen Bahá'ís having been martyred in that Persian city. In the same Tablet quoted above, the Master linked the sacrifice of the lives of these Bahá'ís to the establishment of the Shrine:

> O Friends of 'Abdu'l-Bahá! In These days, through good fortune and the confirmations of the Lord of the Exalted Heavens and the success granted from the Invisible Kingdom, the Sacred Body of His Holiness, the Báb, the Exalted One, was placed on Mount Carmel in that Hallowed Spot. Therefore, sacrifice was required and so, the giving up of life was needed.
>
> Intoxicated by this brimming cup, the friends of Nayríz won the competition in this field with the bat of resolution. May all blessings be unto them! May all pleasure be theirs! May this overflowing Cup of the Wine of the Love of God be delicious to them! May the Glory of the Glories of God rest upon them![30]

Spiritual significance

'Abdu'l-Bahá, as Shoghi Effendi has written, later testified on more than one occasion that the

> removal of the Báb's remains from their place of concealment in Ṭihrán to Mt. Carmel . . . the safe transfer of these remains, the construction of a befitting mausoleum to receive them, and their final interment with His own hands in their permanent resting-place constituted one of the three principal objectives which, ever since the inception of His mission, He had conceived it His paramount duty to achieve.[31]

Shoghi Effendi also wrote that this act 'deserves to rank as one of the outstanding events in the first Bahá'í century',[32] and that it was the Covenant of Bahá'u'lláh that had 'enabled 'Abdu'l-Bahá, 'in the face of formidable obstacles, to effect the transfer and the final entombment of the Báb's remains in a mausoleum on Mt. Carmel'; and further:

> Through His unrelaxing vigilance the holy remains of the Báb, brought forth at long last from their fifty-year concealment, had been safely transported to the Holy Land and permanently and befittingly enshrined in the very spot which Bahá'u'lláh Himself had designated for them and had blessed with His presence.[33]

He described the spiritual significance of the interment:

> With the transference of the remains of the Bab – Whose advent marks the return of the Prophet Elijah – to Mt. Carmel, and their interment in that holy mountain, not far from the cave of that Prophet Himself, the Plan so gloriously envisaged by Bahá'u'lláh, in the evening of His life, had been at last executed, and the arduous labours associated with the early and tumultuous years of the ministry of the appointed Centre of His Covenant crowned with immortal success. A focal centre of Divine illumination and power, the very dust of which 'Abdu'l-Bahá averred had inspired Him, yielding in sacredness to no other shrine throughout the Bahá'í world except the Sepulchre of the Author of the Bahá'í Revelation Himself, had

been permanently established on that mountain, regarded from time immemorial as sacred. A structure, at once massive, simple and imposing; nestling in the heart of Carmel, the 'Vineyard of God'; flanked by the Cave of Elijah on the west, and by the hills of Galilee on the east; backed by the plain of Sharon, and facing the silver-city of 'Akká, and beyond it the Most Holy Tomb, the Heart and Qiblih[34] of the Bahá'í world; overshadowing the colony of German Templars who, in anticipation of the 'coming of the Lord,' had forsaken their homes and foregathered at the foot of that mountain, in the very year of Bahá'u'lláh's Declaration in Baghdad (1863),[35] the mausoleum of the Bab had now, with heroic effort and in impregnable strength been established as 'the Spot round which the Concourse on high circle in adoration'.[36]

16

GATHERINGS AT THE ORIENTAL PILGRIM HOUSE

Soon after the interment of the sacred remains of the Báb in 1909 came the opening of the main building associated with His Shrine, the Oriental Pilgrim House, which had been built within a short walk to the east.[1]

The proposal for the building, later also known as the Eastern or Persian Pilgrim House, had come in 1905 from a pilgrim, Mírzá Ja'far Shírází Raḥmání, who was a tea trader from Jahrum in the Persian province of Fars, and later a resident of Ishqabad and then Khuqand in Turkistan (now Turkmenistan). 'Abdul-Bahá, who had expressed concern about the suitability of where pilgrims were staying and that they might meet Covenant-breakers, accepted his offer after first declining it for fear of the imposition on Mírzá Ja'far.

To pay for the project, Mr Raḥmání used funds that came from a fortunate business deal. He had obtained 600 cases of tea from Calcutta and Bombay. He then learned that a shortage of tea in Russia had caused the prices to multiply sixfold compared to those of three months earlier. He sold his tea at that high price to Russian brokers and used the money to build the Pilgrim House.[2]

In accordance with the wish of the Master, Mírzá Ja'far bought a large piece of land, which had been an orchard owned by an Assyrian. He arranged for 'Abdu'l-Bahá to sign the purchase documents, rather than having the land registered in his own name.[3] In 1907 he arranged for one of the friends in the Holy Land to put in the foundations and to build two rooms.[4] In 1908 he returned and, with the encouragement of 'Abdu'l-Bahá, took charge of the project, staying 100 days and finishing the building, complete with its underground water cistern.[5] In response to a request by the Master, he also furnished and carpeted the building.

Then the day arrived for the opening and for all 80 pilgrims in Haifa to attend a dinner hosted by Mírzá Ja'far in the presence of the Master.

As the guests assembled outside, Mírzá Ja'far approached 'Abdu'l-Bahá with pen and paper asking Him to inscribe something that could be written over the entrance. One of the many great attributes of the Master was his sense of humour, and He first responded in jest: 'What can I write other than '"Áqá Mírzá Ja'far, the mad-man, mad-man", for in these days when everyone is thinking about his own house and comfort and pleasures, Áqá Mírzá Ja'far is mindful to free us from the troubles caused by the Covenant-breakers and has constructed this house.'[6]

But then He wrote: 'This is a spiritual guesthouse and its builder is Mírzá Ja'far Raḥmání Shírází 1327 AH (1909) AD.'[7]

After some impromptu poetry by the poet 'Andalíb,[8] 'Abdu'l-Bahá became the first to enter the completed building. He addressed those attending, the first of many talks that have been delivered in that much loved building in the decades since.

The Master referred to Mírzá Ja'far as a lion in the forest of the love of God and a bird in the garden of his knowledge. He said there would be many Bahá'í guesthouses in the future but this one was different, being the first. It had been built with purity of motive. In one of His Tablets praising Mírzá Ja'far, the Master said that no king has a palace like the pilgrim house, that all palaces will become burial places, but this building would remain forever.[9]

During the subsequent years, 'Abdu'l-Bahá often met with the Eastern pilgrims and local Bahá'ís in the attractive central room of that building, its northern windows providing a striking view over the bay towards Acre.

'The Lord's sustenance'

The combination of the interment and the completion of the Pilgrim House allowed an informal, happy routine which has continued for generations since, where in preparation for visiting the Shrine, Bahá'ís enter the Pilgrim House and return there after prayers at the threshold for talks and socializing. For many years, the Eastern pilgrims stayed there, and, for some time after 1963 when the Universal House of Justice made the Western Pilgrim House its temporary Seat, so did Western pilgrims.[10]

One of the first such events was of great significance, as 'Abdu'l-Bahá pointed out at the time. It was a celebration of the Holy Day held on 15 May 1910 to commemorate the Declaration of the Báb.[11] Late in the afternoon, the Bahá'ís assembled before the door of the Shrine and then entered the outer prayer room and faced the inner chamber while 'Abdu'l-Bahá chanted two prayers. All those present stood except for one, the elderly Vakílu'd-Dawlih (a cousin of the Báb), the man who built the Ishqabad Temple and one dearly loved by the Master.[12] Supported on one side by 'Abdu'l-Bahá and, on the other by a Bahá'í from the United States, Howard Struven,[13] he had been assisted into a chair. The Bahá'ís lit candles in a candelabra in the Shrine.

Afterwards, outside the Shrine, a photograph was taken. Among the group pictured was the father of Shoghi Effendi, Mírzá Hádí, and seated in the important spot in the middle was Vakílu'd-Dawlih.[14]

'Abdu'l-Bahá spoke after a meal near the Shrine[15] which was attended by 70 pilgrims and local Bahá'ís in three sittings – they were from Jewish, Zoroastrian, Christian and Muslim backgrounds. 'Abdu'l-Bahá served the guests food and, as usual, was the last to eat. In eloquent terms. He contrasted the gathering with others in the secular world which render great service to humanity:

> Yet the results [of the secular meetings] are limited, the fruits thereof are finite and the signs are bounded; whereas the traces, the lights and the results of this gathering are unlimited, boundless and infinite, for it is held on the Supreme Spot (the Tomb of the Bab) and under the shadow of the Blessed Beauty.
>
> This feast is one eternal! It has connection with and relation to the soul and body; it shall be continued everlastingly. At least a hundred thousand feasts shall follow this one. All the other gatherings shall be forgotten, whereas the commemoration and celebration of this meeting shall remain and be duly observed forever throughout endless ages; it is under the merciful glances of the Blessed Beauty.

He then referred to the Lord's Supper, also widely known as the Last Supper of Jesus Christ.

> Once His Holiness Christ gathered the disciples together, and having offered to them the Lord's Supper, He advised them, admonished

> them and uttered certain teachings to them, and then He said this was 'The Lord's Supper'. Now, as this meeting is held under the shadow of the Blessed Beauty, it should be called 'The Lord's Sustenance', and as the consequences of 'The Lord's Supper' continued until the present time, so we hope that the results and effects of this 'Lord's Sustenance' may also become permanent and perpetual. In fact, there is no meeting better than this, for it is held in the vicinity of the Supreme Spot and the faces are so brilliant and radiant! What is there superior to this?[16]

That night, Howard Struven and another Bahá'í from the United States, Charles Mason Remey, came back and prayed for an hour in the Shrine, where the candles were still burning.[17]

During that summer of 1910, some young Bahá'ís including Ḥabíb Mú'ayyad, Yúnis Khán Afroukhteh and Badi Bushrui spent time on Mount Carmel. 'Abdu'l-Bahá would come over from Acre to visit the Shrine and speak to them about the martyrdom of the Báb and of the sufferings and hardships sustained by Bahá'u'lláh.[18]

That same summer 'Abdu'l-Bahá moved permanently from the House of 'Abdu'lláh Páshá in Acre to his new home at 7 Haparsim St, Haifa, within easy walking distance to the base of Mount Carmel and with a clear view of the Shrine. He was to make that house His primary dwelling place until the end of His days.

Then in September, 'Abdu'l-Bahá left the Holy Land for visits to establish and promote the Bahá'í Faith in Egypt, Europe and North America.[19] He was to be away for three years. His departure came as a surprise to the pilgrims. On the day He left, the Master had travelled with pilgrims from Acre to Haifa, but did not say anything about His plans.

One of those pilgrims, Isabella D. Brittingham,[20] later reported that during the afternoon 'Abdu'l-Bahá had visited the house of Mírzá Asadu'lláh and then went by horse-drawn carriage to the Tomb of the Báb. That night, the Bahá'ís gathered in front of His house to meet Him as usual, but then one of His sons-in-law came and told them that he had taken the 'Khedivial steamer for Port Said' in Egypt. Some of the Bahá'ís had spotted a steamer, the *Manyih Khadivi*, heading south, and it was said at the time, and later confirmed, that the Master was aboard. Shoghi Effendi left on the next vessel.[21]

In the three years ‘Abdu’l-Bahá was away, His sister Bahíyyih Khánum, the Greatest Holy Leaf, remained in Haifa. As described by her great-nephew, Shoghi Effendi, she acted as ‘Abdu’l-Bahá’s ‘competent deputy, His representative and vicegerent, with none to equal her’. These roles were far from ceremonial. Her functions, according to her biographer, were ‘far reaching and included attending to the administrative and spiritual guidance of the community. She was the one who was empowered to act in His absence.’[22]

Details of her activities have yet to be uncovered, but we know she received dignitaries and officials of both sexes and spoke to the pilgrims on behalf of ‘Abdu’l-Bahá.[23] It seems likely, then, that with the responsibility for the Shrine of the Báb, she would have attended to any extension or beautification of its gardens as much as possible, and directed any maintenance or other issues relating to the building itself.

Her role with respect to the procedure for male pilgrims is as yet unknown, but it is likely that she led female pilgrims to the Shrine of the Báb.

17

WAR, TYRANNY AND LIBERATION

While away in the United States, 'Abdu'l-Bahá turned his mind to how He could better embellish the Shrines of the Báb and Bahá'u'lláh. When visiting the luxurious Hearst Mansion (Hacienda del Pozo de Verona) in California as a guest of Phoebe Hearst, He admired the gardens there and requested that seeds of particular flowers be sent for planting in the gardens of the Shrines.[1]

Although He rarely, if ever, mentioned the Shrine of the Báb in His public talks in North America, at one point in His travels He hinted at the troubles that would await Him (and by extension, the holy Shrines) personally upon his return: 'The Committee of Union and Progress in Constantinople is very good but both internal and external enemies are laying plans to imprison me again on my return to the Holy Land.'[2]

He had health problems while away. In the July heat of 1912 in the United States, He had fallen ill, seemingly susceptible to *tab-i-'asabi* (a fever affecting the nervous system), likely to be a stress–related illness. He may also have been affected by the air pollution in New York City and the lingering effects of his childhood bout of tuberculosis.[3]

After he arrived back in Egypt in June 1913 on his way home to Haifa, His health took a turn for the worse. Insomnia and fever[4] – perhaps malaria – returned. His immune system had been compromised from his exposure to extreme cold as a child. He had nearly died from dysentery upon arriving in Acre and had spent many decades living within the unhealthy confines of that filthy city. He now found his eyes weary, his mind tired and his body exhausted, even after a short walk. Doctors urged total rest upon him. His health ebbed and flowed.

Now aged 69, He remained in Egypt for seven months, away from the demands and threats that would face him at home, yet still meeting with many visitors, including the Ottoman viceroy (the Khedive), answering correspondence and giving advice.

Bahíyyih Khánum visited Him there, arriving on or about 1 August.[5] Shoghi Effendi, who arrived with his aunt that day, wrote that he would not venture to describe her joy and enthusiasm as she greeted Him:

> She was astounded at the vitality of which He had, despite his unimaginable sufferings, proved Himself capable. She was lost in admiration at the magnitude of the forces which His utterances had released. She was filled with thankfulness to Bahá'u'lláh for having enabled her to witness the evidence of such brilliant victory of His Cause no less than for His Son.[6]

She spent several weeks in Egypt, managing His household. Then she returned to Haifa to receive pilgrims and to supervise Bahá'í community activities.[7]

'Abdu'l-Bahá arrived home in Haifa on 5 December 1913, and the next morning proceeded to the Shrine of the Báb. The Bahá'ís who lived in the Holy Land, together with the pilgrims, lined the pathways. He beckoned to them to enter the rear eastern room while He went by himself into the western room opposite.[8]

He had accomplished all three tasks He considered the principal objectives of His ministry: the building of the Shrine of the Báb, the construction of the Temple in Ishqabad, and now the establishment of the Faith in the West.[9] We can only wonder if He rejoiced in the Shrine, if He felt that a huge weight had been lifted off His shoulders.

Two months later, on 14 February 1914, in a talk that has since inspired generations of pilgrims, 'Abdu'l-Bahá, while seated by the window of 'one of the Bahá'í Pilgrim Homes', expressed His vision of a glorious future for Haifa and Acre, the focal points of both places being the holy Shrines.

'The view from the Pilgrim Home is very attractive, especially as it faces the Blessed Tomb of Bahá'u'lláh,' He said.

> In the future the distance between 'Akká and Haifa will be built up, and the two cities will join and clasp hands, becoming the two terminal sections of one mighty metropolis. As I look now over this scene, I see so clearly that it will become one of the first emporiums of the world. This great semi-circular bay will be transformed into the finest harbour wherein the ships of all nations will seek

shelter and refuge. The great vessels of all peoples will come to this port, bringing on their decks thousands and thousands of men and women from every part of the globe. The mountain and the plain will be dotted with the most modern buildings and palaces. Industries will be established and various institutions of philanthropic nature will be founded. The flowers of civilization and culture from all nations will be brought here to blend their fragrances together and blaze the way for the brotherhood of man. Wonderful gardens, orchards, groves and parks will be laid out on all sides. At night the great city will be lighted by electricity. The entire harbour from 'Akká to Haifa will be one path of illumination. Powerful searchlights will be placed on both sides of Mount Carmel to guide the steamers. Mount Carmel itself, from top to bottom, will be submerged in a sea of lights. A person standing on the summit of Mount Carmel, and the passengers of the steamers coming to it, will look upon the most sublime and majestic spectacle of the whole world.

From every part of the mountain the symphony of 'Yá Bahá'u'l-Abhá!'[10] will be raised, and before the daybreak soul-entrancing music accompanied by melodious voices will be uplifted towards the throne of the Almighty.

Indeed, God's ways are mysterious and unsearchable. What outward relation exists between Shíráz and Ṭihrán, Baghdád and Constantinople, Adrianople and 'Akká and Haifa? God worked patiently, step by step, through these various cities, according to His own definite and eternal plan, so that the prophecies and predictions as foretold by the prophets might be fulfilled. This golden thread of promise concerning the Messianic Millennium runs through the Bible, and it was so destined that God in His own good time would cause its appearance. Not even a single word will be left meaningless and unfulfilled.[11]

Defeating the tyrant

After some time back home in Haifa, 'Abdu'l-Bahá regained his health.[12] In the years to come He would need every ounce of the new-found strength to ward off attacks on the Shrine, on Himself, on His family and on the Bahá'í community in general.

He knew there was trouble ahead. At the same time as He had been speaking about the glories of the future, 'Abdu'l-Bahá was making plans to deal with the forthcoming world war that He had predicted, and warned the community about, while He was in North America and Europe.[13]

Pilgrims from the West were in Haifa and were visiting the Shrine of the Báb, but 'Abdu'l-Bahá soon asked that no more come. He rejected a request to allow some Persian pilgrims to visit Haifa and gradually sent home those already there.[14] By the end of July 1914 no pilgrims remained.

'Abdu'l-Bahá had once again demonstrated His foresight. War broke out initially in July and, more substantially, in August. Had there been foreigners in Haifa from the countries comprising the Allied powers, especially after the Ottoman Empire entered the conflict on the side of Germany in October, they could well have been trapped and arrested, along with those with whom they had been associating.

Soon fears began to mount among the population of Haifa and Acre that their cities would be razed to the ground by Allied fire. It didn't help when a warship bombarded the railway bridges between the two cities, one shell landing but not exploding in the Bahá'í property known as the Garden of Riḍván just outside Acre.[15]

The population was in a panic. People spent their evenings in darkness because it was said that people were being hanged without trial just because they had their lights on at night, and so were suspected by the secret police of being spies preparing reports about the Turkish forces.[16]

'Abdu'l-Bahá then instructed the Bahá'í families to leave the Haifa–Acre district and relocate to the Druze village of Abu-Sinan, which was on a hill to the east and whose inhabitants loved the Master as they had His Father before them.[17] He remained in Acre with just one other Bahá'í, leaving the Shrine of the Báb in the custody of Ḥájí Mírzá Ḥaydar-'Alí, a devout and dearly-loved Bahá'í aged 84.[18]

Calm returned and by May 1915 the Bahá'ís had arrived back in Haifa. Although the panic had somewhat abated, times were extremely difficult for the population. British forces were massed in Egypt. The ruling Ottomans were pouring resources into the war effort at the expense of the local population. Olive trees more than a century old in the Carmel district were cut to fuel steam trains.[19] Petrol, matches, rice and sugar became in very short supply. Men between the ages of 19 and 45 were conscripted into the army. The military authorities confiscated animals, including camels, and took grain forage and even the barbed wire protecting crops in the fields.[20] To add to the misery, from March to October 1915 there was a heat wave. Then, as in long-ago events recorded in the Bible, a plague of locusts stripped most of the vegetation in the Holy Land.[21]

'Abdu'l-Bahá took steps to prevent disaster. He provided advice to Bahá'í farmers in the Galilee and made sure they stored grain in case of famine.

In August 1915, despite the difficult circumstances being endured, 'Abdu'l-Bahá described a glorious future for the Shrine. Standing on the steps of His house, He looked up at the edifice and said: 'The sublime Shrine has remained unbuilt. Ten–twenty thousand pounds are required. God willing, it will be accomplished. We have carried its construction to this stage.'[22] He also said: 'The Shrine of the Báb will be built in the most beautiful and majestic style.' At about that time, He ordered a Turk in Haifa to make him a sketch of how the Shrine would appear when completed, a drawing yet to be located.[23]

That year, on the shores of Gallipoli near where Bahá'u'lláh had landed 47 years previously, a battle of great horror was under way, one that led to the deaths of thousands of young men of Christian and Muslim backgrounds. The urgency of Bahá'u'lláh's call to their nations' leaders, kings and emperors alike,[24] to take measures to avert war, had been ignored or dismissed, and the Great War was to mount in intensity and lead to previously unimaginable slaughter in France, one of the loveliest, most scenic countries on earth.

The Shrine protects important documents

During that catastrophic war the Shrine became a place of safekeeping for important documents of great significance to the development of the Bahá'í Faith. Plans by 'Abdu'l-Bahá for the extension of the Bahá'í community around the world had been addressed to the Bahá'ís of the United States and Canada. Five of them, written on postcards, had reached America and had been published.[25]

But communication between the Holy Land and the United States was cut during the war, so 'Abdu'l-Bahá concealed the rest of what were known as the 'Tablets of the Divine Plan' in a vault under the Shrine.[26] The exact location of the hiding place has yet to be identified with certainty, although the likelihood is that it was just below the entrance to the vault, which was in the rear eastern room. That would have enabled them to be retrieved after the war without too much difficulty.

Peril

The years 1915–17 became a time of great peril for 'Abdu'l-Bahá and the Shrine that He was so determined to protect.

Enemies of 'Abdu'l-Bahá whispered slanders against Him in the ear of Jamal Pasha,[27] who was one of a triumvirate known as the 'Three Pashas' who ruled the Ottoman Empire for the duration of World War I. He was to become a formidable foe of the Master.

Jamal Pasha was effectively the dictator of Syria, a region which encompassed the Holy Land, and he was the supreme commander of the Ottoman army in the area.

Arriving in early 1915, he was based for a while in Damascus, and then established his headquarters on the historic Mount of Olives where he became known as the 'tyrant of Jerusalem'.

A vivid description comes from historian Simon Sebag Montefiore: 'Jemal, forty-five years old, squat and bearded, always protected by a camel-mounted squadron of guards, combined brutish, paranoid cruelty with charm, intelligence and grotesque buffoonery.'[28]

Jamal struck terror into the Holy Land, imposing martial law and hanging anybody suspected of being trouble.[29] Montefiore records that Jamal would stage these executions at the gates of the old city of Jerusalem after Friday prayers to ensure the biggest audience for the intimidating displays: '[T]he gates seemed to be permanently festooned with swaying cadavers, deliberately left for days on [Jamal's] orders.'

A Bahá'í student at the time, Ali Yazdi, has vividly described the atmosphere in the Holy Land:

> World War I had been raging for about three years. The Allied blockade had cut Syria and the Holy Land from the outside world – no mail, no trade, no telegrams, and no travellers.
>
> The Turks were ruling the area with an iron hand. The military commander, Jamal Pasha, was ruthless, cruel, unreasonable and inefficient. He destroyed all in his way. Everybody was under suspicion.
>
> Many of the aristocratic families of Syria found their sons

> hanged in the public square. There was a shortage of everything. Nothing could be obtained from aboard. There were no means to produce anything. Even food such as wheat was scarce. Whatever little grain was raised was largely sequestered by the Turkish army without payment to the farmers, and what was left of the crops was decimated by swarms of locusts. Famine was rampant. Poverty was everywhere.[30]

Minorities such as Jews, Christians, Druzes and Bahá'ís were in particular danger. Their legal protection was removed and so many locals took the chance to settle old scores against them.

One Bahá'í, Dr Ḥábib Mú'ayyad, wrote: 'Gallows were active in every town, and all prominent citizens were eliminated . . . As soon as the smallest complaint was raised against anyone, immediately a file would be prepared for him and his demise was assured.'[31]

With his capricious behaviour and his deadly response to any challenge to his authority, Jamal Pasha posed a threat to 'Abdu'l-Bahá and His custodianship and protection of the Shrine of the Báb. His arrival as ruler gave 'Abdu'l-Bahá's disloyal half-brother, Mírzá Muḥammad-'Alí, and his associates – previously discredited and cowed into silence – fresh opportunities to plot against 'Abdu'l-Bahá.

These relatives went to Jamal Pasha with various tales. Majdi'd-Dín told him that his cousin 'Abdu'l-Bahá was hostile to the Committee of Union and Progress, which by 1913 was ruling as a dictatorship. In other words, he was claiming 'Abdu'l-Bahá was against the Turkish State.[32]

The tyrant ordered 'Abdu'l-Bahá to visit him, presumably to assess whether He was a threat. But Jamal Pasha met more than his match. Eloquent in Jamal's own language, 'Abdu'l-Bahá was not one to be intimidated. He knew how to deal with bullies. Balyuzi tells the story:

> Jamál Pá<u>sh</u>á received Him courteously, but told Him that He was a religious mischief-maker, which was the reason He had been put under restraint in the past. It happened that, in the days of [Sultan] 'Abdu'l-Ḥamíd, Jamál Pá<u>sh</u>á himself had been known as a political mischief-maker.
>
> So 'Abdu'l-Bahá now replied that mischief-making was of two kinds: political and religious; and then, pointing at the arrogant

'Abdu'l-Bahá on the eastern side of the Shrine of the Báb with Shoghi Effendi (wearing a white scarf, and behind the elderly Ḥájí Mírzá Ḥaydar-'Alí). This is a rare photograph of Shoghi Effendi at the Shrine

'Abdu'l-Bahá with Shoghi Effendi (third from left, in light-coloured coat) in front of the house of 'Abbás-Qúlí. Dr John Esslemont, in a light-coloured waist-coat, is in the fourth row; Fujita has climbed up the tree; Dr Lotfullah Hakim third from right, front row. Two along to the left from the Master is Ḥájí Mírzá Ḥaydar-'Alí. The Master's room is on the roof. The Shrine is just out of picture to the right

The Pilgrim House as photographed from the roof of the Shrine. In the background is the location of current-day Shifra Street

Mírzá Ja'far Shírází Raḥmání, the builder of the Pilgrim House

'Abdu'l-Bahá and Shoghi Effendi, who is seated second from right in white gown, with the Shrine of the Báb in the background, May 1919. The Western man next to Shoghi Effendi is Hippolyte Dreyfus-Barney; next to him is his wife, Laura Dreyfus-Barney. In a light-coloured suit behind the Master is Badi Bushrui, and to his right 'Abbás-Qúlí

'Abdu'l-Bahá with Bahá'ís at the north-west of the Shrine. Raḥmatu'lláh is in the back row, third from right (black beard and fez), Fujita just below to the left. Directly in front of Raḥmatu'lláh is Badi Bushrui. On the Master's right is Helen Goodall, a Disciple of 'Abdu'l-Bahá. Kneeling at left is Muḥammad Tabrízí, maternal uncle of Mr 'Alí Nakhjavání; seated next to him is Haji Ali Yazdi, paternal uncle of Mr Adib Taherzadeh. Third from left at the rear is 'Abbás-Qúlí. At far left (with white beard and folded hands) is Muḥammad Yazdí, the father of Aziz Yazdi

> Pá<u>sh</u>á, He said that so far the political mischief-maker had not caused any damage, and it was to be hoped that the religious mischief-maker would not do so either.[33]

That deft use of humour and reasoning by 'Abdu'l-Bahá disarmed Jamal Pasha. In another meeting between the two, 'Abdu'l-Bahá once again charmed the tyrant. In early 1916, He attended a lunch also attended by Jamal Pasha, and began speaking in Turkish on philosophical, scientific and spiritual subjects. Jamal Pasha listened with great interest, and soon became deferential, even going to the extent of accompanying 'Abdu'l-Bahá to the bottom of the steps outside as He took his leave.[34]

But tyrants are dangerous and unpredictable, their fears of challenge easily aroused. The enemies of 'Abdu'l-Bahá were in action and did not find it difficult to foment suspicion of Him in the eyes of the authorities. After all, He had visited England and France, now the enemies of the Ottomans, and had met many prominent citizens there. He had hosted pilgrims from those countries on their visits to Haifa and Acre. The enemy British forces were in Egypt not far away, and were planning to advance into the Holy Land from the south.

However, despite the ongoing tension and danger during these years, 'Abdu'l-Bahá kept busy and ensured that at least some events at the Shrine continued. The grain he had advised the farmers to store saved many from starvation when food ran out.[35]

Ali Yazdi described spending the summer of 1917 in Haifa with a fellow student from Beirut, Shoghi Effendi, where they spent time in an 'anteroom to the Shrine of the Báb':

> There were frequent trips to the holy Shrine of the Báb. 'Abdu'l-Bahá rode an old horse-drawn, bus-like vehicle up the mountain.
>
> The rest of us walked the rocky road, past the Persian (or Eastern) Pilgrim House to the terrace overlooking the city of Haifa and the blue bay beyond.
>
> In the distance lay the hazy outline of Akka. We gathered on the terrace until 'Abdu'l-Bahá appeared and entered the Shrine. He generally chanted the Tablet of Visitation, but sometimes He asked Shoghi Effendi to chant it.
>
> When it was over the believers started to come out, He stood at the door with a vial of rose water and put a little in each other's

> hand. I remember following Him as He walked among the pines, past the Holy Shrine on Mt Carmel, deeply absorbed in thought, while the setting sun came down into the Mediterranean Sea.
>
> As I looked down from the Shrine of the Bab on Mt Carmel, I could see the straight, steep path, a succession of flights of stone-and-masonry steps that were in line with the main street of the German colony . . .[36]

During that same summer, Ali Yazdi was in the garden of the house of the Master when he overheard something that demonstrated the pressure 'Abdu'l-Bahá was under:

> Everyone was quiet and I asked why. They said, 'There is a commission of inquiry up in the Master's room.' I listened, and I could hear His clear, commanding voice through the open window right above, talking to the Turkish commission with dignity, as if He were the investigator and they the culprit. Although the Master was humble in many ways, He never really bowed to anyone; He was proud in His nobility. Through sensing His confidence, I acquired confidence and faith that He would be spared.[37]

Towards the end of the war, information reached the British Intelligence Service that, at a meeting of Islamic leaders in Jerusalem, Jamal Pasha had expressed his intention to 'crucify 'Abdu'l-Bahá and His family on Mt Carmel in the event of the Turkish army being compelled to evacuate Haifa and retreat northwards'.[38] In those circumstances, he said, he would also level the Shrine of the Báb and the Shrine of Bahá'u'lláh.

The information about the threat had come from a Major in British Intelligence, Wellesley Tudor Pole.[39] Ali Yazdi provides extra detail:

> In short, the British Intelligence Service, headed by Major Tudor-Pole, one who was very friendly to the Bahá'ís if not a Bahá'í himself, had uncovered a message telling that 'Abdu'l-Bahá was in danger; that Jamal Pasha had vowed to crucify Him, and destroy the Holy tombs and all the sacred buildings of the Baha'i Faith before the British came.[40]

As the Allied forces advanced from Egypt into the Holy Land, there was a real fear among British Bahá'ís that the Ottoman forces, in the chaos of their retreat, would carry out the threat on 'Abdu'l-Bahá's life. In response to a request by Lady Blomfield, a prominent British Bahá'í, Lord Lamington, a British peer who had met 'Abdu'l-Bahá years earlier, made contact at the highest levels of the British Government expressing the urgent need to protect Him.[41]

As a result, the person he had written to, the British Secretary of State for Foreign Affairs, Lord Balfour, cabled the British High Commissioner in Egypt and asked the commander-in-chief of the Egyptian Expeditionary Force, General Sir Edmund Allenby, to ensure 'all possible consideration' for 'Abdu'l-Bahá and His family in the event of a further advance by the British forces in Palestine.[42] Allenby ordered that, once in Haifa, a British guard be posted around 'Abdu'l-Bahá's house and a further guard be placed at the disposal of His family. It was also made known within the Ottoman ranks that there would be stern retribution should there be an attempt to kill or injure 'Abdu'l-Bahá or His family.[43]

The advancing British troops feinted as they pushed further into the Holy Land. Rather than sending their forces up the Jordan Valley as the enemy would have predicted, they burst through the Ottoman defences on the coastal plain and surged towards Haifa. Only then did they cut inland. They moved through the Musmus Pass, just before the point where Mount Carmel extends out to the Mediterranean shoreline.

From their position on the inland side of Mount Carmel, they faced Haifa and the Mediterranean Sea. Ahead and to the right were the thick stone walls of Acre. As they approached Haifa on 23 September 1918 they came under enemy fire from high on their left. It came from the summit of Mount Carmel where there were two German naval cannons as well as machine guns.[44]

Soon some Indian soldiers under the British command, members of the Mysore Lancers, supported by a squadron of British Sherwood Rangers, surged up Mount Carmel and destroyed those emplacements, including one overlooking the Shrine of the Báb.[45] British artillery then fired from the top of Mount Carmel, unintentionally frightening the townsfolk of Haifa. But the gunners were not aiming at them, but rather at Turkish positions amidst palm trees on the coast.

Indian cavalry forces, the Jodhpur Lancers accompanied by British engineers from 15th Field Troop, Royal Engineers, also on horseback, galloped into Haifa. There was brief resistance and fighting from some Turkish soldiers but it faded quickly. Soon Brigadier General A. D'A. King arrived. He asked about 'Abdu'l-Bahá and was informed He was safe. British troops, 'Indian army outriders', quickly found His house and placed a guard there.[46] A message about Him reached General Allenby, who cabled London: 'Have today taken Palestine. Notify the world that 'Abdu'l-Bahá is safe.'[47] Also safe at last was the unutterably sacred Shrine of the Báb.

Next evening, the new British military governor of Jerusalem, Sir Ronald Storrs, paid 'Abdu'l-Bahá a visit:

> I renewed in Haifa my friendship with Abbas Effendi Abd al-Baha' [sic] and his Bahai [sic] followers, whom I had last seen imprisoned in Acre on my visit in 1909. I found him sitting in spotless white, noble as a prophet of Michael Angelo [sic]. He placed at my disposal the training and talents of his community, one or two of whom I appointed to positions of confidence which they still continue to deserve.[48]

Sir Ronald had first met the Master in Acre in 1909 after driving along the beach from Haifa, his companion taking unsuccessful potshots with his revolver at eagles along the way. As he wrote in his memoirs, and referring to Professor Edward Granville Browne: 'We visited Abbas Effendi, the head of the Bab religion, Johnny Browne's name being a passé partout [providing a means of passage] with Persians. He ['Abdu'l-Bahá] had been exiled and imprisoned there about forty-two years, but seemed cheerful enough.'[49]

General Allenby first met 'Abdu'l-Bahá in January 1919 when he visited the Master's house, telling 'Abdu'l-Bahá that He was 'a person whom I esteem and honour more than any one else in the region'. The Master congratulated him for liberating the Holy Land 'with the least shedding of blood'.[50]

Some time after the liberation, 'Abdu'l-Bahá briefly outlined the threat that had been made against him by Jamal Pasha in the war years, and His reaction to it:

> When Jamál Pá<u>sh</u>á came to Jerusalem he made some remarks about me. He said: 'I will go and conquer Egypt. I will drive England out

of Egypt. I will conquer all the Suez Canal. Victorious I shall return. My first command will be this, that I will hang 'Abdu'l-Bahá at the gate of 'Akká.'

The German Consul was in that meeting. He was an acquaintance of mine.[51] He came and told me that Jamál Páshá had said this . . .

I said: 'Let Jamál Páshá go and conquer Egypt. Then I will give myself up. Let him conquer Egypt, I am ready.'

. . . As soon as the battle began he fled. He rode in his automobile and fled . . . He would not say: 'I am defeated.' I said: 'It must be so.'

Two or three days later, the German Consul came and said: 'He (Jamál Páshá) is defeated.' Jamál Páshá returned here. He began to twist his moustaches and said: 'This was a reconnoitring attack. I wanted to test the strength of the enemy.'

'But', wrote 'Abdu'l-Bahá in conclusion, 'I understood.'[52]

The tyrant Jamal Pasha was conquered.[53] The British now ruled the Holy Land. 'Abdu'l-Bahá and His family had survived unharmed. The Shrine of the Báb was intact, as was the Shrine of Bahá'u'lláh and the other holy places. 'Abdu'l-Bahá was to be knighted for His humanitarian services during the war in providing food to prevent famine, and His advice to the incoming administration.[54]

Shoghi Effendi wrote:

The past four years have been years of untold calamity, of unprecedented oppression, of indescribable misery, of severe famine and distress, of unparalleled bloodshed and strife, but now that the dove of peace has returned to its nest and abode a golden opportunity has arisen for the promulgation of the Word of God. This will be now promoted and the Message delivered in this liberated region without the least amount of restriction. This is indeed the Era of Service.[55]

18

POST-WAR GATHERINGS AT THE SHRINE OF THE BÁB

In the safe, happy and free days in Haifa after the end of World War I, there were many wonderful gatherings at the Shrine of the Báb and the Pilgrim House to the east. Descriptions of those events convey the special spirit of this time when the threat to the Shrine and to the One who built it had disappeared.

Usually, it was 'Abdu'l-Bahá who was giving the talks and leading the way to the Shrine, which He usually visited twice a day, but one day in January 1919 He was absent.[1] His grandson, Shoghi Effendi, then 22 years old, took a leadership role, unusual in that as secretary to the Master he usually remained in the background.

The future Guardian[2] later wrote in his diary what happened in the 'long, warm and spiritual' gathering. It began with a message from 'Abdu'l-Bahá and was followed with a recital by three singers. Then Shoghi Effendi delivered a talk on 'the significance of this celebration in view of the rapid progress of the Cause and the fulfilment of Bahá'u'lláh's explicit prophecies'. Shoghi Effendi's short description of the subsequent experience in the Shrine captures an atmosphere that many others have felt in the years since.

> When we visited the Holy Shrine, it had grown dark, and the visit at this silent hour of twilight was indeed imbued with a deep sense of fervour and respect. The whole day was marked with a sense of triumph, merriment and gratitude and was in accordance with the wish and recommendation of the Beloved ['Abdu'l-Bahá].[3]

At a gathering nearly a week later attended by 'Abdu'l-Bahá and Shoghi Effendi, the Master gave a warm greeting to about thirty believers and some British soldiers on leave. After the soldiers left, He gave the friends a talk on faithfulness and trust. Shoghi Effendi wrote in his diary:

> As the meeting came to a close, we were all led to visit the Blessed Shrine, at the door of which stood as usual the Beloved in the utmost of humility and respect. That spot was exceptionally cold and exposed, yet there was the Servant of Bahá giving the good example to his friends and servants.[4]

Hostilities in the Great War had finished only two months previously and Shoghi Effendi was keenly waiting for the flow of pilgrims to fully resume:

> What we eagerly look forward to, however, is the practical opening of ways and the removal of all travel restrictions so that pilgrims and friends may pour in, may set foot on the Holy Land, may visit the Holy Mount, may look again at the Beloved's face and may circumambulate the Holy Shrine.
>
> This day we trust will not be indefinitely postponed.[5]

The flow resumed, and by December 1919 Shoghi Effendi was able to write: 'We are exceedingly busy here. Some fifty pilgrims, Arabs, Kurds, Persians, Americans, European and Japanese.'[6]

One of the best descriptions of a visit to the Shrine and its environs in those magical years when the Master was still alive came from George Latimer, a Bahá'í from Oregon in the United States, who had met 'Abdu'l-Bahá in 1912 in New Hampshire. He arrived as a pilgrim in November 1919. In the account he later wrote of his experiences he noted how 'Abdu'l-Bahá visited the pilgrims before they ascended the steep road up Mt Carmel. Prior to seating the pilgrims for a luncheon, He sprinkled on the table cloth jasmine blossoms from the gardens near the Shrine, a perfumed hint of the special atmosphere they would shortly experience.

Every Sunday the pilgrims would gather at the Shrine of the Báb. Latimer described such an occasion, which was preceded by 'Abdu'l-Bahá driving up early with another pilgrim from the United States, Harry Randall,[7] to have a quiet discussion with him before that meeting was to begin.

The other pilgrims, including George Latimer, went on foot. On the way up they overtook one of 'Abdu'l-Bahá's secretaries, Mírzá Núru'd-Dín Zayn, who uttered what many pilgrims have observed in different languages and different ways of expression in the years that followed:

'Tis hard,' he said, 'to climb the Mountain of God but very easy to come down.'

Mr Latimer agreed: 'It did seem hard, the rocks rose so abruptly one above the other. But when we thought of our Beloved just above us on the mountain, wings rose beneath our feet.'

He then describes the 'fathomless stillness surrounding the Tomb' and 'its ravishingly beautiful view':

> The city of Haifa lies below, white stone houses with red-tiled roofs, planted amid walled gardens; the great bay swings in a perfect semi-circle around to the north. 'Akka, white, dazzlingly bright in the resplendent sunlight of that holy land, lies like a jewel on the blue sea.

Latimer tells how the pilgrims entered the central northern room of the Shrine via the door with 'the symbol of the Cause of God, two stars standing at each side of the Tree of Life'.[8] He then gives his readers a vicarious experience of visiting the Shrine in the company of 'Abdu'l-Bahá. His account is special because it is one of the first of a visit by Western pilgrims after the interment of the sacred remains of the Báb.

First they entered a room at the front of the Shrine:

> In one corner, sitting on the beautiful Persian rug that covers the floor and part of the wall, was the blessed Hayder-'Ali . . .[9] When the Master entered the room, now filled with friends, Persians, Arabs, Egyptians, Americans, joy swept our hearts. Hayder-'Ali, like an eager child in the presence of the Master, tried to rise but 'Abdu'l-Bahá prevented him . . .
>
> Presently we all rose and followed the silent steps of the Master out and around the terrace to the holy room where the body of the Blessed Báb lies in its age-long rest. The Master stood at the door and anointed our hands with rose-water as we entered[10] . . .
>
> We lifted the rose-water to our foreheads and then bowed with our Persian brothers just inside the Threshold.[11] The atmosphere

of that holy place was marvellous. The air was vibrant with a living presence . . .

One by one, silently, the Persians, those pure, wonderful servants of the God who is Most Glorious, approached the inner room and dropped their heads on the shining Threshold, while Shoghi chanted impressively the Tablet of Visitation[12] . . . and when 'Abdu'l-Bahá . . . with sublime tenderness helped Hayder-'Alí down the centre of that room, supporting and leading him, and then with kingly majesty walked back again – the effect was indescribable.

After we left the Tomb we watched the majestic figure of the Master, with black flowing abbá, shining white turban and silver hair, finding his way down the winding stony path. The friends followed in silent love and wonder.[13]

Another pilgrim, Genevieve Coy, also used elevated and uplifting language to describe her experience in September 1920.[14] Her account is valuable not only to convey the atmosphere but also to describe some physical aspects of the Shrine, and for that reason much of it is best read verbatim.

She and fellow pilgrims rode up, in a horse-drawn carriage, at about 4 p.m.:

Finally we turned off from the main road, and the carriage drove down a steep[15] incline toward the Mossafer Kaneh [*musáfir-kháánih*], – the Persian Hospice for men.[16] There we alighted and Mrs. Hoagg[17] led us along a wide path, which is bordered with cypress trees on one side and with fig trees on the other. We passed the house of the care-taker, with the little room on top where the Master sometimes sleeps when He is on the mountain, and walked around to the front of the Tomb.

In front of the Tomb of the Bab we found perhaps thirty of the men pilgrims sitting. One of the most majestic was a tall man, dressed in a long black robe, – one of the Baha'i teachers from Ishkabad . . .

We were shown to seats in front of the Tomb, on the edge of the beautiful garden of the terrace . . .

Suddenly all of the believers rose and faced the East. Then, from around the corner of the Tomb came the Master with two of the young men walking a little behind him. He came slowly toward us, – and said, 'Welcome, welcome!' in English; and then, 'Sit down, sit down!' Sylvia [Paine] sat next to him; then Mabel Paine, myself, Cora [Grey], and Mrs. Hoagg. The other friends were beyond her, in two rows . . .

The Master began to speak in Persian, and Rouhi Effendi[18] translated into English. He asked several questions; he talked of principles of living. Sometimes he would be silent for several minutes, – with His eyes looking far, far away . . .

. . . Afterward we walked about the garden at the front of the Tomb. We saw the big reservoir for rain-water, built into the terrace, which supplies water for the garden and for many of the people of the neighbourhood. Mirza Lotfullah[19] brought us figs from one of the trees in the garden. We looked across the beautiful blue waters of the bay, to Acca, shining in the distance. We caught a suggestion of luxuriant growth of trees, and were told that it marked the Tomb of Baha'u'llah . . .

The care-taker opened a door at the southwest corner of the Tomb, and spread a piece of matting in front of it. Mrs. Hoagg went with us to show us the custom used in entering the Tomb. We removed our shoes, and then the care-taker poured rose-water on our hands, from a little glass cruet. We followed Mrs. Hoagg into the first room. It was perhaps fifteen feet square, and the floor was covered with a beautiful dark Persian carpet. There was no furniture of any kind. Directly in line with the outer door was a second door[20] that led into an inner room. That was also covered with beautiful rugs. Standing on the floor were exquisite glass vases with candles burning in them. They were in groups, perhaps of three, and they gave the impression of flowers of living flame. I think there must have been other objects, a few, in the room. But the whole impression was one of exquisite beauty, simplicity and peace. The inner room was raised several inches above the outer, and the raised threshold was covered with an embroidered cloth.

Mrs. Hoagg walked slowly up to the threshold, knelt there a moment in prayer and then came back to a corner of the room. Cora followed her, and then came my turn. I had heard of the custom of prostrating oneself at the threshold of the Tomb, and I had wondered whether it would not seem stilted and formal. But it did not

> in the least! Perhaps it was the dignity and majesty of the Tomb, perhaps it was because we had been with the Master so recently . . .[21]

Then Genevieve Coy recounts an experience that was wondrous for her.

> Finally Mrs. Hoagg, Cora and I had left the Tomb. Mabel and Sylvia had not yet come out. We were about to put on our shoes, when suddenly the Master came around the corner! He smiled at us, and took up the cruet of rose-water. He held it out toward us, and I realized in a few moments that he wished to pour some on our hands. But I did not dream of going into the Tomb again, and so I did not realize what he meant! So he poured some on his own hands, put some on his face, and again held out the rose-water, giving us a glorious smile as he did so. That time we understood that he was waiting to anoint our hands, – and we gladly held them out for the fragrant drops. Mrs. Hoagg whispered, 'We will go in again' – and just then the men believers came in a long line from the front of the Tomb. The Master anointed the hands of each, and they passed into the Tomb. Each knelt at the inner threshold a moment, until all had risen, and stood in a circle about the room. Then the Master spoke to Rouhi Effendi, who began to chant a long prayer, one of the Prayers of Visitation. His chanting was the sweetest, the most melodious of any I have ever heard. After the prayer the believers knelt at the threshold, and then passed quietly out.[22]

In a description of a conclusion of another visit, Genevieve Coy referred to a view from the base of Mount Carmel of the lighting of the Shrine: 'Soon above us, on the mountain, there shone out the light in front of the Tomb, which is lighted every night unless there is very brilliant moonlight.'[23]

She also described a personal visit that she undertook on 4 September, 1920 with her fellow pilgrim Cora Grey:

> On Saturday morning, Cora and I rose in the darkness of 4:30 a.m., dressed, and by 5:15 we were on our way up the mountain toward the Tomb of the Bab. That early hour was a bit too late, for even then we found the climb warm, and the sun rose before we had reached the Tomb . . . As we passed the care-taker's house, he saw us, and

by a gesture, asked whether we wished to enter his house. Perhaps he thought we had come up to see the Master, whom we knew was either in the house or at the Tomb. But we motioned toward the Tomb. He smiled, and preceding us, opened the west door into the room where we had been on Thursday. Then he quietly departed.

The candles were not lighted and the central room was not quite so beautiful on that account. But a soft light filtered in through the doors, – and the exquisite peace filled our hearts. We stayed for perhaps an hour, in meditation and prayer.

It must have been after seven when we went out into the garden. We walked about a bit, and then Rouhi Effendi and Mirza Lotfullah came out to wish us good-morning . . .

The two young men talked to us for a few minutes, and then asked whether we would like to see the circle of cypress trees where Baha'u'llah used to sit . . .

Mirza Lotfullah led us up a path, onto a terrace back of the Tomb, and there we saw the circle of cypress trees. There are ten of them, planted quite close together so that their boughs interlace, forming an almost solid wall. They are on a bit of ground which is raised about three feet from the surrounding field, and is held up by a stone wall. We went up into the circle of ground between the trees. Above our heads was a small circle of blue sky. The ground was brown with needles from the trees . . . But we had been there only a few minutes, when Rouhi Effendi came toward us, calling that the Master wished to see us! And we went on eager feet, following Rouhi Effendi to Abbas Kuli's house. (Abbas Kuli is the caretaker of the Tomb of the Bab.)

Cora was ahead of me, and she told me afterward that when she entered the room where the Master was sitting on a divan, she was not sure what to do! He bade her welcome, but still she stood in the doorway! Then he rose, held out his hands and motioned her to a chair. She went and sat down. Just then I came in, and the Master motioned me to a chair beside Cora . . .

The room we were in had a north window, which looked out over the Bay of Acca. Like all windows in the eastern houses, it had several iron bars across it to keep out intruders. The house is high on the hillside and there was a wonderful view across the bay. The Master sat on a divan in front of the window . . .

> Abbas Kuli brought to the Master a little tray with a teapot full of what looked like tea. The Master poured out some and drank it, explaining that it was a kind of herb drink. Then Abbas Kuli brought us tea in the lovely little Persian glasses. Afterward he came in with a tray full of things to eat and placed it on a chair in front of us. The Master told us to eat. 'He says you must eat your breakfast here,' Mirza Lotfullah interpreted . . . The tray had on it ripe figs, ripe olives, honey, and slices of white bread, – and the latter were the only slices of white bread we saw on our whole journey! I ate one or two figs, and a few olives . . . Thus we had breakfast with the Master at the Tomb of the Bab! . . .
>
> . . . We followed him from the house to where Esfendiar was waiting with the carriage. We had expected to walk down the mountain, but after the Master had ascended to the middle seat, he motioned to us to get in the back seat . . . At the gate of his house he alighted, and, saluting us with uplifted hand, he left us and entered his home![24]

One day at the Shrine, 'Abdu'l-Bahá gave His vision of the future of the environs of the Shrine of the Báb, as He had so often done before: 'The day will come when this mountain will be resplendent with light – light from top to bottom,' adding that in the area there would also be a hotel, a university, a Temple, a home for incurables, the poor and orphans. 'I foresee that this harbour will be full of vessels. And from here to the Blessed Shrine (Bahje) there will be wide avenues, on both side of which there will be trees and gardens.'[25]

Shoghi Effendi recorded that 'Abdu'l-Bahá said that in the future Haifa would have a predominant position in the Near East, and that He

> praised highly the unique position of [Mount Carmel], the spirituality which pervades it, the view of the neighbouring blue sea, a clear and azure sky, a lovely coastal plain and a magnificent range of hills, sand dunes and mountains which it unfolds and particularly the historic and religious memory which clusters around it. Tourists, remarked the Beloved, on their pilgrimage to the Holy Land will make it their favourite Shrine, will tarry a time on its glorious summit and will sojourn on its lovely slopes. Etymologically taken, Carmel separates into two words 'Carm' and 'Il' which denote the Vineyard of God, and moreover said the Beloved it has

been recorded in the Scriptures, 'The Lord verily is the Splendour of Carmel.' On this blessed Mount, monuments, temples, asylums, hospitals, pilgrim-houses, orphanages, hospices, educational institutions, Mashrekul-Azkars shall be erected. Its universities will flourish and its educational, cultural centre shall attract hundreds and thousands of scholars and of truth-seekers. Every span of it shall thrive and prosper, the melody of praise and thanksgiving, the hymns of prayer and supplication will rise from it and shall ascend the Supreme Concourse. Carmel will become a centre of material, cultural and spiritual activities.[26]

Shoghi Effendi visits the Shrine

Of all the descriptions of the Shrine, the one that seems to capture the essence of the experience the most at that time came from the pen of the future head of the Faith, Shoghi Effendi, who wrote of a visit he made in 1919:

Just before sunset, I was ordered by the Beloved to walk up to the Holy Tomb and offer a prayer of devotion and thanksgiving on His behalf. I instantly put on my walking boots, took hold of my cane and ascended the Holy Mount. The wind that was violently blowing softened down to a pure and fragrant breeze which heralded the approach of springtime; the mighty, and I venture to add matchless, view that was unfolded to my eyes as I ascended higher and higher the green and verdant slopes of Carmel; the spirituality that imbued the atmosphere; the stillness, save the distant roar of the waves, that added greatly to the Majesty and the imposing serenity of the surroundings; the beautiful sight of the blossoming almond trees that surround the Holy Tomb; the fragrant smell of the rain-drenched roses that reminded the pilgrim of his approach to the door of the Tomb; all made me forget my care, my concerns and my anxieties. The environment was elevating, the thought that amid such a scene, I was to offer a prayer on behalf of the Beloved thrilled and moved me from within and made me realise what an insignificant speck of dust did I figure at the foot of His Throne. I prayed the best I could and begged guidance, protection and capability from Him who had sent me to this hallowed Spot.[27]

19

THE WESTERN PILGRIM HOUSE

From about 1913, western pilgrims coming to visit the Shrine would stay at 4 Haparsim Street, over the road from 'Abdu'l-Bahá's house. The house was owned by Mírzá Muḥsin Afnán, husband of the Master's second daughter, Ṭúbá Khánum, and he gave the use of it to his Father-in-law.[1] A beautiful pen portrait of the place and its atmosphere comes from Genevieve Coy, who stayed there as a pilgrim in September, 1920.

> To waken in the Pilgrim House in Haifa is a very, very happy experience! From our west windows would catch a glimpse of the Tomb of the Bab, and how eagerly we looked up at it, knowing that there the Master was dwelling;[2] there was the memorial to the wonderful herald of our Faith, the Supreme Bab . . .[3]

Fujita, the Japanese Bahá'í who had come from the United States to serve 'Abdu'l-Bahá, was the caretaker. 'He gets the breakfast; he serves the lunch, the food for which is brought over from the Master's house; he washes the dishes, he cleans the lamps, he is always busy in serving us.'[4] The pilgrims would cross the road and visit the family of the Master in His house.

'Abdu'l-Bahá would also visit the pilgrim house and talk with those there. He said to Genevieve Coy and the others: 'Your food and rooms are very simple here, but your purpose in coming here makes them seem good to you. When a man is good, all things about him are good. When a man is bad, all things about him are bad. It is necessary that man be very good.'[5] Genevieve wrote: 'I do not know how or why, but in his presence, all life is *lifted* higher; it acquires freshness and beauty.'[6]

As pilgrim numbers mounted, a bigger pilgrim house was needed. A Persian Bahá'í offered land in Haparsim Street, a site where Bahá'u'lláh had once pitched His tent.[7] It seems this land was sold by that Bahá'í, rather than donated, because a wealthy American pilgrim, William Henry (Harry) Randall wrote in his diary on 20 November 1919 that his wife Ruth

> asked the Master if we might buy a piece of land and erect a Pilgrim House for the friends to occupy, some twenty rooms, garden, kitchen, etc. He replied, 'Yes, very good, most excellent.' At lunch the Master said, 'See 'Abbás Kulí about it, and I will approve.' So this is the land we may now get for the Pilgrim House, trod by the Blessed Feet of the Blessed Perfection, once the dwelling of God.[8]

Harry Randall, who was to become a generous donor to the Faith and to individual Bahá'ís, had met the Master in Boston in 1912 and became a Bahá'í at Green Acre in the following year.[9] On pilgrimage in 1919, he rode in a carriage with 'Abdu'l-Bahá up Mount Carmel where, in the house of 'Abbás-Qulí just a few metres away from the Shrine, the Master spoke to him about various matters, drinking tea and looking towards Bahjí from the rear balcony that faced north. Then they entered the Shrine, with the Master putting rose water on the hands of the Bahá'ís at the door. Harry wrote in his diary: 'One is spellbound in this presence. The body fades and the hour of the Spirit rules the heart of nearness.'[10]

Later, 'Abbás-Qulí suggested that Harry might donate the curtains to put over the entrance to the Holy Tomb, then a doorway as opposed to the arch it became in future years.[11] It would be, 'Abbás-Qulí said, the first gift from America for the Shrine and the Master would be pleased.

The Master was to call Harry 'my spiritual associate . . . my participator and co-sharer!'[12] On 16 May 1921, the Master cabled Harry, saying that he had bought two adjacent pieces of land for the pilgrim house at a cost of seven hundred pounds and that Harry and Ruth were to pay for them as part of the gift. The pilgrim house was not to be completed for some years.

Also in the vicinity were the houses of the German Templers. 'Abdu'l-Bahá loved the German children and they loved Him, as one of that community recalled:

> When he left his beautiful house for a walk, all the children,

Liberator of the Holy Land in 1917, General Edmund Allenby, and his wife, Lady Adelaide Mabel (Chapman) Allenby. General Allenby told 'Abdu'l-Bahá He was 'a person whom I esteem and honour more than anyone else in the region'.

The tyrant Jamal Pasha

In 1918 the Shrine was easily visible from the air. It is just below the approximate halfway point of Mountain Road that crosses the middle of the slope of Mount Carmel above Haifa

The Shrine of the Báb and the room of 'Abdu'l-Bahá on top of the house of 'Abbás-Qúlí are seen, upper right, in this view of the Master accompanied by two attendants (one mostly obscured) along Persian Street (now Haparsim Street), as He rides towards His house

Harry Randall, right, who with his wife Ruth donated the purchase price for the site of the Western Pilgrim House. With him is Shrine custodian 'Abbás-Qúlí, who suggested that Harry make the first donation from North America for the Shrine, the cost of curtains to hang at the entrance of the inner Shrine

Murgh Maḥallih (Abode of the Birds), a garden near Tehran, was loved by Bahá'u'lláh and inspired 'Abdu'l-Bahá's plan to have terraces associated with the Shrine of the Báb

A lighting generator occupied a building separate from the Shrine

Curtis Kelsey, who installed the lighting for the Shrine

New York coffee entrepreneur Roy Wilhelm, later appointed a Hand of the Cause, sent a lighting plant for the Shrine

> especially the pre-school children, gathered near the 'Persian God' who was walking in a white flowing gown with a white scarf around his white hair, with friendly blue eyes and holding a white rose from his garden in his hand. Then he would stop and speak to the children in fairly good German. Of course, he also had his darlings, obviously it was light blond and blue-eyed children. For example my younger sister Gerda received a golden coin.[13]

The author of this anecdote, who had black hair, received a tin coin and as a child was a little envious.[14]

Recalling the days when she was a child in her grandfather's house in the Templer community, Cornelia Wortz said that 'Abdu'l-Bahá would come by and, from outside the property, call out: 'Is there anyone to give some water to this old man?' He would then enter the courtyard where the two men would chat – she remembered her grandfather consulting with 'Abdul-Bahá about a wheat crop. Once when Cornelia was ill, 'Abdu'l-Bahá brought her some apple juice. Most afternoons she would go next door and, on the flat roof of the home of another German Templer (the mother of a Templer child, Gerhard Bubeck, who later become a Bahá'í), she would do embroidery with 'Abdu'l-Bahá's daughters, the start of a long friendship. She also went to Bahjí where she met Bahíyyih Khánum. She recalled that in 1917, when the first aeroplane landed in Haifa, 'Abdu'l-Bahá asked His gardeners to pick some beautiful flowers from which a bouquet was made and gave it to Cornelia to present to the pilots on His behalf.[15]

The brother of the late Gerhard Bubeck remembered as a child sitting on the knee of 'Abdu'l-Bahá, Who was feeding him sweets.[16]

Bahá'í children may also have attended the Templer school, as a modern Templer archivist has advised: 'As a rule, Templer schools in Palestine were open to all nationalities willing to be instructed in the German language'.[17] If so, they may have included the Master's grandchildren.

Clara Klingeman, a Templer who was 14 years old when the Master passed away, recalled in later years that He had lived 'in a very simple house, overgrown with bougainvillea'. She wrote:

> Abbas Effendi was an outstanding figure in his long white gown, with his long white beard and his long white hair covered by a white

turban. A very impressive sight were his frequent walks through our colony street, with his faithful followers a few steps behind him. Two or three of my cousins, boys of 10–12 years, often watched this solemn procession. They soon found out that, if they would demurely stand by the side of the street and politely greeted Abbas Effendi, he would put his hand into the pocket of his gown and take out some sweets or small coins for them. One of the fabulous gifts he had for our family was a peacock pair that we children admired and venerated very much. The entire kindergarten was allowed to come to us and watch how the peacock spread its tail.[18]

20

TERRACES AND LIGHTS

On 15 August 1919, 'Abdu'l-Bahá gave a talk in which he spoke of His inspiration for His plan to have terraces associated with the Shrine.[1] He said he was reminded of the Darband of Shimiran, a lovely area to the north of Tehran where there was a location called Murgh Maḥallih (Abode of Birds). Using the beautiful and meaningful images of mythology, He said it was not the abode of ordinary birds, but rather it was the nest of the eastern phoenix and the abode of the griffin of the Caucasus Mountain – the Kúh-i-Qaf, the mountain which surrounds the world. He was alluding to Bahá'u'lláh.

In the early years of the Cause in about 1849, the Master explained, Bahá'u'lláh spent a complete summer there in the garden of Ḥájí Báqir, where He would speak on spiritual topics to gatherings of some 150 believers. The garden comprised three levels overlooking a lake. In the middle of the lake, which was fed by a river, there was a big stone platform and in the middle of the platform there was a tent. Around the platform there were flower beds. 'Abdu'l-Bahá said it was a delightful period, and that Bahá'u'lláh would often remember and mention that place.

The Master said He thought the environs of the Shrine of the Báb, as at Murgh Maḥallih, should also have different levels all the way up its slope. However, the first comprehensive plan to develop terraces from the bottom of Mount Carmel up to the Shrine came not from the Bahá'ís but from the city engineer of Haifa.

It had its origins back in 1913 in Edinburgh, when 'Abdu'l-Bahá had met Sir Patrick Geddes (1854–1932),[2] a Scot who was an innovative thinker in urban planning. After the World War had come to an end, they were reunited when Sir Patrick became a town planner in Palestine. In 1920 he presented to 'Abdu'l-Bahá a request by members of 'Pro-Carmel', an interfaith organization aimed at improving the city.

They asked that He become the organization's president.[3] 'Abdu'l-Bahá agreed and also consented to the impact on the Bahá'í property on Mount Carmel of a town planning scheme proposed by Sir Patrick and the city engineer, Dr Assaf Ciffrin.[4] In addition, He granted land without compensation for two new public roads through Bahá'í property, and donated 4,000 square metres for a public school in the vicinity.[5]

As part of the town plan, there was a scheme for Terraces up the steep slope towards the Shrine. Sir Patrick wrote:

> Dr. Ciffrin, in his architectural capacity has produced a fine scheme for a monumental stairway and cypress avenue leading uphill from the Templar Boulevard upon the level plain, to the central meeting place of the Bahai community in Haifa, which as all Bahais doubtless know, contains the Tomb of the Bab.
>
> For this scheme, (of which the design is a gift by Dr. Ciffrin) between £2,000 and £3,000 will be required; but he and I and other friends and sympathizers are confident that this sum will readily be subscribed within a reasonable time by the many members and friends of the Bahai Cause throughout the world. Sir Abbas[6] at once expressed himself as approving the design, and gratified by it, as at once a useful and needed access, and a beautiful and dignified memorial. He granted the land, and promised also to compensate from his own ground, the small portion of a Moslem neighbour's ground which is also required to complete the scheme. He further gave a subscription of £100 to begin the list; but while authorizing us to open a subscription list, and send it to friends and sympathizers, he charged us to be careful to explain this as a purely voluntary matter, and not to represent him as in any way pressing his followers or friends to subscribe, and this we of course promised to do.
>
> We are thus however free to say that all subscriptions may be sent to *The Treasurer, Bab Memorial Stairway, c/o Dr. Ciffrin, Municipal Engineer, Haifa, Palestine.*[7]

However, for a reason or reasons not yet determined, no such stairway or terraces were built during the lifetime of 'Abdu'l-Bahá.

In the years after the war, work began to illuminate the Shrine. 'Abdu'l-Bahá had earlier described His concept of the finished structure of the Shrine, saying it should have an arcade surrounding the original nine rooms He had planned, and be surmounted by a dome.[8] He also expressed his wish to have the Shrine of the Báb 'bathed in light' and at the same time provide a view across the bay to see the Shrine of Bahá'u'lláh illuminated.[9]

The lighting project had its origins across the oceans. In New York, Roy Wilhelm, a Bahá'í who was a millionaire coffee entrepreneur,[10] had read the words of the Báb in which He lamented the lack of a lamp in His prison cell in the fortress of Maku:

> In His presence, which is My presence, there is not at night even a lighted lamp! And yet, in places [of worship] which in varying degrees reach out unto Him, unnumbered lamps are shining.[11]

Inspired into action, Mr Wilhelm wrote to 'Abdu'l-Bahá and asked for permission to send a lighting plant to Haifa to illuminate the Shrine. A cable came back from Him saying three plants were necessary. Within weeks the machinery was on its way. However, the equipment remained in Haifa for a year without being installed. A Californian Bahá'í sent a young electrical engineer to do the work, but 'Abdu'l-Bahá sent him back home saying the time was not right yet. Then a Persian Bahá'í, Ḥusayn Kahrubá'í,[12] travelled to Haifa and asked if he could work on the project. 'Abdu'l-Bahá said he would be called upon to assist at the appropriate time.

Mr Wilhelm then suggested that Curtis Kelsey,[13] a 26-year-old Bahá'í and World War I veteran from the United States, go to Haifa to help get things moving. The mission was to design and install electrical systems at the Shrine of the Báb, the Shrine of Bahá'u'lláh, and at 'Abdu'l-Bahá's house, none of which had electricity. Curtis had experience in construction projects but thought an electrical engineer would have been more useful than him. However, he agreed to take on the job and 'Abdu'l-Bahá cabled acceptance of the idea.

When Curtis arrived in Haifa in September 1921 he felt he had stepped back in time. Arab women were carrying jars of water while men sat in the shade smoking bubble pipes, and camels were tied up in the streets.[14]

Curtis was a competent mechanic, having worked at the Ford Motor Plant in Detroit.[15] He repaired the big Cunningham and Ford cars that had been sent by American Bahá'ís to 'Abdu'l-Bahá but had not been functioning. That job completed, he drove 'Abdu'l-Bahá up Mount Carmel.[16]

The project for the Shrine of the Báb began early one morning when 'Abdu'l-Bahá showed Curtis the small building He had selected to house the lighting plant. It was half-way between the Pilgrim House and the Shrine, a structure that would help cushion the noise of the electric motor.[17] 'Abdu'l-Bahá told him to spend two weeks at that Shrine alternating with two weeks at the Shrine of Bahá'u'lláh. He introduced him to Ḥusayn Kahrubá'í, and soon the two young men began to work together learning words in each other's language as they went. Curtis spent some ten days exploring the vicinity of the Shrine figuring out how he was going to light the tomb. He bought pipe and other supplies in the town.

It was not all work, though. On Sundays, he experienced the special event that regularly occurred there. 'Abdu'l-Bahá would gather with about fifty Bahá'ís and speak about some topic to do with the Faith, and would then stand by the door of the Shrine and pour a little rose water in the hands of the Bahá'ís as they entered to pray.

Curtis soon decided that rather than installing the thick black lighting wire Roy Wilhelm had sent from the United States, he would use a different kind that could be hidden behind the walls. That required a journey to Cairo to obtain supplies so off he went, accompanied by 'Abdu'l-Bahá's Japanese aide, Fujita, and obtained what was needed.

'Abdu'l-Bahá was clearly pleased with Curtis and his work. He wrote to Roy Wilhelm, who showed the letter to Curtis's proud mother, Valeria, also a Bahá'í. It read: 'The electrician, Mr Kelsey, arrived. He is a real man. Really, that dear friend is confirmed with utmost energy in the service of the Cause of God. This is from the Heavenly blessings.'[18]

'Abdu'l-Bahá described the project:

> We ordered electric power for the Holy Precinct and the Shrine of the Exalted One so that they are luminous inside and out.
>
> We even ordered a line for the Pilgrim House. This is all the bounty of the Blessed Beauty, may my soul be a sacrifice for His loved ones. All nations and governments of the world showed prejudice and enmity towards us. Yet we are gathered with such spirituality and joy visiting such a Holy Place as if we have no enemy. Electric lights are no comparison to gas and oil lights: they are far superior.[19]

But 'Abdu'l-Bahá was never to see the Shrines of the Báb and Bahá'u'lláh electrically illuminated.

21

THE SHRINE BECOMES THE TOMB OF 'ABDU'L-BAHÁ

Until 1921 the Shrine had been reserved for important Bahá'í events. There was no reason for local residents who were not members of the Bahá'í community to visit the building on the steep northern slope of Mount Carmel.[1] That was all to change with the sudden and unexpected death of 'Abdu'l-Bahá in the early hours of Monday, 28 November 1921.

In the presence of a charismatic, larger-than-life presence, ordinary people often do not focus on the inevitability that such a public figure will eventually die, and this was the case with the passing of 'Abdu'l-Bahá. He had not shown signs of any grievous illness, so nobody expected Him to pass away so soon. He had spoken about visiting Ishqabad,[2] China, Japan, the mid-Pacific islands and India. He was carrying on His usual activities of helping the poor, attending to His vast correspondence, meeting with officials and giving inspirational talks to the pilgrims.

His death was a big shock to the Bahá'í community. Many were distraught. It was difficult initially for them to believe that it had happened, and then to cope with it emotionally. 'Abdu'l-Bahá was not only their spiritual and community leader, admired for His wisdom and many other qualities, but they had felt personally deeply loved by Him and they reciprocated that feeling.[3]

In retrospect, some Bahá'ís came to believe that 'Abdu'l-Bahá had in fact been preparing to pass away.[4] In July 1921 near the Shrine of the Báb, He had revealed a prayer which read in part:

> My bones are weakened, and the hoar hairs glisten on My head . . . and I have now reached old age, failing in My powers . . . No strength is there left in Me wherewith to arise and serve Thy loved

> ones . . . O Lord, My Lord! Hasten My ascension unto Thy sublime Threshold . . . and My arrival at the Door of Thy grace beneath the shadow of Thy most great mercy.[5]

And in a last Tablet written to the Bahá'ís in America in October of 1921, He wrote: 'In the cage of this world I flutter like a frightened bird and long for the flight to Thy Kingdom.'[6]

Shoghi Effendi and Lady Blomfield, in their account in 1922 of the passing of 'Abdu'l-Bahá, wrote:

> We have now come to realize that the Master knew the day and hour when, His mission on earth being finished, He would return to the shelter of heaven. He was, however, careful that His family should not have any premonition of the coming sorrow. It seemed as though their eyes were veiled by Him, with His ever-loving consideration for His dear ones, that they should not see the significance of certain dreams and other signs of the culminating event. This they now realize was His thought for them, in order that their strength might be preserved to face the great ordeal when it should arrive, that they should not be devitalized by anguish of mind in its anticipation.[7]

On Saturday morning, 26 November, 'Abdu'l-Bahá said He felt very cold and put on a favourite fur-lined coat which had once belonged to His Father. He then went to his room, took off the coat, lay down on His bed and asked to be covered up, saying that He had not slept well the night before. 'This is serious, it is the beginning,' He said to His daughter Munavvar. He asked for the fur coat to be added to the blankets that had been placed over Him. He was feverish in the afternoon, and in the evening had a worrisome temperature of 104 Fahrenheit (40 Celsius),[8] which then lowered during the night as the fever left Him. After midnight, He had some tea.[9]

On the Sunday morning, He said He felt quite well and got up and dressed, but was persuaded to remain on the sofa in His room. A Parsi pilgrim from India organized an event at the Shrine – in the north-east room – to commemorate the holy day of the Declaration of the Covenant, a commemoration which had been instituted by 'Abdu'l-Bahá rather than agreeing to requests that His own birthday (23 May) be observed in a formal event.

'Abdu'l-Bahá sent his family and the pilgrims to the gathering but did not attend Himself. When told later that the host had been disappointed by His absence, He made a remark that seemed especially meaningful in retrospect: 'The friends must not attach any importance to the absence of my body. In spirit I am, and shall always be, with the friends, even though I be far away.'[10] Dr Habíb, a Christian Arab physician, gave Him an injection of quinine for malaria.[11] He had been suffering from bronchitis,[12] so may have been treated for that as well.

'Abdu'l-Bahá had afternoon tea with His sister and the family, and then met with the Mufti of Haifa, the mayor, a Muslim judge, and the chief of police, an Englishman to whom He gave some silk hand-woven Persian handkerchiefs as a gift.[13] At 8 p.m. or shortly after,[14] after taking a little nourishment and saying He was quite well, 'Abdu'l-Bahá went to bed in a room on the southern side of the house. His two daughters successively attended to Him because they were concerned about His health. He went to sleep very calmly and was fever-free.

Normally He slept in a room which was upstairs in a small building separate from the main house and adjoining the gate to the property. However, He had given the use of that room to pilgrims from the United States, Dr Florian Krug, a medical practitioner, and his wife, Grace, who had arrived nine days earlier.[15] They had been struck by 'Abdu'l-Bahá's 'extreme fatigue and weariness',[16] and Dr Krug had soon asked, from a medical standpoint, that the Master save His strength and not join them in the pilgrim house for lunch – the stairway was a challenge, and He ate very little anyway.[17]

'Abdu'l-Bahá awoke about 1.15 a.m., got up and walked across to a table where he drank some water. He took off an outer night garment, saying: 'I am too warm.' He went back to bed. When his daughter Rúhá Khánum approached, she found Him lying peacefully and, as He looked into her face, He asked her to lift up the net curtains, saying: 'I have difficulty in breathing, give me more air.' At some stage His daughter administered some remedies that had been left by physicians that day.[18] Some rose water was brought. Without needing any help, He sat up in bed to drink some. He again lay down. When some food was offered him, He remarked in a clear and distinct voice: 'You wish me to take some food, and I am going?' He gave them a beautiful look.

His face was so calm, His expression so serene, the two daughters thought him asleep. His daughter Munavvar, who was also there at the end, later wrote: 'There was not the least agitation or agony. It was so calm that we could not realize that he was going.'[19] 'Abdu'l-Bahá had quietly passed away at 1.30 a.m. He was 77 years old.

Dr Krug arrived and confirmed that 'Abdu'l-Bahá had indeed died, and closed His eyelids.[20] Five other pilgrims were invited into the room. They were Dr Krug's wife Grace, Curtis Kelsey, Louise and John Bosch (from Switzerland but California residents), and Johanna Hauff from Germany.[21] According to Johanna Hauff the Master looked 'unspeakably beautiful'.[22] Louise Bosch later wrote that doctors (other doctors had been called) had told the pilgrims, in response to their question, that His heart had ceased to beat and it would be useless to try to revive Him.[23]

In later years, John Bosch recalled that he had seen people weeping as he entered the Master's bedroom and knelt by the bed. Bahíyyih Khánum then took his hand and sat him beside her on the divan that was built-in alongside the window. Munírih Khánum took Louise's hand in hers. There they stayed from two to four a.m. At about three o'clock, John got up and went over and held the Master's hand, which was still warm, and said, 'Oh, 'Abdu'l-Bahá!' To John, He had seemed alive, as John hoped He was. But that was not the case.[24]

The mosquito netting was lowered over the bed on which lay 'Abdu'l-Bahá and the pilgrims left for an adjacent room. The door of the Master's room was then closed.

John Bosch recalled that although Bahíyyih Khánum wept far less than the others, and remained dignified and composed, she sighed often during that night and many times said: 'Ya Ilahi – O God, my God!'[25]

Curtis Kelsey also witnessed the pandemonium of grief in the main central room of the house, and, in counterpoint, the calming influence of Bahíyyih Khánum. At 2.30 a.m., at her request, he left to drive the Master's Ford motor car, with Fujita next to him and another Bahá'í, a servant named Khusraw, in the back, to Bahjí to convey the shocking news to the Bahá'ís there and to call them to Haifa for the funeral. The cool evening had turned balmy. The drive was dramatic, fraught with difficulties that had to be overcome.[26]

In the midst of the utter shock and anguish, a decision had to be made. It was, and remains, a widespread custom in the Middle East that funerals are held soon after a death, so a burial place had to be selected as soon as possible.

Family members searched 'Abdu'l-Bahá's papers to see if He had left any instructions as to where He should be buried. His Will was soon found but there were no directions as to His preferred burial place.[27] It then fell to His sister, Bahíyyih Khánum, to make the decision. She selected a place under the central northern room of the Shrine of the Báb. One report describes how this decision was made:

> Jináb-i-Khádim [the custodian of the Shrine, 'Abbás-Qulí] went to the Greatest Holy Leaf and said: 'On the day you came up to the shrine for the interment of the remains of the Báb, 'Abdu'l-Bahá indicated a place for Himself. After He interred the holy remains in their eternal place, He stepped from the vault into a passageway and ordered the opening to be closed and, pointing to the passageway, said, 'And this should be a place for Us.' The Greatest Holy Leaf said, 'Very well.' She blessed him for what he said and stated: 'This is where it will be.'[28]

Taking a leadership role and making this decision at a time of the death of her beloved Brother, the most significant figure in her life since the passing of Bahá'u'lláh 29 years previously, demonstrated her enormous strength and wisdom.

What could have been a more suitable burial place for Him at this stage in history? 'Abdu'l-Bahá had loved the Shrine and understood its spiritual power more than anybody else. He had spent as much time as possible near it, and had made sure pilgrims visited it at their first opportunity.

It was He who had directed the latter stages of the concealment of the sacred remains of the Báb in Persia, He who had supervised the perilous mission of conveying, with all due respect and honour, the casket from Persia to the Holy Land. In obedience to a direction from Bahá'u'lláh He had endured great difficulties in purchasing the necessary land, and then taken on the task to build the Shrine, a near-impossible project due to conditions that would have daunted any other human being.

Living an abstemious life, He had relied on donations to pay the builders and, when desperately short of funds, prayed ardently that they might arrive in time.[29] But through His mysterious spiritual power, His constant prayers, and almost superhuman levels of such attributes as persistence, patience, detachment, courage and wisdom, He had achieved His goal. His sister and His wife had accompanied Him as He experienced anguish and joy throughout the 18 years it took to carry out what Bahá'u'lláh had required of Him.[30] They prayed for the success of this mission, and they rejoiced when He achieved it. For them, surely the Shrine was a highly suitable resting place for the Master until His own Shrine would be built.[31]

After 'Abdu'l-Bahá's body was washed, it was wrapped in five separate folds of white silk. A black mitre, given to 'Abdu'l-Bahá by Bahá'u'lláh, was placed on His head.[32] He remained on the bed until an hour before the funeral began.[33]

A white coffin[34] of plain white wood was hurriedly obtained. A description of the casket comes from Charles Mason Remey, who wrote that he obtained the information in an interview with 'Abbás-Qulí, and was given 'a description and the exact dimensions of the present casket . . . It is built of fine white wood four centimetres thick and has a zinc lining, the lid of which is fitted into a groove running about the box, and before the wooden lid was screwed down this groove was filled with olive oil in order to insure a good contact all around.'[35]

On Monday night, the Western pilgrims were permitted to see the body again – the only ones besides the family. Johanna Hauff wrote: 'How beautiful it was! Such peace! Such rest! I do not believe that I shall ever in my life see again such an unspeakably beautiful face as that of 'Abdu'l-Bahá in life and in death.'[36]

Meanwhile, telegrams with the shocking news of the death of 'Abdu'l-Bahá had been transmitted within the Holy Land and sent around the world. Messages of condolence flowed back. Telegrams came from the British authorities, a professor at the University of Oxford, Bahá'í communities and the Theosophical Society in London. There were reports in such newspapers as the *Morning Post,* the *New York World* and the *Times* of India. Among the telegrams received was one bringing a message from Winston Churchill, then British Secretary of State for the Colonies. Advised of the death by Lord Lamington, Churchill had telegraphed the High Commissioner for Palestine, Sir Herbert Samuel, giving instructions to 'please convey to the Bahai community suitable expression of condolence of His Majesty's Government'.[37]

From Egypt where he was High Commissioner, Viscount Allenby, the general who had befriended 'Abdu'l-Bahá, contacted Sir Herbert and asked him to 'convey to the relatives of the late Sir 'Abdu'l-Bahá

Abbas Effendi and to the Bahá'í Community' his sincere sympathy. After catching a special train at midnight on Monday, Sir Herbert together with the Governor of Jerusalem, Sir Ronald Storrs, and their officials arrived at Haifa in the early hours on the day after the death.[38]

It had been a stormy week but the weather for the funeral on that Tuesday morning was fine, with not a cloud in the sky. By 7 a.m. soldiers had lined up on both sides of Persian (now Haparsim) Street where 'Abdu'l-Bahá's house was located. Some other soldiers were stationed within the actual compound. The whole town was virtually at a standstill. Grieving people were everywhere. As John Bosch entered the property, he noticed on the left going up the steps an Arab soldier standing guard. The man was leaning on his gun with tears streaming down his face.[39]

Johanna Hauff arrived with fellow pilgrims Mr and Mrs Bosch at 8 a.m. In a letter to her parents, she said that she was with Mr and Mrs Bosch in the big hall of the house when the sons-in-law of 'Abdu'l-Bahá passed by to get the casket and then called upon Mr Bosch to help them carry it into the bedroom and help lift the body into it.[40] The coffin was placed on two chairs by the bed. To lift the body of 'Abdu'l-Bahá, John Bosch held His knees, Mírzá Jalál held His feet and others lifted His head and shoulders.[41]

There is no record yet found of a Bahá'í funeral service having been conducted within the home of 'Abdu'l-Bahá. However, as Mr 'Alí Nakhjavání has written, 'it is entirely logical to assume that the special Prayer for the Dead and other Bahá'í prayers would have been read in the main hall of the Master's house, with the participation of the household, including the ladies.'[42] Although the pilgrims are likely to have been invited to such a service, Johanna Hauff does not mention it but writes about other prayers: 'For a short time the casket was left in the hall and Mohammedan priests, who had asked permission to come, as did Jews and Christians, said a short prayer.'[43]

The coffin, covered by a simple paisley shawl,[44] was then carried out of the house on the shoulders of eight Bahá'ís amidst a throng of mourners. The pallbearers were to frequently change during the procession.[45]

The funeral was 'the like of which Palestine had never seen – no less than ten thousand people participated representing every class, religion and race in that country.'[46]

The procession up to the Shrine of the Báb began at 9 a.m.[47] Leading the cortège was a guard of honour provided by the City Constabulary Force. Behind them were Muslim and Christian Boy Scout troops, holding their banners and accompanied by their bands. Then came Muslim choristers chanting from the Qur'án. Also in that forward section of the procession were the Mufti (the senior Muslim jurist) and other Muslim leaders, as well as Christian clergy from the Roman Catholic, Greek Orthodox and Anglican traditions.[48]

Although there were 40 carriages waiting to take mourners to the Shrine, only five made the journey because the mourners wanted to honour Him by walking after the casket.[49]

Immediately behind the coffin were family members and next to them walked Sir Herbert Samuel, Sir Ronald Storrs and the Governor of Phoenicia, Lieutenant-Colonel Stewart Symes[50] and their staff.

Following them were 'consuls of various countries resident in Haifa, notables of Palestine, Muslim, Jewish, Christian and Druze, Egyptians, Greeks, Turks, Arabs, Kurds, Europeans and Americans, men, women and children. The long train of mourners, amid the sobs and moans of many a grief-stricken heart, wended its slow way up the slopes of Mt. Carmel to the Mausoleum of the Báb'.[51] It is likely that among the prominent mourners were senior members of the German Templer colony, including the leader, Friedrich Lange.[52]

The cortège headed up Persian Street and turned left along Weinstrasse, now Hagefen Street.[53] Above them, high over Abbas Street,[54] was a boarding school called Dames de Nazareth (Sisters of Nazareth). One of the students was Gertrud Struve, a daughter of the American Vice Consul in Haifa, Theodore Jonathan Struve (1868–1936). Her sister, Clara, later wrote an account in her memoirs that is in effect a testimony to the great love the Templers had for the Master:

> it was arranged that all pupils should gather on the roof terrace of the school from where the cortège could be well observed. The pupils were kneeling and praying from the moment the cortége left the house of 'Abdu'l-Bahá until the moment it had reached its destination on Mt Carmel two hours later.
>
> This was the greatest demonstration of respect the boarding school had ever shown to a human being. Even the death of the Pope a few years later was not mourned to such an extent.[55]

After moving eastward to the intersection with Mountain Road (now Hatzionut Avenue), the procession turned right and went up the steep slope, along the roadway 'Abdu'l-Bahá had helped fund.[56] During the procession, flags over government offices in Haifa were lowered to half-mast. The sounds were confined to the 'soft, slow, rhythmic chanting of Islam in the Call to Prayer, or the convulsed sobbing moan of those helpless ones, bewailing the loss of their one friend, who had protected them in all their difficulties and sorrows'.[57]

Halfway along the journey, a troop of Boy Scouts placed a wreath on the coffin.[58] The cortège continued along the steep road, up the mountain and then turned right off Mountain Road into the path leading to the Pilgrim House. Before it got to that building it turned left 90 degrees, continued for a while and then paused along the way before passing a few metres in front of the south-facing frontage of the house of 'Abbás-Qulí, which faced Mountain Road. It then went down the path on the western side of that house and came to a halt at a spot a few metres to the north-east of the Shrine.[59] The procession had taken some two hours.[60]

The pallbearers placed the coffin on a plain table, covered with a white linen cloth, in the garden at the eastern side of the Shrine, and the mourners stood in a circle around it. Seven people, including two boys, were photographed looking down at the proceedings from the roof of the Shrine.[61] They probably gained access to the roof via a ladder from the slope of the mountain at the rear.

Then began nine funeral orations of striking eloquence.[62] The first was by Yúsuf al-Khaṭíb, a well-known Muslim orator, who said in part:

> Whom are ye bewailing? Is it he who but yesterday was great in his life and is today in his death greater still? Shed no tears for the one that hath departed to the world of Eternity, but weep over the passing of Virtue and Wisdom, of Knowledge and Generosity. Lament for yourselves, for yours is the loss, whilst he, your lost one, is but a revered Wayfarer, stepping from your mortal world into the everlasting Home . . . What am I to set forth the achievements of this leader of mankind? They are too glorious to be praised, too many to recount. Suffice it to say, that he has left in every heart the most profound impression, on every tongue most wondrous praise. And he that leaveth a memory so lovely, so imperishable, he, indeed, is not dead. Be solaced then, O ye people of Baha!

Dr Florian Krug, a Bahá'í from the United States, confirmed that 'Abdu'l-Bahá had passed away, and closed His eyelids

© Denny Allen

The room where 'Abdu'l-Bahá passed away

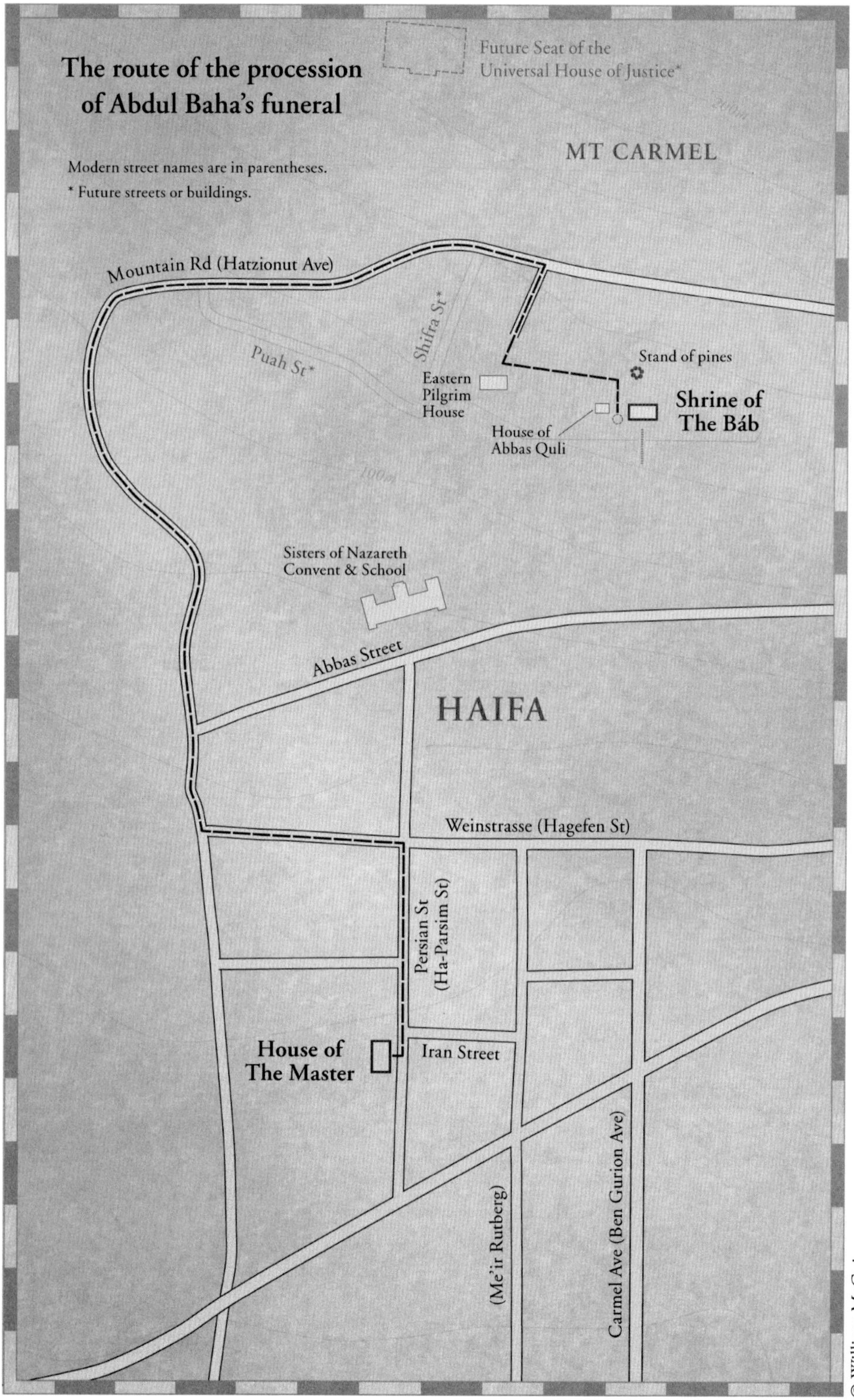

Map of funeral route

Pallbearers carry the Master's casket down the steps from His house

Crowds accompany the cortège along Persian Street (Haparsim) as the Master's coffin is carried in the direction of Mount Carmel

Mourners follow the procession along Mountain Road before turning right into the path heading towards the Pilgrim House

The coffin of the Master can be seen near the circle of cypress pines as the funeral cortège pauses in front of the house of ʻAbbás-Qúlí before proceeding down the path between the house and the Shrine

Boys and men watch from the roof of the Shrine as mourners stand near the coffin of 'Abdu'l-Bahá and listen to tributes paid to Him

The coffin of the Master being carried into the north-east room of the Shrine before being taken into the one behind it and down to the space prepared for it

Sir Herbert Samuel, the British High Commissioner for Palestine, who attended the funeral of 'Abdu'l-Bahá

Shoghi Effendi, about two years before he became head of the Faith

That orator was followed by a celebrated Christian writer, Ibráhím Nassár:

> O bitter is the anguish caused by this heart-rending calamity! It is not only our country's loss but a world affliction . . . He hath lived for well-nigh eighty years the life of the Messengers and Apostles of God. He hath educated the souls of men, hath been benevolent unto them, hath led them to the Way of Truth . . . Fellow Christians! Truly ye are bearing the mortal remains of this ever lamented one to his last resting place, yet know of a certainty that your ‘Abbas will live forever in spirit amongst you, through his deeds, his words, his virtues and all the essence of his life . . .

Then came the Mufti of Haifa, Muḥammad Murád, who had spoken with ‘Abdu'l-Bahá in His home just two days earlier.

> This great funeral procession is but a glorious proof of thy greatness in thy life and in thy death. But O, thou whom we have lost! Thou leader of men, generous and benevolent! To whom shall the poor now look? Who shall care for the hungry? and the desolate, the widow and the orphan?

A distinguished Muslim, ‘Abdu'lláh Mukhliṣ, said this:

> I beg your pardon if I fail in doing my duty as far as faithfulness is concerned or if I am unable to pay the generous one who has departed what he deserves of the best and highest praise, because what my tongue utters has emanated from a tender memory and broken heart. Indeed, they are wounds and not words; they are tears and not phrases . . .

After a Muslim poet, Shaykh Yúnus al-Khaṭíb, recited a poem he had composed, Bishop Bassilious, the head of Haifa's Greek Catholic Church, described ‘Abdu'l-Bahá's ‘humanitarian deeds, His generosity to the poor, His charm and majesty of mien'.[63] A young Christian, Wadí‘ Bustání, then recited a poem, which included these lines:

> O ‘Abdu'l-Bahá, O son of Bahá'u'lláh! May my life be a sacrifice to

> one like thee. Thou art the all-wise, and all else beside thee are only learned. What can the poets say in thy day?
>
> O 'Abdu'l-Bahá, O son of Bahá'u'lláh! Thou wert just as God wanted thee to be and not as others wished. Thou hast departed in the Holy Land wherein Christ and the Virgin Mary lived. The land that received Mohammed; the land the dust of which is blessing and wealth . . . We shall be sustained by this Tomb and the One it contains.

Among the final speakers was Salomon Bouzaglo, 'one of the leading figures of the Jewish population of Haifa, who spoke most eloquently in French'.[64] Here is a translation of excerpts:

> In a century of exaggerated positivism and unbridled materialism, it is astonishing and rare to find a philosopher of great scope, such as the lamented 'Abdu'l-Bahá 'Abbás, speak to our hearts, to our feelings, and especially seek to educate our soul by inculcating in us the most beautiful principles, which are recognized as being the basis of all religion and of all pure morality. By His Writings, by His spoken Word, by His intimate conversations as well as by His famous dialogues with the most cultivated and the most fervent adepts of sectarian theories, He knew how to persuade; He was always able to win our minds. Living examples have a special power. His private and public life was an example of devotion and of forgetfulness of self for the happiness of others . . .
>
> 'Abbás died in Haifa, Palestine, the Holy Land which produced the prophets. Sterile and abandoned for so many centuries, it is coming back to life and is beginning to recover its rank and its original renown. We are not the only ones to grieve for this prophet; we are not the only ones to testify to His glory. In Europe, in America, yea, in every land inhabited by men conscious of their own mission in this base world, athirst for social justice, for brotherhood, He will be mourned as well . . .
>
> May one not see herein a divine will and a marked preference for the Promised Land which was and will be the cradle of all generous and noble ideas? He who leaves after Him so glorious a past is not dead. He who has written such beautiful principles has increased His family among all His readers and has passed to posterity, crowned with immortality.

Colonel Symes also spoke at the funeral.[65] There were no speeches by Bahá'ís.[66] Which Bahá'í could possibly sum up the life of the Master? Local customs would have prevented Bahíyyih Khánum or Munírih Khánum from delivering a funeral oration. Shoghi Effendi was still in England. His tribute was to come later.

After the speeches were over, Sir Herbert Samuel, the first Jew to govern in the Land of Israel in 2,000 years,[67] bowed in front of the coffin as he paid homage. He held his hat in his left hand as he knelt and kissed the shawl covering the coffin, an act repeated by others.[68] 'A great throng,' Sir Herbert later wrote, 'had gathered together, sorrowing for His death, but rejoicing also for His life.'[69] Sir Ronald Storrs wrote: 'I have never known a more united expression of regret and respect than was called forth by the utter simplicity of the ceremony.'[70]

Then the coffin was taken into the north-east chamber of the Shrine.[71] Only when the large crowd had dispersed did Raḥmatu'lláh carry the casket down to the level of the vault. This was most probably done by taking it back out the door of the north-east room, and into the south-east chamber, and then descending via the re-opened entrance in that room, the one the Master had used for the interment of the sacred remains of the Báb. A description of the placement of the casket in the vault has come from Curtis Kelsey:

> This man [the caretaker of the Shrine, Raḥmatu'lláh] had been told where to open the floor of the Shrine for the body of 'Abdu'l-Bahá to be placed in the lower part of the Shrine. So he had opened the floor at that time and I took a picture of this particular place.[72] But when they lowered the coffin of 'Abdu'l-Bahá down through this opening in the floor it was this man that 'Abdu'l-Bahá had told to carry him to a place where he would rest. He was so strong he bore the whole weight of the coffin as it was carried down through the floor some 30 or 40 feet below the floor.[73]

The depth given by Kelsey is unlikely to be accurate. It is probably about four metres, judging by the drawing of Charles Mason Remey now on display at Mazra'ih and calculations about the steps required. In the memoirs he wrote 31 years later,[74] Raḥmatu'lláh said there was only room for one person to take the coffin down into the vault but nobody else could lift it. But he found he could lift it up very easily, as if it were lifted by itself. He then carried it down on his back. After the funeral, Raḥmatu'lláh said, he had come to understand why before He died, 'Abdu'l-Bahá had asked him a question that had puzzled him: 'You are a strong man. Could you not carry me away to a place where I could rest? I'm tired of this world.'[75]

He placed the Master's coffin facing Bahjí under the south-east part of the central chamber at the north of the building, not under the centre of that room. It was not directly in front of the sarcophagus of the Báb, which was behind the vault wall to the rear, under the centre of the chamber above.

A description of the last resting place comes from Charles Mason Remey. He had not been present at the funeral, but later went to Haifa and interviewed 'Abbás-Qulí about aspects of it. He also consulted, as an architect, with Shoghi Effendi about the future developments of the Shrine and other matters, including the future location of the permanent Shrine of 'Abdu'l-Bahá between Haifa and Acre.[76]

> It seems there is a large and deep crypt under the north-eastern chamber of the building, while adjoining it on the subterranean level is a small crypt, which is under the south-eastern portion of the central chamber of the north side of the building.
>
> It was in this small crypt beneath the central chamber on the north side that the Master's body was laid. I was told that as soon as M. Abbas Gholi heard of the Master's ascension, he went to work to open up this crypt below the north-eastern chamber.
>
> The work was continued through the day and the entire night previous to the funeral, so thick was the floor[77] and the vault of masonry which had to be pierced. At present the casket rests upon two pieces of wood upon the floor of the smaller crypt, while directly above on the carpeted floor of the central chamber is spread an embroidered green cloth marking the exact spot.
>
> It was three o'clock in the afternoon before the casket was lowered into the crypt, and during this interim of three hours or more Lotfullah and Baddie [Badí?] remained alone in the chamber with the blessed remains. Lotfullah spoke at some length of that vigil, and of what it meant to him.[78]

One report slightly differs in some details. It says that so hurriedly had the coffin been made that its lid could not be properly secured and that the night following the interment, Dr Luṭfu'lláh (Lotfullah) Ḥakím remained in the vault and kept watch until the deficiency could be righted.[79]

One of the first descriptions of the room above, the interior of the Shrine of 'Abdu'l-Bahá, came from a pilgrim from London, Ethel Jenner Rosenberg, who had viewed it on 3 December 1921. It was, she said: 'most bright and beautiful. There are wonderful carpets spread upon the floor and a ten-branched candlestick on either side, besides all the other lights . . . it is all so bright and joyous.'[80] She said she 'felt a deep and abiding joy . . . When we think of his great happiness and freedom, we cannot help but be happy, can we?' Each day she was in Haifa, she accompanied the women of 'Abdu'l-Bahá's household to the Shrine for prayers.[81] After the passing of 'Abdu'l-Bahá, a nine-day mourning period ensued.

Because of passport problems,[82] it was not until 29 December that 'Abdu'l-Bahá's beloved grandson, Shoghi Effendi, was able to arrive back in Haifa from England, where he had been a student at Oxford University. After he had learned of the shocking news of his grandfather, reading about it in a telegram in the London office of Major Tudor-Pole, he was 'in a state of collapse, dazed and bewildered by the catastrophic news'.[83] He was accompanied on his journey home by prominent English Bahá'í Lady Blomfield and his sister Rúḥangiz, who had been studying in Scotland. When he arrived he was almost prostrate with grief.

He knew a letter to him was waiting for him in Haifa but he did not know the contents, although his aunt, the Greatest Holy Leaf, and perhaps one or two others would have known because the letter was part of the Will of the Master which they had read in their search for burial instructions.[84]

When it was read to him, Shoghi Effendi discovered that even as far back as his childhood, 'Abdu'l-Bahá had named him as His successor.[85] Shoghi Effendi had no foreknowledge of that appointment and it came as a great shock. As his biographer, his future wife, Amatu'l-Bahá Ruḥíyyih <u>Kh</u>ánum,[86] later wrote: 'The burden which had rested first on the Báb, then on Bahá'u'lláh, and then on his beloved grandfather, 'Abdu'l-Bahá, had fallen with all its weight on his shoulders. He told me once, "The day they read me the Will and Testament I ceased to be a normal human being."'[87]

On 3 January 1922, Shoghi Effendi visited the Shrine of the Báb and the adjacent tomb of His grandfather. Later that day, in another place, and without Shoghi Effendi being present, the Will and Testament of 'Abdu'l-Bahá was read to nine Bahá'í men, mostly senior members of His family.[88] In His Will 'Abdu'l-Bahá had clearly and unmistakeably appointed His 24-year-old grandson as His successor as head of the Faith, with the title of 'Guardian'.

But there was to be another reading of the Will and it came after yet another tribute by a public official to the sterling qualities of its Author. On 6 January 1922, there was a memorial feast for 'Abdu'l-Bahá, marking the 40th day after His passing, an event in which Lieutenant-Colonel Stewart Symes was one of those to pay tribute to the Master:

> Most of us here have, I think, a clear picture of Sir 'Abdu'l-Bahá 'Abbás, of His dignified figure walking thoughtfully in our streets, of His courteous and gracious manner, of His kindness, of His love for little children and flowers, of His generosity and care for the poor and suffering. So gentle was He, and so simple, that in His presence one almost forgot that He was also a great teacher, and that His writings and His conversations have been a solace and an inspiration to hundreds and thousands of people in the East and in the West.[89]

It is recorded that during the commemoration, Shoghi Effendi led those attending to the Shrine of 'Abdu'l-Bahá, where he chanted a prayer,[90] and later, in the Eastern Pilgrim House, asked the American women pilgrims to sing the hymn 'Nearer My God to Thee'.[91]

'Thus,' Shoghi Effendi later wrote in a passage after his description of that event, 'was brought to a close the ministry of One Who was the incarnation, by virtue of the rank bestowed upon Him by His Father, of an institution that has no parallel in the entire field of religious history . . .'[92]

The next day, in the Master's house, 'Abdu'l-Bahá's Will and Testament was read in its entirety to Bahá'ís from Persia, India, Egypt, England, Italy, Germany, America and Japan.[93] Whenever the name of Shoghi Effendi, who was not present, was mentioned, everybody there rose in a mark of respect.[94] It was clear to all present that the responsibilities of leading the Faith, including the supervision of everything to do with the Shrine of the Báb, had now fallen upon his youthful shoulders.

ANNEX 1

THE BÁB

To know the Báb: A brief history

Childhood

The Báb was born in Shiraz, in the southern part of Persia (Iran) on 20 October 1819. His given name was Siyyid 'Alí-Muḥammad. The Báb (Arabic for 'Gate') is a title adopted later. His father passed away when He was young, and He was raised by His maternal uncle. As a child at school, He appeared to His teachers to have innate knowledge.

Young adulthood

In His late teens, the Báb began work with another uncle, who was a merchant in Bushihr, a city southwest of Shiraz. When He was 23, He married Khadíjih-Bagum (1822–82). They had one child, a boy named Ahmad, who died in 1843, the year he was born. In about 1839–40, the Báb went to Iraq on a spiritual pilgrimage, spending most of the time in and near Karbila.[1]

This was a time when the people of Iran, followers of Shi'ah Islam, were awaiting the coming of a great spiritual figure, the promised Mahdi or Qa'im, a station later claimed by the Báb.

His Declaration

In the evening of 23 May 1844, the Báb declared to a young man named Mullá Ḥusayn that He was the Báb ('the Gate'), the Promised One. He announced that another Messenger of God with a greater mission was soon to appear. Mullá Ḥusayn became His first disciple. Within five months, seventeen other disciples independently recognized the Báb as a Messenger of God, and they began spreading His Faith.

Among His followers was Mírzá Ḥusayn-'Alí, a member of a prominent family. He was later to take the title Bahá'u'lláh ('the Glory of God') and to become the Founder of the Bahá'í Faith.[2]

Persecution

As the disciples of the Báb (known as 'Bábís') started spreading the Faith, the authorities began to persecute them. In 1846 the Báb gained refuge in the city of Isfahan with the Governor, who became a follower. The fame of the Báb spread. The Shah ordered Him to the capital Tehran, but the Prime Minister convinced the Shah to change that demand and to send Him to the north-west of the country, to the city of Tabriz in the province, as it was then, of Azerbaijan. The Báb was then imprisoned in the remote fortress of Maku where He won the respect of the local people, members of the Sunni branch of Islam. His faith continued to spread in Iran and the persecutions intensified. The Báb was then transferred to another remote fortress, that of Chihriq near Urumiyyih, known today as Riza'iyyih. As in Maku, the local Sunni people were attracted to His magnetic personality. Some distinguished clergy in Iran became His followers.

Trial

In 1848 the Báb was brought to Tabriz where He was examined on His spiritual claims by clergy and government officials. Also present was the Crown Prince, later to be the Shah[3] of Persia. At that gathering, the Báb openly proclaimed His mission and His status as Mahdi. He was then tortured and sent back to Chihriq.

Death

In 1850 a new Prime Minister ordered the execution of the Báb, Who was again brought to Tabriz and imprisoned with His secretary and a young follower, Anís.[4] The next day, 9 July 1850, the Báb and Anís were suspended together on the wall of a military barracks and faced a firing squad. Despite a volley from the soldiers, they both survived. The Báb was found back in his cell. A different regiment then carried out the execution. Both died. The Báb was 31 years old.

Where He lived: A corrupt and stagnant society

The Báb lived in a society of decadence and degeneration.

A 20th-century historian

Hasan Balyuzi, a biographer of the Báb, provides a graphic description of the Persia of those times:

> . . . by the middle of the nineteenth century, Persia was materially impoverished, intellectually stagnant, spiritually moribund. The condition of the peasantry was appalling. Corruption had eaten deep into the vitals of the nation and oppression and tyranny were widespread . . . Offices of State and governorships were shamelessly bought and sold. Taxes and customs revenues were farmed. Bribery, peculation and extortion were legitimized . . . Historic cities and buildings were falling into ruin . . . The toll of disease and neglect and insecurity had reduced the population of a country with an area the size of Western Europe to well below ten million . . . collectively the divines abused the power they had obtained with the advent of the Ṣafavid dynasty.[5]

A 19th-century observer

Lord Curzon, British Viceroy of India, visited Persia and included this chilling description in a book he wrote about the country:

> The Persian character has ever been fertile in device and indifferent to suffering; and in the field of judicial executions it has found ample scope for the exercise of both attainments. Up till quite a recent period, well within the borders of the present reign, condemned criminals have been crucified, blown from guns, buried alive, impaled, shod like horses, torn asunder by being bound to the heads of two trees bent together and then allowed to spring back to their natural position, converted into human torches, flayed while living.
>
> . . . Under a twofold governing system . . . namely, an administration in which every actor is, in different aspects, both the briber

> and the bribed; and a judicial procedure, without either a law or a law court – it will readily be understood that confidence in the Government is not likely to exist, that there is no personal sense of duty or pride of honour, no mutual trust or co-operation (except in the service of ill-doing), no disgrace in exposure, no credit in virtue, above all no national spirit or patriotism. Those philosophers are right who argue that moral must precede material, and internal exterior, reform in Persia. It is useless to graft new shoots on to a stem whose own sap is exhausted or poisoned.[6]

An ordained divine station

A clear and polished mirror

What is the spiritual station of the founders of the great world religions? A question like this came from Laura Barney (later Laura Dreyfus Barney), an American Bahá'í who was a pilgrim in the ancient city of Acre in the Holy Land in the early years of the 20th century.

Over the centuries, a variety of unsatisfactory answers have been given to that question, answers that have tested the faith of millions. One such answer equated Jesus with God himself. Many of those who followed the Prophet Muhammad said He was the final messenger from God, the last who would ever instruct humanity. Then there were those who said that Buddha was special only because He achieved enlightenment.

When Laura Barney put the question to her host, 'Abdu'l-Bahá used the analogy of a mirror to explain the connection to God of the founders of the great religions. He introduced his explanation by saying that God, as the creator, is a pure essence which cannot be completely described.

> [T]he divine Essence is an all-encompassing reality, and all created things are encompassed. The all-encompassing must assuredly be greater than that which is encompassed, and thus the latter can in no wise discover the former or comprehend its reality.[7]

So if we humans cannot comprehend God, how can we learn about the Creator?

These great religious figures, 'Abdu'l-Bahá explained, are 'a clear and spotless mirror' reflecting the attributes of God: 'the true mirrors of the sanctified Essence of the Divinity'.[8] He compared God with the sun, and said that these great figures reflect the qualities of God as a mirror reflects the sun. The sun does not descend into the mirror, nor does God descend into and become one of these figures.

'Abdu'l-Bahá explained that the great religious figures[9] are not God. Rather they are physical beings with a rational everlasting soul, just like everybody else on the planet. However, they have another station. They manifest – that is, 'demonstrate' or 'reveal' – the qualities of God.

'Abdu'l-Bahá's explanation illustrates why Bahá'ís often use the term 'Manifestations of God' for these figures. Other terms include Messenger of God, Divine Messenger, Prophet, and, in the case of the Báb, Martyr-Prophet.[10]

The knowledge of the Manifestations as 'Abdu'l-Bahá pointed out 'is divine and not acquired – that is, it is a heavenly grace and a divine discovery'.[11] Bahá'u'lláh Himself refers to the Manifestations of God as having two stations: the station of 'pure abstraction and essential unity', and the station of 'distinction'. In the latter station, they are distinct servants of God. In the former station, they are all identically the Manifestation of God.[12] Although they all reflect the one 'sun' (God), they all have their own individuality and mission.

His twofold mission

The Báb had a twofold mission, as the bearer of a wholly independent revelation and the herald of one still greater than His own.

He was the Founder of the Bábí religion (1844–52). At the same time He was also the forerunner announcing the coming of Bahá'u'lláh, Who brought the Bahá'í Revelation with its message of world unity.

Among the many spiritual titles and roles of the Báb is one that has strong links to Mount Carmel. He was, wrote Shoghi Effendi, the 'Return of Elijah'[13] a prophet who lived on the mountain and whose reappearance was anticipated by the Jews.

A self-description

The Báb described Himself in these words:

> I am, I am, I am the Promised One! I am the One Whose name you have for a thousand years invoked, at Whose mention you have risen, Whose advent you have longed to witness, and the hour of Whose Revelation you have prayed God to hasten. Verily I say, it is incumbent upon the peoples of both the East and the West to obey My word, and to pledge allegiance to My person.[14]

In Bahá'u'lláh's words

In a prayer recited by Bahá'ís during the Faith's fasting month, Bahá'u'lláh pays tribute to His forerunner, the Báb.

> Magnify Thou, O Lord my God, Him Who is the Primal Point, the Divine Mystery, the Unseen Essence, the Dayspring of Divinity, and the Manifestation of Thy Lordship, through Whom all the knowledge of the past and all the knowledge of the future were made plain, through Whom the pearls of Thy hidden wisdom were uncovered, and the mystery of Thy treasured name disclosed . . . Whom Thou has called 'Alí-Muḥammad in the kingdom of Thy names, and the Spirit of Spirits in the Tablets of Thine irrevocable decree . . .[15]

In 'Abdu'l-Bahá's words

According to Shoghi Effendi, 'Abdu'l-Bahá described the Báb as the

> *'Morn of truth'* and the *'Harbinger of the Most Great Light'*, Whose advent at once signalized the termination of the 'Prophetic Cycle': and the inception of the "Cycle of Fulfillment' . . . and proclaimed the impending rise of that Incomparable Orb [Bahá'u'lláh] Whose radiance was to envelop the whole of mankind.[16]

Comparison to Jesus Christ

Shoghi Effendi draws attention to the remarkable similarity in distinguishing features of the spiritual careers of Jesus Christ and the Báb:[17]

- in the youthfulness and meekness of the Inaugurator of the Bábí Dispensation

- in the extreme brevity and turbulence of His public ministry
- in the dramatic swiftness with which that ministry moved towards its climax
- in the apostolic order which He instituted
- in the primacy which He conferred on one of its members
- in the boldness of His challenge to the time-honoured conventions, rites and laws which had been woven into the fabric of the religion He Himself had been born into
- in the role which an officially recognized and firmly entrenched religious hierarchy played as chief instigator of the outrages which He was made to suffer
- in the indignities heaped upon Him
- in the suddenness of His arrest
- in the interrogation to which He was subjected
- in the derision poured, and the scourging inflicted upon Him
- in the public affront He sustained
- in His ignominious suspension before the gaze of a hostile multitude

Shoghi Effendi also identified some clear differences between the roles of the Báb and Jesus Christ.

1. The Báb is not only to be regarded (as was Jesus) the 'independent Author of a divinely revealed Dispensation, but must also be recognized as the Herald of a new Era and the Inaugurator of a great universal prophetic cycle'.
2. While the 'chief adversaries of Jesus Christ, in His lifetime, were the Jewish rabbis and their associates, the forces arrayed against the Báb represented the combined civil and ecclesiastical powers of Persia'.

Personal appearance

The portrait

The stately International Bahá'í Archives building on Mount Carmel, its design inspired by the Parthenon, is just a short walk from the Shrine of the Báb. Inside, at the far end, in front of a blue and crimson stained glass window, is a cabinet containing a 19th-century portrait of the Báb. It is the only likeness on display to Bahá'ís (there are no photographs) and, apart from rare occasions, the Báb's portrait is only displayed in the Archives building. The usual procedure for viewing the portrait is that guides open the cabinet for pilgrims who invariably gaze intently and silently at the image before them.

Only later do the pilgrims speak about their reactions. For many the painting, in Persian miniature style, confirms the written testimonies by the contemporaries of the Báb: a serene and symmetrical face of somebody widely regarded by his contemporaries as handsome. Others describe how viewing the portrait had a spiritual effect upon them.

A cabinet nearby displays clothing once worn by the Báb. The elegant garments are beautifully made with carefully-chosen, refined materials, patterns and colours.

The image of a handsome young man who is well presented fits with descriptions of those who saw Him.

Through the eyes of a Westerner

The only Westerner[18] to encounter and describe the Báb was Dr William Cormick (1819–77) who met Him several times in July 1848.[19] This is how he described the Báb's physical appearance:

> He was a very mild and delicate-looking man, rather small in stature and very fair for a Persian, with a melodious voice which struck me very much. . . . In fact, his whole look and deportment went far to dispose one in his favour.[20]

The Báb, he said, was dressed in the clothes of a Siyyid, a descendant of Muhammad, with the right to wear a green turban.

But in his report Dr Cormick provided much more than a physical description. That July 1848, two years before the Báb's execution, Dr Cormick had been sent with two Persian doctors to His cell in Tabriz to assess if the Báb were sane. This assessment was for the purposes of the authorities, who were deciding 'whether to put Him to death or not'.

Asked later about the occasion by a Presbyterian missionary from the United States, Rev. Benjamin Labaree, Dr Cormick said 'nothing of any importance' happened in the interview.[21] However, from a modern perspective the doctor's report of the events is intriguing.

> To all enquiries he merely regarded us with a mild look, chanting in a low melodious voice some hymns, I suppose . . . He only once deigned to answer me, on my saying that I was not a Musulman and was willing to know something about his religion, as I might perhaps be inclined to adopt it. He regarded me very intently on my saying this, and replied that he had no doubt of all Europeans coming over to his religion.

As a result of the report of the doctors, the Báb's life was temporarily spared but He was administered the bastinado, a particularly painful torture involving being beaten on the soles of His feet. A severe injury to His face, which occurred at the time, required treatment. Dr Cormick continues:

> On being asked whether a Persian surgeon should be brought to treat him, he expressed a desire that I should be sent for, and I accordingly treated him for a few days but in the interviews consequent on this I could never get to have a confidential chat with him, as some Government people were always present, he being a prisoner.
>
> He was very thankful for my attentions to him.

As for spiritual matters: 'Of his doctrine I heard nothing from his own lips, although the idea was that there existed in his religion a certain approach to Christianity.' Dr Cormick said that some Armenian carpenters (who might possibly have been Christians) when making some repairs in his prison, had seen Him openly 'reading the Bible, and he took no pains to conceal it, but on the contrary told them of it'.

'Most assuredly,' Dr Cormick concluded, 'the Musulman fanaticism does not exist in his religion, as applied to Christians, nor is there that restraint of females that now exists.'

Dr Cormick may have obtained the information about the lack of fanaticism and the absence of restraint on women from the Armenian carpenters. Born in Persia and a medical graduate from England, he was the son of an Irishman and an Armenian woman. He was also married to an Armenian.[22] It is likely, then, that he spoke Armenian as well as being fluent in English and Persian. He may possibly also have known another Armenian, Colonel Sám Khán, a Christian who was the officer in charge of the regiment originally assigned to execute the Báb. This officer, who had spoken with the Báb, later withdrew from the assignment.[23]

There is also another description, which may have been obtained directly from Dr Cormick.[24] It comes from a British diplomat's wife, Lady Sheil, who did not meet the Báb.

She wrote: 'Báb possessed a mild and benignant countenance, his manners were composed and dignified, his eloquence was impressive, and he wrote rapidly and well.'[25] If Lady Sheil's information came from Dr Cormick, the doctor may have been witnessing the revelation of verses by the Báb.

The first disciple[26]

The best-known description of the Báb comes from Mullá Ḥusayn, the one who witnessed His declaration in Shiraz on 23 May 1844 that He was a divine messenger.[27]

Mullá Ḥusayn, who became the Báb's first disciple, described his meeting with Him. It occurred on a street in the city. The Báb, he said, was a young man of radiant countenance, Who wore a green turban and Who, advancing towards him, greeted him with a smile of loving welcome. He embraced Mullá Ḥusayn with tender affection as though he had been his intimate and lifelong friend and overwhelmed him with expressions of affection and loving-kindness.

He had a 'gentle yet compelling manner', Mullá Ḥusayn said. 'As I followed Him, His gait, the charm of His voice, the dignity of His bearing, served to enhance my first impressions of this unexpected meeting.'[28]

Mullá Ḥusayn and the Báb arrived at the Báb's house, where their conversation began in earnest. At one point during the evening, the Báb asked him a question. The response provides interesting descriptive details:

'Has your teacher given you any detailed indications as to the distinguishing features of the promised One?'

'Yes,' Mullá Ḥusayn replied. 'He is of a pure lineage, is of illustrious descent, and of the seed of Fáṭimih.[29] As to His age, He is more than

A painting of the Báb and a photograph of Bahá'u'lláh are among the items in these cabinets in the International Archives building at the Bahá'í World Centre. Pilgrims may view these images during their time in Haifa

Dr William Cormick (1819–77), the only Westerner to meet and describe the Báb, who told him He had no doubt of all Europeans coming over to his religion. Four years earlier in 1844, the Báb had called on Westerners to 'issue forth' from their 'cities' to aid God, and 'become as brethren' in His 'one and indivisible religion'

Before the Báb's last days in Tabríz, pictured below, He was imprisoned in a castle above the town of Maku (right) near the border between Persia and the Ottoman and Russian Empires, and later in the fortress of Chihriq (above) near Urumiyyih, known today as Riza'iyyih. Most of His writings were revealed during His confinement in these two places

This colourized photograph of the terrace of the Shrine and the cypress circle behind was published in Views of Acca, Haifa, Mt. Carmel, and Other Places (Chicago, 1911). The images were said by Edward Getsinger to have been approved by ʻAbduʼl-Bahá

twenty and less than thirty. He is endowed with innate knowledge. He is of medium height, abstains from smoking, and is free from bodily deficiency.'

At this response, the Báb 'paused for a while and then with vibrant voice declared: "Behold, all these signs are manifest in Me!"'

During their meeting, the Báb also wrote and chanted one of his major works, responding to Mullá Ḥusayn's questions. An enthralled Mullá Husayn later said: 'The overpowering effect of the manner in which He wrote was heightened by the gentle intonation of His voice which accompanied His writing . . . I sat enraptured by the magic of His voice and the sweeping force of His revelation . . . I sat spellbound by His utterance, oblivious of time and of those who awaited me.' He described the 'state of ecstasy into which I seemed to have fallen' and how he was 'enthralled by the music of that voice which rose and fell as He chanted', describing ethereal, subtle harmonies as the Báb revealed prayers.[30]

Effects on contemporaries

The first disciple

The first disciple, Mullá Ḥusayn, spoke of the effect the Báb had on him at their first meeting:

> Sleep had departed from me that night . . . This Revelation, so suddenly and impetuously thrust upon me, came as a thunderbolt which, for a time, seemed to have benumbed my faculties. I was blinded by its dazzling splendour and overwhelmed by its crushing force. Excitement, joy, awe, and wonder stirred the depths of my soul. Predominant among these emotions was a sense of gladness and strength which seemed to have transfigured me. How feeble and impotent, how dejected and timid, I had felt previously! Then I could neither write nor walk, so tremulous were my hands and feet. Now, however, the knowledge of His Revelation had galvanized my being. I felt possessed of such courage and power that were the world, all its peoples and its potentates, to rise against me, I would, alone and undaunted, withstand their onslaught. The universe seemed but a handful of dust in my grasp . . .[31]

And in the following days, he said, 'Wakeful until the dawn, I sat at His feet fascinated by the charm of His utterance and oblivious of the world and its cares and pursuits.'[32]

Townsfolk near the jail

In 1848 the Báb was consigned as a prisoner to a remote and forbidding castle near the summit of a mountain above the town of Maku near the border between Persia and the Ottoman and Russian Empires. The residents were Kurds, who were members of the Sunni sect of Islam. They detested people who were members of the rival Shi'ah sect.[33] But they came to adopt a different view of the Báb.

A follower of the Báb, Shaykh Ḥasan-i-Zunúzí, describes what the townsfolk of Maku heard:

> The voice of the Báb, as He dictated the teachings and principles of His Faith, could be clearly heard by those who were dwelling at the foot of the mountain. The melody of His chanting, the rhythmic flow of the verses which streamed from His lips caught our ears and penetrated into our very souls. Mountain and valley re-echoed the majesty of His voice. Our hearts vibrated in their depths to the appeal of His utterance.[34]

The effect of the Báb upon them was profound, as writes Shoghi Effendi:

> An unruly, a proud and unreasoning people were gradually subdued by the gentleness of the Báb, were chastened by His modesty, were edified by His counsels, and instructed by His wisdom. They were so carried away by their love for Him that their first act every morning, notwithstanding the remonstrations of the domineering 'Alí Khán [the chief jailer], and the repeated threats of disciplinary measures received from Ṭihrán, was to seek a place where they could catch a glimpse of His face, and beseech from afar His benediction upon their daily work. In cases of dispute it was their wont to hasten to the foot of the fortress, and, with their eyes fixed upon His abode, invoke His name, and adjure one another to speak the truth.[35]

The jailer

The chief jailer at Maku was 'Alí Khán. Initially he was very strict on the Báb. Then one day he had a dream which changed his attitude completely, as described by one who observed his reaction:

> I found 'Alí Khán standing at the threshold in an attitude of complete submission, his face betraying an expression of unusual humility and wonder. His self-assertiveness and pride seemed to have entirely vanished. Humbly and with extreme courtesy, he returned my salute and begged me to allow him to enter the presence of the Báb. I conducted him to the room which my Master occupied. His limbs trembled as he followed me. An inner agitation which he could not conceal brooded over his face.[36]

'Ali Khán described his dream to the Báb, and was welcomed by Him and forgiven: 'You belittled this Revelation and have contemptuously disdained its Author. God, the All-Merciful, desiring not to afflict you with his punishment, has willed to reveal to your eyes the Truth.'[37] Siyyid Ḥúsayn continued:

> This marvellous experience completely changed the heart of 'Alí Khán. Those words had calmed his agitation and subdued the fierceness of his animosity. By every means in his power, he determined to atone for his past behavior . . .
>
> 'Alí Khán set out, within the limits imposed upon him, to provide whatever would tend to alleviate the rigour of the captivity of the Báb. At night the gate of the castle was still closed; in the daytime, however, those whom the Báb desired to see were allowed to enter His presence, were able to converse with Him and to receive His instructions.[38]

The authorities

Shoghi Effendi describes the response to the Báb by the Persian authorities:

> Government, clergy and people arose, as one man, to assault and exterminate their common enemy. In remote and isolated centres

the scattered disciples of a persecuted community were pitilessly struck down by the sword of their foes, while in centres where large numbers had congregated measures were taken in self-defense, which, misconstrued by a cunning and deceitful adversary, served in their turn to inflame still further the hostility of the authorities, and multiply the outrages perpetrated by the oppressor.[39]

The Persian populace

Hundreds of thousands of Persians adopted the faith of the Báb, the most important being Bahá'u'lláh Himself, but they also included distinguished scholars, religious leaders and the famous poet Ṭahirih.[40] As described above by Shoghi Effendi, some followers rose to defend themselves and their faith using arms; to defend the chosen one on His appearance was a requirement of every faithful believer under the Shi'ah tradition. Most of them perished. Many thousands of others were tortured and killed because of their beliefs.[41]

Some understanding of the extraordinary effect the Báb had on parts of the populace can be seen by this account by Rev. J. H. Shedd, an American missionary in Persia, who wrote:

> When the Bab passed through Oroomiah [Urumiyyih] on his way to his execution, the missionaries watched the excitement with great interest. The crowds of people were ready to receive him as the long-expected Imam, even the water in which he bathed was regarded as holy water.[42]

The following description comes from a critic of the Báb, the Rev. Dr Isaac Adams, who was a Nestorian Persian.

> We are told that vast numbers flocked to see him, and even the governor did not conceal his sympathy with the prisoner of such engaging manners; the crowd shed tears as they looked upon the interesting young man, and more than half believed that he might be the very 'Imam Mahdi,' the great desire of Moslem nations. Traditions about the town relate that when he went to the bath the people carried away the water in vessels, in which he had bathed as if it were holy.[43]

Effects on contemporary life

A Bahá'í scholar has noted that Shoghi Effendi identified in the following words the vast spiritual forces of our time, so intimately connected with the Báb.

> Citing the words of the Báb, [Shoghi Effendi] explains that the Báb's spirit is 'vibrating in the innermost realities of all created things'. He then describes this spirit as 'impelling', 'moving', 'world-shaking, world-energising, world-redeeming', 'world-directing', 'world-vitalising', and 'all-conquering'. It is a 'God-born force', 'generative', 'purifying' and 'transmuting' in its 'influence'. Such a force is 'cleansing', 'propelling', 'onrushing', 'intensely alive and all-pervasive'. It is 'irresistible in its sweeping power, incalculable in its potency, unpredictable in its course, mysterious in its working, and awe-inspiring in its manifestations'.[44]

The West

Within 18 months of the Báb announcing His mission to His first follower, the world's most prominent foreign newspaper, *The Times* of London, described events in Persia associated with the new religion. On 1 November 1845, *The Times* reported that that 'a Persian merchant' in Bushihr was 'endeavouring here to prove that he was one of the successors of Mahomet' and that He 'had already collected a good number of followers'.[45] The report also described the torture and execution of some followers of the Báb, and the arrest and examination of the Báb in Shiraz.[46]

The article was republished in January 1846 in the United States and in March 1846 in Australia.[47] These were the first mentions of the Báb and His new religion on both continents.

The spread of the teachings of the Báb and the gruesome persecutions in response prompted reports by diplomats in Persia – mainly British, Russian and French, some of whom were sympathetic to the new movement. Those accounts were drawn upon in later public descriptions of the Faith by Western writers.[48]

Information provided by the Persian authorities would have been biased, and the European view was also distorted because of the ferment on their continent, which was experiencing revolutions. Influenced by those tumultuous upheavals, the Europeans in Tehran mistakenly thought of the Bábís as socialists, communists and anarchists.[49] In general the reports by Westerners were characterized by errors and distortions. The savage persecution meted out to the followers of the Báb meant that first-hand accounts of their beliefs were difficult to obtain by outsiders. The errors in the reports that were written in these circumstances were repeated and taken to be the truth.

The martyrdom of the Báb in 1850 was not reported by the contemporary European press, except for a short report in the Venetian official gazette two months later.[50] However, there are reports of the execution by Russian and British diplomats based on information given to them and confirmed in many respects by Bahá'í historians and by descriptions provided by two people who claimed to be eyewitnesses.

The diplomats erred as to the fate of the sacred remains of the Báb and those of the disciple who died with Him. They accepted the incorrect official position that the remains were devoured by animals. As a result of the work of Edward Granville Browne, the distinguished Cambridge University orientalist, it was learned much later in the West that the remains had been rescued and hidden.

ANNEX 2

THE SPIRITUAL SIGNIFICANCE OF THE SHRINE

A focal point of spiritual power

The foundation spiritual document for the Shrine of the Báb is the Tablet of Carmel, revealed by Bahá'u'lláh in 1891. In this Tablet, Bahá'u'lláh ordained the mountain as the spiritual and administrative centre of the Faith, the heart of which was to be the Shrine.

For the complete impact, the whole Tablet[1] is best read with a commentary to explain the allusions and style. This paragraph is an example:

> Rejoice, for God hath in this Day established upon thee His throne, hath made thee the dawning-place of His signs and the day spring of the evidences of His Revelation. Well is it with him that circleth around thee, that proclaimeth the revelation of thy glory, and recounteth that which the bounty of the Lord thy God hath showered upon thee.

The Shrine of the Báb has significance because it is a mausoleum for a Divine Messenger. It was, as stated by Shoghi Effendi, not only 'the first and most holy edifice' reared at the World Centre of the Faith, but also 'the initial international institution heralding the establishment of the supreme legislative body of the World Administrative Centre . . .'[2]

Bahá'ís see the Shrine as the focal point of the spiritual power which drives the international administration of the Faith.

As explained in the biography of Shoghi Effendi by his widow, Ruḥíyyih Rabbani, the sacred remains of Bahá'u'lláh in the Shrine across the bay at Bahjí, which is just outside Acre, are too sacred in essence, and 'His station too infinitely exalted, to act as the spiritual dynamo galvanizing the institutions of His World Order. The Dust of the Báb, however . . . had been chosen by Bahá'u'lláh Himself to be the Centre around which His Administrative Institutions would cluster and under Whose shadow they would function . . .'[3]

For Bahá'ís, these administrative institutions are vitally important because they will play a leading role in the spiritualization of humanity leading to the world becoming one global society that will guarantee peace for all mankind. Shoghi Effendi wrote:

> I cannot at this juncture over emphasize the sacredness of that holy dust embosomed in the heart of the Vineyard of God, or overrate the unimaginable potencies of this mighty institution founded sixty years ago,[4] through the operation of the Will of, and the definite selection made by, the Founder of our Faith, on the occasion of His historic visit to that holy mountain, nor can I lay too much stress on the role which this institution, to which the construction of the superstructure of this edifice[5] is bound to lend an unprecedented impetus, is destined to play in the unfoldment of the World Administrative Centre of the Faith of Bahá'u'lláh and in the efflorescence of its highest institutions constituting the embryo of its future World Order.[6]

In elevated prose, He describes the sacred remains as constituting the heart and centre of nine concentric circles. After describing the outer circles, He describes, in a passage of great literary and spiritual beauty, the Shrine as built by 'Abdu'l-Bahá:

> Embosomed in these lovely and verdant surroundings stands in all its exquisite beauty the mausoleum of the Báb, the shell designed to preserve and adorn the original structure raised by 'Abdu'l-Bahá as the tomb of the Martyr-Herald of our Faith. Within this shell is enshrined that Pearl of Great Price, the holy of holies, those chambers which constitute the tomb itself, and which were constructed by 'Abdu'l-Bahá. Within the heart of this holy of holies is the tabernacle, the vault wherein reposes the most holy casket. Within this vault rests the alabaster sarcophagus in which is deposited that inestimable jewel, the Báb's holy dust. So precious is this dust that the very earth surrounding the edifice enshrining this dust has been extolled by the Centre of Baha'u'llah's Covenant ['Abdu'l-Bahá], in

one of His Tablets in which He named the five doors belonging to the six chambers which He originally erected after five of the believers associated with the construction of the Shrine, as being endowed with such potency as to have inspired Him in bestowing these names, whilst the tomb itself housing this dust He acclaimed as the spot round which the Concourse on high[7] circle in adoration.[8]

He describes the Shrine in these wonderful words:

an edifice at once so precious, so holy; consecrated to the memory of so heroic a Soul; whose site no one less than the Founder of our Faith has selected; whose inner chambers were erected by the Centre of His Covenant with such infinite care and anguish; embosomed in so sacred a mountain, on the soil of so holy a land; occupying such a unique position; facing on the one hand the silver-white city of 'Akká, the Qiblih of the Bahá'í world; flanked on its right by the hills of Galilee, the home of Jesus Christ, and on its left, by the Cave of Elijah; and backed by the plain of Sharon and, beyond it, Jerusalem and the Aqṣá mosque, the third holiest shrine in Islám . . .[9]

Why Bahá'ís visit the Shrine

The remains of Báb are regarded by Bahá'ís as sacred because they were the physical vehicle of One Who manifested the attributes of God. However, these remains, or articles associated with Him such as His clothes, are not regarded as magic talismans or fetish objects with magical properties as are found in some traditions of other belief systems. A visit to the Shrine is for spiritual upliftment, as 'Abdu'l-Bahá explained:

Holy places are undoubtedly centres of the outpouring of Divine grace, because on entering the illumined sites associated with martyrs and holy souls, and by observing reverence, both physical and spiritual, one's heart is moved with great tenderness.[10]

A Bahá'í who was the project manager for the last stages of the construction of the superstructure of the Shrine, Leroy Ioas, a Hand of the Cause of God, would say that the Shrines are not places of the dead, though they shelter the remains of the Manifestations of God. Rather, he said, they are places of dynamic life because the spirit of the age flows through them. He said that one evening Shoghi Effendi had remarked that when visiting the Shrine of the Báb, one should remember that the spirits of all the Prophets of God are revolving around that Shrine, as they do around the Shrine of Bahá'u'lláh, with the addition of that of the Báb.[11]

Bahá'ís exercise reverence by dignity and modesty in dress, silence in the Shrine,[12] and respect and consideration for others. It is a custom, though not obligatory, to leave the Shrine by walking backwards, still facing the raised threshold of the central room, which is above the vault containing the sarcophagus.

As a result of the spiritual experience in the Shrine, Bahá'ís can be inspired in their future lives of service. A letter written on behalf of Shoghi Effendi and approved by him reads:

> Assemblies[13] get a new life and spirit when they come in touch with a pilgrim newly coming from a visit to the Sacred Shrines. The pilgrim can impart to those he meets some of the spirit he obtained himself while kneeling in absorbed prayer and meditation at the Thresholds.[14]

Another such letter says:

> There is no doubt that after this pilgrimage and your prayers for aid and grace at the sacred Threshold of the Abhá Beauty – the Point round which the concourse on high revolves – and the Shrines of the Báb, and of 'Abdu'l-Bahá, you will be privileged to render greater and more glorious services.[15]

Bahá'ís may visit the Shrine of the Báb while on a private visit or on a formal nine-day pilgrimage.[16] Although pilgrimage to the Shrine is not obligatory for Bahá'ís, this paragraph in the Tablet of Carmel may be taken as an injunction by Bahá'u'lláh to visit the Shrine if at all possible:

> Hasten forth and circumambulate the City of God that hath descended from heaven, the celestial Kaaba round which have circled in adoration the favoured of God, the pure in heart, and the company of the most exalted angels.[17]

Individual Bahá'ís describe their experience in the Shrines in a variety of ways. Some report immediate spiritual exhilaration, while others find the expected inspiration does not come until later.

There are special prayers by Bahá'u'lláh and 'Abdu'l-Bahá to say in the Shrines of the Báb and 'Abdu'l-Bahá. The framed text of the prayers appears in the Shrines.[18] The prayers are highly encouraged. However, they are not obligatory for anybody. A pilgrim or visitor may say any prayer, or none, as they wish.

An eminent Bahá'í poet, Roger White (1929–93) described his experience in verse.

The visit to the Shrine takes place
in an easy but awesome silence.
The crunching of tile shards underfoot as
he moves in file with the others towards the goal
helps anchor him to his purpose from which
he might be pulled by exquisite details of the garden
or even the unself-conscious trill of a bird
that clothes in song his mounting ecstasy.
His senses collude with the beauty to delay his pace
and postpone the rewarding confrontation.
But then he is there with the others – too soon
and far from soon enough – and the door,
giant-tall and heavy and swung on its hinges,
extends its irresistible invitation.
Attar of roses becomes his oxygen.

The pattern in the carpet provides
occupation to his insatiable eyes
till he raises them to see the petal-strewn threshold
and, beyond, the inner chamber screened by golden mesh.
Are the prayers offered here invested with
a special potency? He wonders, but his words
seem impertinent in this setting and
leave no imprint on his mind. He blushes,
concerned that he might have spoken aloud,
and cannot tell, so articulate is this silence,
so resonant of all the anguish deposited there.

He hears a fellow pilgrim weep
and longs to have his own heart break
or conflagrate that he might rush forward,
ashes dribbling from his cupped hands,
to scatter them upon the threshold.
A scornful voice in his head causes him to squirm
in discomfort, but shrugging it away
he finds it possible to recite prayers
and then he slowly takes his leave
wondering what he may have left on the threshold
where the petals gave their lives.[19]

Avoiding misinformation

Bahá'ís are encouraged to consult the Bahá'í writings as they develop their own understandings about the Shrine. There is guidance not to rely on notes taken on pilgrimage nor any other unofficial information, nor upon unauthenticated stories about the Shrine. Bahá'u'lláh wrote:

> We entreat Our loved ones not to besmirch the hem of Our raiment with the dust of falsehood, neither to allow references to what they have regarded as miracles and prodigies to debase Our rank and station, or to mar the purity and sanctity of Our name.[20]

ANNEX 3

THE HOLY LAND AND MOUNT CARMEL

The Holy Land

The arrival in 1868 of Bahá'u'lláh in Acre was the result of an order by the Ottoman Sultan 'Abdu'l-Azíz that the Bahá'í leader spend the rest of His days there. His death and burial in the vicinity of Acre fixed the permanent location of the spiritual and administrative centre of His Faith in what Bahá'ís and followers of Judaism, Christianity, Islam and some other faiths refer to as 'the Holy Land' and was once called Palestine, now Israel.

The burial place of Bahá'u'lláh is regarded by Bahá'ís as the holiest place on earth. It is in that direction that they turn when they say their daily obligatory prayers.

In his history of the Faith, Shoghi Effendi described the Holy Land as

> the Land promised by God to Abraham, sanctified by the Revelation of Moses, honoured by the lives and labours of the Hebrew patriarchs, judges, kings, and prophets, revered as the cradle of Christianity, and as the place where Zoroaster, according to 'Abdu'l-Bahá's testimony, had 'held converse with some of the prophets of Israel,' and associated by Islám with the Apostle's night-journey, through the seven heavens, to the throne of the Almighty. Within the confines of this holy and enviable country, 'the nest of all the prophets of God', 'the Vale of God's unsearchable Decree, the snow-white Spot, the Land of unfading splendour' was the Exile[1] of Baghdád, of Constantinople and Adrianople condemned to spend no less than a third of the allotted span of His life, and over half of the total period of His Mission.[2]

Shoghi Effendi also recorded what Bahá'ís see as the fulfilment of Biblical and Islamic prophecies, and referred to 'Abdul-Bahá's assurance that Bahá'u'lláh's arrival was prophesied 'through the tongues of the Prophets two or three thousand years before'. Elsewhere Shoghi Effendi wrote:

> Within the heart of this planet lies the 'Most Holy Land,' acclaimed by 'Abdu'l-Bahá as 'the Nest of the Prophets' and which must be regarded as the centre of the world and the Qiblih[3] of the nations.[4]

Mount Carmel

Facing the Bay of Haifa

When Bahá'ís refer to Mount Carmel they are talking about the headland looking over the Bay of Haifa[5] rather than the complete mountain range to the southeast of Haifa. Its Hebrew name, Carmel, means 'Vineyard (*carm*) of God (*el*)', and its Arabic name is Mount Saint Elijah (*Jabal Mar Elyas*).

At the time Bahá'u'lláh selected the site for the Shrine of the Báb, Mount Carmel was covered in gravel and giant boulders and there were caves and underground pockets. In its lower section there were vineyards and orchards planted by the German Templer immigrants.

The trees on the mountain, though relatively sparse at that time, were oak, pine, olive and laurel. It had once been more heavily forested but many trees were felled by the Ottomans.

Stretching back in time

Archaeological research has established that humans first occupied an area south of Haifa in the Mount Carmel range about 500,000 years ago. According to the UNESCO World Heritage Committee, at one site in the range ninety years of archaeological research have revealed a cultural sequence of unparalleled duration:

> This 54 [hectare] property contains cultural deposits representing at least 500,000 years of human evolution demonstrating the unique existence of both Neanderthals and Early Anatomically Modern

Humans within the same Middle Palaeolithic cultural framework, the Mousterian.

Evidence from numerous Natufian[6] burials and early stone architecture represents the transition from a hunter-gathering lifestyle to agriculture and animal husbandry. As a result, the caves have become a key site of the chrono-stratigraphic framework for human evolution in general, and the prehistory of the Levant in particular.[7]

Spiritual history

Mount Carmel has been considered an important and sacred site for many centuries.

Egypt, Greece and Rome

In the middle of the second millennium BC (15 centuries before Christ), in a list of places conquered by the Egyptian King Thotmes III, the mountain is referred to as the 'sacred promontory'.[8]

In the 4th century BC the neo-Platonic philosopher Iamblicus described Carmel as 'sacred above all mountains and forbidden of access to the vulgar'. He describes Pythagoras visiting the mountain, attracted to it by its sacred reputation.

The Roman historian Tacitus (56–117 AD) stated there was an oracle there which Vespasian visited for a consultation. Tacitus said there was an altar there but without any image upon it and without a temple around it.

Jewish tradition

Carmel is renowned in Jewish history, and occurs frequently in the imagery of the Prophets.

The Prophet Elijah, believed to have lived in the mid-9th century BC during the reign of Ahab and his successor Ahaziah, fought the priests of Baal in order to maintain the integrity of monotheistic Judaism.

As recounted in the Bible,[9] Elijah called all the peoples of Israel to gather on Mount Carmel at a site on its eastern face. This group included the 450 prophets of Baal and the 400 prophets who served Queen Jezebel. Elijah asked them to choose whom they worshipped, either God or Baal.

As the crowd fell silent, Elijah called for two bulls to be brought to him. He asked the Baal prophets to choose one, butcher it, build an altar for it, and call upon Baal to light the fire for the sacrifice. The priests prayed, appealed, and danced to no avail.

Then Elijah built his altar and prepared his sacrifice, asking that water be poured onto the mound until the trench he had dug around it was filled. In the Biblical account, Elijah prayed to God, asking Him to prove to the people that there is only one God. God caused the sacrifice to burn until even the water was evaporated. The false prophets were put to death.

Elijah is reported to have lived in two caves during his time on Mount Carmel, one of which is at the crest of the hill and is sheltered by the Carmelite monastery there. The lower cave is directly below, at the base of the mountain and is regularly visited for prayer, although Jewish interest arose only in recent centuries – more attention was paid to the eastern face of the mountain. The lower cave is carved out of the rock. Bahá'í historian David Ruhe writes:

> In Greek times, it may have been a centre of worship of Adonis or of Tammúz (God of Green Things), and the cave was certainly used as the centre of a fertility cult as indicated by some 150 inscriptions, pagan graffiti scratched into the chalky walls, and dating probably to the second century BC in the Hellenic period. In Roman times Vespasian, then commanding general of the legions in the East during the war against the Jews, sacrificed here seeking auguries on his contemplated strike for imperial power . . .[10]

During the Crusades Christians showed interest, and new legends appeared during Arab times. Druze[11] and Arabs venerate the site. Bahá'u'lláh visited the cave, as did 'Abdu'l-Bahá, Who spent some time living in a building near the cave mouth.

Christianity

A Catholic monastery was founded on Mount Carmel in 1156 by Berthold, Count of Limoges. Traditions derived from that time, and among the Druzes of the neighbouring villages, indicate that the scene for events relating to Elijah was the eastern end of the ridge at a spot called El-Maharrakah ('the burning').

In 1226 Crusaders received permission from Rome to form what is now the Carmelite Order. The first institution of Carmelite nuns was founded in 1452. In 1826 the monastery was rebuilt at this ancient site on Mount Carmel, where it stands today.

Others from Europe were enticed to settle on Carmel's fertile plains. In the mid-1800s Christoph Hoffmann, Georg David Hardegg and Christoph Paulus founded the Temple Society in Germany. Their dream was to establish communities that would realize the idea of creating God's kingdom on earth. Hoffmann and Hardegg arrived in Haifa in 1868, leading an influx of families that settled in Haifa and Jaffa between 1868 and 1875. Research on the dates of their arrival is ongoing.

Islam

The upper chapel of the monastery became either a mosque or *maqám* (small shrine) during the Arab period, when a *mihrab*, or a prayer niche, faced Mecca. Today the Ahmadiyya Muslim community has a mosque on Mount Carmel, known as the Mahmood Mosque.

The Bahá'í Faith

Many Bahá'ís believe that a well-known extract from the Bible refers to Mount Carmel:

> And it shall come to pass in the last days, that the mountain of the Lord's house shall be established in the top of the mountains, and shall be exalted above the hills; and all nations shall flow unto it.
>
> And many people shall go and say, Come ye, and let us go up to the mountain of the Lord, to the house of the God of Jacob; and he will teach us of his ways, and we will walk in his paths: for out of Zion shall go forth the law, and the word of the Lord from Jerusalem.
>
> And he shall judge among the nations, and shall rebuke many people: and they shall beat their swords into plowshares, and their spears into pruning hooks: nation shall not lift up sword against nation, neither shall they learn war any more.[12]

Today Mount Carmel has significance for the Bahá'ís because it is the site of the Shrine of the Báb and of the world administrative centre of the Faith, including the seat of its world governing council, the Universal House of Justice.

'Abdu'l-Bahá was interred in a vault in the Shrine of the Báb in 1921, and his burial place is referred to as His Shrine, although a permanent resting-place will be established for Him in the future.

The remains of Navváb, wife of Bahá'u'lláh, as well as His daughter Bahíyyih Khánum (the Greatest Holy Leaf) and His son Mírzá Mihdí – mother, sister and brother of 'Abdu'l-Bahá – are also interred on Mount Carmel.

Bahá'í Writings and Mount Carmel

Bahá'u'lláh

In His writings, Bahá'u'lláh describes a special spiritual relationship with Mount Carmel dating from the time He was in Haifa for a few hours in 1868 on His way to Acre across the bay. He declared:

> Verily His Temple was established upon the Mountain of God at the beginning of His arrival; to this testify whatever has been written in the Books of the Messengers. Verily both sea and land were privileged by His footsteps and seeing Him and inhaling the scent of His luminous robe.[13]

In His visits to Haifa in the last years of His life, Bahá'u'lláh spent time on and near the mountain, including at a spot to the east of the entrance to the Terraces of the Shrine and now preserved by the Bahá'í World Centre as a garden. It was on Mount Carmel in 1891, during a visit of about three months, that Bahá'u'lláh chose the site for the Shrine of the Báb. In 1891 He revealed the Tablet of Carmel, the spiritual charter for the Bahá'í World Centre.[14] This excerpt refers to the mountain:

> Haste thee, O Carmel for lo, the light of the countenance of God, the Ruler of the Kingdom of Names and Fashioner of the heavens, hath been lifted upon thee. Rejoice, for God hath in this Day established

> upon thee His throne, hath made thee the dawning-place of His signs and the day-spring of the evidences of His Revelation.

And elsewhere He writes: 'Carmel, in the Book of God, hath been designated as the Hill of God, and His Vineyard. It is here that, by the grace of the Lord of Revelation, the Tabernacle of Glory hath been raised.'[15]

'Abdu'l-Bahá

Among the many references made by 'Abdu'l-Bahá to Mount Carmel are these:

> Many Israelitish prophets either lived here or passed a portion of their lives or sojourned for a while or spent the last days of their existence on this mountain . . . Abraham, Isaac, Joseph, David, Solomon, Moses, Isaiah, Zechariah and, last of all, Christ. Elijah lived on Mount Carmel . . . His Holiness Christ came to this holy mountain many times.[16]

> Thou seest me, O my God, in this lofty Mountain, this high and exalted place..., this abode of the prophets, the haven of Elijah, the sanctuary of Isaiah, the heights which the Spirit of God, Jesus Christ – upon Him rest salutation and praise – hath traversed, this most exalted Spot blessed by the footsteps of the Lord of Hosts. O Lord! This is the Mountain that Thou has named Carmel in the Torah, and hast related unto Thyself within the treasury of the holy Scripture and Tablets. In the midst of the darksome nights, O Lord, I earnestly pray unto Thee in this most exalted Spot.[17]

> This mountain (Carmel) is where Israel's prophets passed their nights in prayers. Every step of it has been blessed by the footsteps of the prophets . . . This land will be the envy of the world, the centre of arts and sciences. 'Akká and Haifa will be connected and all the vacant lands will be cultivated. All these caves that you see have been the abode of the prophets, step by step. Every atom of this soil is holy. All the prophets, while praying, longed to reach this day and give the glad tidings of the coming of the Lord. They prophesied

> that the Lord of Hosts would come and the tent of the Lord would be pitched on Mount Carmel . . . in all these mountains and caves the prophets of God prayed at night, shed tears, and longed to be with us in the days of the Blessed Beauty.[18]

'Abdu'l-Bahá's affection for the mountain was recorded by the American pilgrim Julia M. Grundy: "Abdul-Baha loves Mount Carmel and has often visited, sometimes staying overnight in caves which overlook the sea . . .'[19] She reports 'Abdu'l-Bahá as saying:

> I once lived in a cave on Mount Carmel. One day I went to the Carmelite Monastery and asked to see someone, saying I had a message to deliver. They refused to see me or hear my message. I said, 'I will put in in writing if you will read it.' They still refused, so I returned to Akka in great sadness, walking the whole distance of nine miles.

Shoghi Effendi

The Guardian's writings include many references to Mount Carmel, among which are these:

> . . . Carmel, the 'Vineyard of God'; flanked by the Cave of Elijah on the west, and by the hills of Galilee on the east; backed by the plain of Sharon, and facing the silver-city of 'Akká, and beyond it the Most Holy Tomb, the Heart and Qiblih of the Bahá'í world . . .[20]

> Within this Most Holy Land rises the Mountain of God of immemorial sanctity, the Vineyard of the Lord, the Retreat of Elijah, Whose return the Báb Himself symbolizes.[21]

> In that same year Bahá'u'lláh's tent, the 'Tabernacle of Glory,' was raised on Mt. Carmel, 'the Hill of God and His Vineyard,' the home of Elijah, extolled by Isaiah as the 'mountain of the Lord,' to which 'all nations shall flow.' Four times He visited Haifa, His last visit being no less than three months long. In the course of one of these visits, when His tent was pitched in the vicinity of the Carmelite Monastery, He, the 'Lord of the Vineyard,' revealed the Tablet of Carmel, remarkable for its allusions and prophecies. On another

> occasion He pointed out Himself to 'Abdu'l-Bahá, as He stood on the slopes of that mountain, the site which was to serve as the permanent resting-place of the Báb, and on which a befitting mausoleum was later to be erected.[22]
>
> For it must be clearly understood, nor can it be sufficiently emphasized, that the conjunction of the resting-place of the Greatest Holy Leaf with those of her brother and mother incalculably reinforces the spiritual potencies of that consecrated Spot which, under the wings of the Báb's overshadowing Sepulchre, and in the vicinity of the future Mashriqu'l-Adhkár,[23] which will be reared on its flank, is destined to evolve into the focal center of those world-shaking, world-embracing, world-directing administrative institutions, ordained by Bahá'u'lláh and anticipated by 'Abdu'l-Bahá, and which are to function in consonance with the principles that govern the twin institutions of the Guardianship and the Universal House of Justice. Then, and then only, will this momentous prophecy which illuminates the concluding passages of the Tablet of Carmel be fulfilled: 'Ere long will God sail His Ark upon thee (Carmel), and will manifest the people of Bahá who have been mentioned in the Book of Names.'[24]

Hand of the Cause Zikrullah Khadem recalled what Shoghi Effendi told him when he was on pilgrimage:

> Have you read the Tablet of Carmel? . . . The Tablet is there in the Pilgrim House. The Blessed Beauty revealed this Tablet when His tent was first raised on Mount Carmel near the Deyr (Carmelite Monastery) . . . It contains the divine mysteries of God. Bahá'u'lláh said, 'Call out to Zion, O Carmel,' which means, O Carmel, address Jerusalem, 'and announce the joyful tidings: He that was hidden from mortal eyes is come! . . . Hasten forth and circumambulate the City of God . . .' The City of God refers to the establishment of the Shrine of the Báb on Mount Carmel. The City of God in this Tablet is Bahá'u'lláh's promise to entomb the sacred body of the Báb. A 'celestial Kaaba' is a mystery [which he did not disclose and I did not dare to ask]. These are mysteries. Bahá'u'lláh proceeds in this Tablet, 'Ere long will God sail His Ark upon thee,' a further mystery

which means the Universal House of Justice will be established here on Mount Carmel under the shadow of the Shrine of the Báb. The Ark in this Tablet is the Ark of God's civilization. And the 'people of Bahá,' the occupants of the Ark, are members of the House.[25]

In interpreting the meaning of this extract from the Tablet of Carmel: 'Ere long will God sail His Ark upon thee', Shoghi Effendi said that it was a reference to the establishment of the Universal House of Justice from which the laws of God would flow to all mankind.[26]

He also referred to the Shrine of the Báb in these Arabic terms in Arabic: *Maṭla'-i-Anwár* (the Dawning Place of Light), and *Kúh-i-Núr* (the Mountain of Light).[27]

In an exquisite tribute to the Shrine of the Báb, Shoghi Effendi describes its location and it spiritual station. It was part of his Naw-Rúz (New Year) 1955 Message to the Bahá'ís of Persia, and includes references to the dome and superstructure, completed in 1953:

This magnificent Edifice stands facing Bahá'u'lláh's Most Great Prison, extolled by the Pen of Glory as the 'Heaven of heavens,' and looks toward the Qiblih of the people of Bahá, that Spot within the Vale of Security and Peace, the Plain of 'Akká, round which circle in adoration the Concourse on high. To her right are the hills of Galilee in which nestles the childhood home of the beautiful Christ, and the locality by the banks of the Jordan River where He who is the Spirit [Jesus] was called to prophethood; and on her left, on the crest of Carmel, are to be found the Cave of Elijah and the exalted Spot which was blessed by the footsteps of the Most Holy Abhá Beauty and was ennobled through the revelation of the Tablet of Carmel from the treasury of the Pen of Glory . . .

High, immeasurably high is this Shrine, the lofty, the most great, the most wondrous. Exalted, immeasurably exalted is this Resting-place, the fragrant, the pure, the luminous, the transcendent. Glorified, immeasurably glorified is this Spot, the most august, the most holy, the most blessed, the most sublime . . .

Upon thee, O Queen of Carmel, be the purest, the most tender salutations, the fairest, the most gracious blessings! Glorified is He Whose footsteps have ennobled the spot whereon thou standest,

Who ordained thy Seat, and Who extolled thee in His Tablet and Book. How great is the potency of thy might, a might which has bewildered the souls of the favored ones of God and His Messengers.

Methinks I behold thee in my dreams established upon thy glorious throne, attired in thy white raiment, crowned with thy golden crown, resplendent with the lights shining within thee and around thee, calling aloud in ringing tones and raising thy voice between earth and heaven.

Methinks I perceive the souls of the holy ones and of the dwellers of the realms above hastening toward thee with utmost joy, eagerness and ecstasy, pointing to thee, circling round thee, inhaling the perfume of thy flowers and roses, seeking blessing from the earth of thy precincts, bowing their foreheads to the ground before thee in recognition of the majesty and glory which surround the Holy Dust reposing within thee, the Pearl which is enshrined in thy bosom.

Blessed, immeasurably blessed is the person who visits thee and circles around thee, who serves at thy threshold, waters thy flowers, inhales the fragrance of holiness from thy roses, celebrates thy praise and glorifies thy station for the love of God, thy Creator, in this hallowed and radiant, this great, august and wondrous age.[28]

ANNEX 4

THE TABLET OF CARMEL

All glory be to this Day, the Day in which the fragrances of mercy have been wafted over all created things, a Day so blest that past ages and centuries can never hope to rival it, a Day in which the countenance of the Ancient of Days hath turned towards His holy seat. Thereupon the voices of all created things, and beyond them those of the Concourse on high, were heard calling aloud: 'Haste thee, O Carmel, for lo, the light of the countenance of God, the Ruler of the Kingdom of Names and Fashioner of the heavens, hath been lifted upon thee.'

Seized with transports of joy, and raising high her voice, she thus exclaimed: 'May my life be a sacrifice to Thee, inasmuch as Thou hast fixed Thy gaze upon me, hast bestowed upon me Thy bounty, and hast directed towards me Thy steps. Separation from Thee, O Thou Source of everlasting life, hath well nigh consumed me, and my remoteness from Thy presence hath burned away my soul. All praise be to Thee for having enabled me to hearken to Thy call, for having honored me with Thy footsteps, and for having quickened my soul through the vitalizing fragrance of Thy Day and the shrilling voice of Thy Pen, a voice Thou didst ordain as Thy trumpet-call amidst Thy people. And when the hour at which Thy resistless Faith was to be made manifest did strike, Thou didst breathe a breath of Thy spirit into Thy Pen, and lo, the entire creation shook to its very foundations, unveiling to mankind such mysteries as lay hidden within the treasuries of Him Who is the Possessor of all created things.'

No sooner had her voice reached that most exalted Spot than We made reply: 'Render thanks unto thy Lord, O Carmel. The fire of thy separation from Me was fast consuming thee, when the ocean of My presence surged before thy face, cheering thine eyes and those of all creation, and filling with delight all things visible and invisible. Rejoice, for God hath in this Day established upon thee His throne, hath made thee the dawning-place of His signs and the day spring of the evidences of His Revelation. Well is it with him that circleth around thee, that proclaimeth the revelation of thy glory, and recounteth that which the bounty of the Lord thy God hath showered upon thee. Seize thou the Chalice of Immortality in the name of thy Lord, the All-Glorious, and give thanks unto Him, inasmuch as He, in token of His mercy unto thee, hath turned thy sorrow into gladness, and transmuted thy grief into blissful joy. He, verily, loveth the spot which hath been made the seat of His throne, which His footsteps have trodden, which hath been honored by His presence, from which He raised His call, and upon which He shed His tears.

'Call out to Zion, O Carmel, and announce the joyful tidings: He that was hidden from mortal eyes is come! His all-conquering sovereignty is manifest; His all-encompassing splendor is revealed. Beware lest thou hesitate or halt. Hasten forth and circumambulate the City of God that hath descended from heaven, the celestial Kaaba round which have circled in adoration the favored of God, the pure in heart, and the company of the most exalted angels. Oh, how I long to announce unto every spot on the surface of the earth, and to carry to each one of its cities, the glad-tidings of this Revelation – a Revelation to which the heart of Sinai hath been attracted, and in whose name the Burning Bush is calling: 'Unto God, the Lord of Lords, belong the kingdoms of earth and heaven.' Verily this is the Day in which both land and sea rejoice at this announcement, the Day for which have been laid up those things which God, through a bounty beyond the ken of mortal mind or heart, hath destined for revelation. Ere long will God sail His Ark upon thee, and will manifest the people of Bahá who have been mentioned in the Book of Names.

Sanctified be the Lord of all mankind, at the mention of Whose name all the atoms of the earth have been made to vibrate, and the Tongue of Grandeur hath been moved to disclose that which had been wrapt in His knowledge and lay concealed within the treasury of His might. He, verily, through the potency of His name, the Mighty, the All-Powerful, the Most High, is the ruler of all that is in the heavens and all that is on earth.[1]

ANNEX 5

TABLETS OF VISITATION[1]

(This Tablet is read at the Shrines of Bahá'u'lláh and the Báb. It is also frequently used in commemorating Their anniversaries.)

The praise which hath dawned from Thy most august Self, and the glory which hath shone forth from Thy most effulgent Beauty, rest upon Thee, O Thou Who art the Manifestation of Grandeur, and the King of Eternity, and the Lord of all who are in heaven and on earth! I testify that through Thee the sovereignty of God and His dominion, and the majesty of God and His grandeur, were revealed, and the Daystars of ancient splendour have shed their radiance in the heaven of Thine irrevocable decree, and the Beauty of the Unseen hath shone forth above the horizon of creation. I testify, moreover, that with but a movement of Thy Pen Thine injunction 'Be Thou' hath been enforced, and God's hidden Secret hath been divulged, and all created things have been called into being, and all the Revelations have been sent down.

I bear witness, moreover, that through Thy beauty the beauty of the Adored One hath been unveiled, and through Thy face the face of the Desired One hath shone forth, and that through a word from Thee Thou hast decided between all created things, causing them who are devoted to Thee to ascend unto the summit of glory, and the infidels to fall into the lowest abyss.

I bear witness that he who hath known Thee hath known God, and he who hath attained unto Thy presence hath attained unto the presence of God. Great, therefore, is the blessedness of him who hath believed in Thee, and in Thy signs, and hath humbled himself before Thy sovereignty, and hath been honoured with meeting Thee, and hath attained the good pleasure of Thy will, and circled around Thee, and stood before Thy throne. Woe betide him that hath transgressed against Thee, and hath denied Thee, and repudiated Thy signs, and gainsaid

Thy sovereignty, and risen up against Thee, and waxed proud before Thy face, and hath disputed Thy testimonies, and fled from Thy rule and Thy dominion, and been numbered with the infidels whose names have been inscribed by the fingers of Thy behest upon Thy holy Tablets.

Waft, then, unto me, O my God and my Beloved, from the right hand of Thy mercy and Thy loving-kindness, the holy breaths of Thy favours, that they may draw me away from myself and from the world unto the courts of Thy nearness and Thy presence. Potent art Thou to do what pleaseth Thee. Thou, truly, hast been supreme over all things.

The remembrance of God and His praise, and the glory of God and His splendour, rest upon Thee, O Thou Who art His Beauty! I bear witness that the eye of creation hath never gazed upon one wronged like Thee. Thou wast immersed all the days of Thy life beneath an ocean of tribulations. At one time Thou wast in chains and fetters; at another Thou wast threatened by the sword of Thine enemies. Yet despite all this, Thou didst enjoin upon all men to observe what had been prescribed unto Thee by Him Who is the All-Knowing, the All-Wise.

May my spirit be a sacrifice to the wrongs Thou didst suffer, and my soul be a ransom for the adversities Thou didst sustain. I beseech God, by Thee and by them whose faces have been illumined with the splendours of the light of Thy countenance, and who, for love of Thee, have observed all whereunto they were bidden, to remove the veils that have come in between Thee and Thy creatures, and to supply me with the good of this world and the world to come. Thou art, in truth, the Almighty, the Most Exalted, the All-Glorious, the Ever-Forgiving, the Most Compassionate.

Bless Thou, O Lord my Lord, the Divine Lote-Tree and its leaves, and its boughs, and its branches, and its stems, and its offshoots, as long as Thy most excellent titles will endure and Thy most august attributes will last. Protect it, then, from the mischief of the aggressor and the hosts of tyranny. Thou art, in truth, the Almighty, the Most Powerful. Bless Thou, also, O Lord my God, Thy servants and Thy handmaidens who have attained unto Thee, Thou, truly, art the All-Bountiful, Whose grace is infinite. No God is there save Thee, the Ever-Forgiving, the Most Generous.

Bahá'u'lláh

(This prayer, revealed by 'Abdu'l-Bahá, is read at His Shrine. It is also used in private prayer.)

Whoso reciteth this prayer with lowliness and fervour will bring gladness and joy to the heart of this Servant; it will be even as meeting Him face to face.

He is the All-Glorious!

O God, my God! Lowly and tearful, I raise my suppliant hands to Thee and cover my face in the dust of that Threshold of Thine, exalted above the knowledge of the learned, and the praise of all that glorify Thee. Graciously look upon Thy servant, humble and lowly at Thy door, with the glances of the eye of Thy mercy, and immerse him in the Ocean of Thine eternal grace.

Lord! He is a poor and lowly servant of Thine, enthralled and imploring Thee, captive in Thy hand, praying fervently to Thee, trusting in Thee, in tears before Thy face, calling to Thee and beseeching Thee, saying:

O Lord, my God! Give me Thy grace to serve Thy loved ones, strengthen me in my servitude to Thee, illumine my brow with the light of adoration in Thy court of holiness, and of prayer to Thy kingdom of grandeur. Help me to be selfless at the heavenly entrance of Thy gate, and aid me to be detached from all things within Thy holy precincts. Lord! Give me to drink from the chalice of selflessness; with its robe clothe me, and in its ocean immerse me. Make me as dust in the pathway of Thy loved ones, and grant that I may offer up my soul for the earth ennobled by the footsteps of Thy chosen ones in Thy path, O Lord of Glory in the Highest.

With this prayer doth Thy servant call Thee, at dawntide and in the night-season. Fulfil his heart's desire, O Lord! Illumine his heart, gladden his bosom, kindle his light, that he may serve Thy Cause and Thy servants.

Thou art the Bestower, the Pitiful, the Most Bountiful, the Gracious, the Merciful, the Compassionate.

'Abdu'l-Bahá

BIBLIOGRAPHY

Ábádih'í, Layla. Unpublished memoirs. Excerpts provided by the Bahá'í World Centre.

'Abdu'l-Bahá. *Memorials of the Faithful*. Wilmette, IL: Bahá'í Publishing Trust, 1971.

— *A Traveler's Narrative Written to Illustrate the Episode of the Báb* (1891). Trans. E. G. Browne. Wilmette, IL: Bahá'í Publishing Trust, rev. ed. 1980.

— *Selections from the Writings of 'Abdu'l-Bahá*. Comp. Research Department of the Universal House of Justice. Trans. Committee at the Bahá'í World Centre and Marzieh Gail. Haifa: Bahá'í World Centre, 1978.

— *Some Answered Questions* (1908). Comp. and trans. Laura Clifford Barney. Haifa: Bahá'í World Centre, rev. ed. 2014.

— *Majmú'iy-i-Makátib-i Ḥaḍrat-i 'Abdu'l-Bahá* (Collected Tablets of 'Abdu'l-Bahá). Iranian National Bahá'í Archives (INBA). Partially reprinted Tehran, 1976.

— *Muntakhabátí az Makátib-i-Ḥaḍrat-i-'Abdu'l-Bahá* (Selections from the Tablets of 'Abdu'l-Bahá). Hofheim: Bahá'í Publication Committee in Persian and Arabic, 2000.

Abu'l-Faḍl, Mírzá (Abu'l-Faḍl-i-Gulpáygání). *The Bahá'í Proofs (Ḥujaja'l-Bahíyyih) and A Short Sketch of the History and Lives of the Leaders of This Religion*. Trans. Ali-Kuli Khan. Facsimile of the 1929 edition. Wilmette, IL: Bahá'í Publishing Trust, 1983.

Afnán, A.-Q. *Ahd-i-A'lá Zindigániy-i-Ḥaḍrat-i-Báb* (The Bábí Dispensation: The Life of the Báb). Oxford: OneWorld, 2000.

Afnán, Ḥabíbu'lláh. *Memories of the Báb, Bahá'u'lláh and 'Abdu'l-Bahá*. Trans. Ahang Rabbani. Electronic publication. Los Angeles: Kalimát, 2005.

Afroukhteh, Youness. *Memories of Nine Years in 'Akká*. Trans. Riaz Masrour. Oxford: George Ronald, 2003.

Áhang-i-Badí'. Bahá'í periodical published in Iran.

Ahdieh, Hussein; Chapman, Hillary. *Awakening: A History of the Bábí and Bahá'í Faith in Nayríz*. Wilmette, IL: Bahá'í Publishing, 2013. Expanded version (2016) available at: www. nayriz.org.

Alkan, Necati. *Dissent and Heterodoxy in the Late Ottoman Empire: Reformers, Babis and Baha'is*. Istanbul: The Isis Press, 2008.

The Báb. *Selections from the Writings of the Báb.* Comp. Research Department of the Universal House of Justice. Trans. Habib Taherzadeh with the assistance of a Committee at the Bahá'í World Centre. Haifa: Bahá'í World Centre, 1976.

Bahá'í International Community. *Bahá'í Holy Places in Haifa and the Western Galilee.* Haifa: Bahá'í World Centre, 2005.

— *Bahá'u'lláh.* New York: Bahá'í International Community Office of Public Information, 1992. Available at: http://www.bahai.org/library/other-literature/official-statements-commentaries/bahaullah/.

Bahá'í Prayers: A Selection of Prayers Revealed by Bahá'u'lláh, The Báb, and 'Abdu'l-Bahá. Wilmette, IL: Bahá'í Publishing Trust, rev. ed. 2002.

The Bahá'í World: An International Record. Vol. III (1928–1930); vol. IX (1940–1944); vol. X (1944–1946). Wilmette, IL: Báhá'í Publishing Trust; vol. XVIII (1979–1983). Haifa: Bahá'í World Centre, 1986.

Bahá'u'lláh. *Epistle to the Son of the Wolf.* Trans. Shoghi Effendi. Wilmette, IL: Bahá'í Publishing Trust, rev. ed. 1976.

— *Gleanings from the Writings of Bahá'u'lláh.* Trans. Shoghi Effendi. Wilmette, IL: Bahá'í Publishing Trust, 2nd ed. 1976.

— *The Kitáb-i-Aqdas: The Most Holy Book.* Haifa: Bahá'í World Centre, 1992.

— *The Summons of the Lord of Hosts: Tablets of Bahá'u'lláh.* Haifa: Bahá'í World Centre, 2002.

— *Tablets of Bahá'u'lláh Revealed after the Kitáb-i-Aqdas.* Comp. Research Department of the Universal House of Justice. Haifa: Bahá'í World Centre, 1978.

Bahá'u'lláh; The Báb; 'Abdu'l-Bahá; Shoghi Effendi. *Mountain of the Lord.* London: Bahá'í Publishing Trust, 1993.

Bahíyyih Khánum: The Greatest Holy Leaf. Comp. Research Department of the Bahá'í World Centre. Haifa: Bahá'í World Centre, 1982.

Ballenger, Robert. 'The master humorist', in *Dialogue*, vol. 2, no. 2–3 (1988), pp. 25–9. Available at: http://bahai-library.com/ballenger_master_humorist.

Balyuzi, H. M. *'Abdu'l-Bahá.* Oxford: George Ronald, 1971.

— *The Báb: The Herald of the Day of Days.* Oxford: George Ronald, 1973.

— *Bahá'u'lláh, the King of Glory.* Oxford, George Ronald, 1980.

— *Eminent Bahá'ís in the Time of Bahá'u'lláh.* Oxford: George Ronald, 1985.

Ben-Artzi, Yossi. *The Case of the German Templers in Eretz-Israel.* Bentleigh, Vic.: TSA Heritage Group, Temple Society Australia, 2006.

Blaich, Irene, in conjunction with Horst Blaich. *The Wennagel Story: The Fate of the Wennagel Families of Master Builders from the Black Forest, Germany, The Templer Settlements in the Holy Land and onto Australia from 1699–2007.* Trafford Publishing, 2007.

Blomfield, Lady. *The Chosen Highway.* London: Bahá'í Publishing Trust, 1940. RP Oxford: George Ronald, 2007.

Bowle, John. *Viscount Samuel: A Biography.* London: Victor Gollancz, 1957.

Bushrui, Badi. 'Kúh-i-muqaddas Karmil va istiqrar-i arsh-i-Mubárak dar Maqám-i-A'lá' (The Holy Mountain of Carmel and the Interment of the Blessed Remains in the Shrine of the Most High) in *Áhang-i-Badí'*, vols. 3 & 4 (2008).

Butt, Abbasali. 'An account of the services of Siyyid Muṣṭafá Rúmí', in *The Bahá'í World*, vol. X (1944–1946), pp. 517–20.

Cameron, Glenn; Momen, Wendi. *A Basic Bahá'í Chronology.* Oxford: George Ronald, 1996.

Carmel, Alex. *Ottoman Haifa: A History of Four Centuries under Turkish Rule.* London: Tauris, 2011.

Chapman, Anita Ioas. *Leroy Ioas: Hand of the Cause of God.* Oxford: George Ronald, 1998.

Chase, Thornton. *In Galilee.* Chicago: Bahai Publishing Society, 1921. Published with Arthur S. Agnew, *In Wonderland.* RP Los Angeles: Kalimát Press, 1985.

Cole, J. R. 'Foreword to facsimile edition', in Abu'l-Faḍl, *The Bahá'í Proofs*, pp. v–xiii.

Coy, Genevieve L. 'A week in Abdul-Baha's home', in *Star of the West*, 4 instalments: vol. 12, nos. 10–13 (September–November 1921). Republished as Wilhelm, Roy; Cobb, Stanwood; Coy, Genevieve L: *In His Presence: Visits to 'Abdu'l-Bahá.* Los Angeles: Kalimát Press, 1989.

Dalman, D. Gustaf. *Hundert deutsche Fliegerbilder aus Palastina.* Gutersloh: Bertelsmann, 1925.

The Dawn-Breakers: Nabíl's Narrative of the Early Days of the Bahá'í Revelation. Trans. Shoghi Effendi. Wilmette, IL: Bahá'í Publishing Trust, 1932, 1999.

Djemal Pasha. *Memoirs of a Turkish Statesman, 1913–1919.* London: Hutchinson, 1922.

Dunbar, Hooper C. *Forces of Our Time: The Dynamics of Light and Darkness.* Oxford: George Ronald, 2010.

Esslemont, John. *Bahá'u'lláh and the New Era* (1923). Rev. ed. Wilmette, IL: Bahá'í Publishing Trust, 1980.

Faizi, M.-A. *Malakíy-i-Karmil.* Tehran: National Spiritual Assembly of the Bahá'ís of Iran, 132 BE (1975 AD).

—*Ḥaḍrat-i-Nuqtiy-i Úlá* (The Life of the Báb). Tehran:Bahá'í Publishing Trust, 1973.

Faizi-Moore, May. *Faizi.* Oxford: George Ronald, 2013.

Fáḍil-i-Mázindarání. *Asráru'l-Á<u>th</u>ár.* A glossary of Bahá'í terms. Tehran: Bahá'í Publishing Trust, 5 vols. 124–9 BE (1967–72 AD).

—*Ẓuhúru'l-Ḥaqq*. Vol. 8, part 2. Tehran: Bahá'í Publishing Trust, 132 BE (1975 AD).

Flannery, Vincent. 'Dr. William Cormick', in Brendan McNamara (comp.): *Connections: Essays and Notes on Early Links Between the Bahá'í Faith and Ireland.* Cork: Tusker Keyes Publications, 2007. Available at: http://connectionsbmc.wordpress.com/2011/01/17/dr-william-cormick/.

Furútan, 'Alí-Akbar. *The Story of My Heart*. Oxford: George Ronald, 1984.

Ghadimi, Riaz. *The Báb: The King of Messengers.* Trans. Riaz Masrour. Hong Kong: Juxta, 2009. Available at: http://juxta.com/wp-content/uploads/king_of_messengers_online_1.0.pdf.

Gail, Marzieh.,"Abdu'l-Bahá: Portrayals from East and West', in *World Order* (1971), vol. 6, no. 1, pp. 29–41; reprinted in Gail, *Dawn Over Mount Hira*, pp. 194–216. Also available at: http://bahai-library.com/gail_abdul-baha_portrayals.

— *Arches of the Years.* Oxford: George Ronald, 1991.

— *Dawn over Mount Hira.* Oxford: George Ronald, 1976.

— *Khánum: The Greatest Holy Leaf.* Oxford: George Ronald, 1981.

— *Summon Up Remembrance.* Oxford: George Ronald, 1987.

Geddes, Patrick. 'Notes after a visit to Sir Abdul-Baha (Abbas Effendi)', in *Star of the West*, vol. 12, no. 7 (13 July 1921), pp. 136–7, reprinted from *Bahai News* (Bombay).

Ghirshman, Roman; Minorsky, Vladimir; Sanghvi, Ramesh. *Persia: The Immortal Kingdom*. Photographs by William MacQuitty. London: Orient Commerce Establishment, 1971.

Giachery, Ugo. *Shoghi Effendi: Recollections*. Oxford: George Ronald, 1973.

Goldman, Dan. *The Architecture of the Templers in their Colonies in Eretz-Israel, 1868–1948, and Their Settlements in the United States, 1860–1925.* Cincinnati, OH: The Union Institute and University, Graduate College, School of Interdisciplinary Arts and Sciences, 2003.

Gollmer, U. *Mein Herz ist bei Euch: 'Abdu'l-Bahá in Deutschland.* Hofheim-Langenhain: Bahá'í Verlag 1988. Werner Gollmer, *My Heart is With You: 'Abdu'l-Bahá in Germany*. Trans. Martha Otto.

Grundy, Julia M. *Ten Days in the Light of 'Akká.* Wilmette, IL: Bahá'í Publishing Trust, 2000.

Harper, Barron. *Lights of Fortitude.* Oxford: George Ronald, 2007.

Ḥaydar-'Alí, Ḥájí Mírzá. *Bihjatuṣ-Ṣudúr*. Bombay, 1913. *Stories from the Delight of Hearts: The Memoirs of Ḥájí Mírzá Ḥaydar-'Alí.* Trans. and abridged by A-Q. Faizi. Los Angeles: Kalimát Press, 1980.

Herbert, Gilbert; Sosnovksy, Silvina. *Bauhaus on the Carmel and the Crossroads of Empire.* Jerusalem: Yad Izhak Ben-Zvi, 1993.

Hobhouse, Penelope. *Gardens of Persia.* Glebe, NSW: Florilegium, 2003.

Hogenson, Kathryn Jewett. *Lighting the Western Sky*. Oxford: George Ronald, 2010.

Ioas, Sylvia. 'Interview of Sachiro Fujita', 1975. Available at: http://bahai-library.com/ioas_fujita_interview.

Irwin, Beatrice. 'Shrines and gardens', in *The Bahá'í World*, vol. III, pp. 349–53.

Johnson, Paul. *The History of the Jews*. New York: Harper and Row, 1987.

Ishráq Khávarí, 'Abdu'l-Ḥamíd. *Qámús-i-Tawqí'-i 108 (BE).* A commentary on Shoghi Effendi's General Letter to the Bahá'ís of the East, Naw-Rúz 108 BE, vol. 3 in the series *Aṣrár-i-Rabbání*. Ed. Vahid Rafati. Darmstadt: 'Asr-i-Jadíd, 2001.

Izadinia, Fuad. *The Major Opus: The German Templers and the Bahá'í Faith.* Unpublished.

Khadem, Javidukht. *Zikrullah Khadem: The Itinerant Hand of the Cause of God.* Wilmette, IL: Bahá'í Publishing Trust, 1990.

Khadem, Riaz. *Prelude to the Guardianship*. Oxford: George Ronald, 2014.

Khadem, Zikrullah. 'Carmel: The Mountain of God and the Tablet of Carmel', in Javidukht Khadem, *Zikrullah Khadem: The Itinerant Hand of the Cause of God.* Wilmette, IL: Bahá'í Publishing Trust, 1990.

Khan, Janet A. *Prophet's Daughter: The Life and Legacy of Bahíyyih Khánum, Outstanding Heroine of the Bahá'í Faith.* Wilmette, IL: Bahá'í Publishing, 2005.

Khasawneh, Diala. *Memoirs Engraved in Stone: Palestinian Urban Mansions.* Riwaq Centre for Architectural Conservation, 2007.

Kinross, Lord. *The Ottoman Centuries.* New York: Morrow Quill, 1977.

Klingeman, Clara (née Struve). *Some Childhood Stories Remembered,* manuscript provided by Templer Society archivist Peter Lange, trans. Martha Otto.

Latimer, George Orr. *The Light of the World.* Boston: George Orr Latimer, 1920. Available at: http://bahai-library.com/latimer_light_world.

Ma'ani, Baharieh Rouhani. *Leaves of the Twin Divine Trees*. Oxford: George Ronald, 2008.

Maḥmúd's Diary: The Diary of Mírzá Maḥmúd-i-Zarqání Chronicling 'Abdu'l-Bahá's Journey to America. Trans. Mohi Sobhani with the assistance of Shirley Macias. Oxford: George Ronald, 1998.

Manuchehri, Sepehr. 'Further extracts concerning the remains of the Báb in Tehran', translations from the Persian of Fáḍil-i-Mázindarání, *Tarikh Ẓuhúru'l-Ḥaqq*, vol. 6, pp. 490–492, and Ávárih, *Kavakebu'l Dorriah,* pp. 369–372. Available at: http://bahai-library.com/mazandarani_remains_bab_tehran.

Maude, Roderic.; Maude, Derwent. *The Servant, The General and Armageddon.* Oxford: George Ronald, 1998.

McNamara, Brendan. 'The man who met the Báb: Some new facts about his life', online article, available at: https://connectionsbmc.wordpress.com/2013/01/14/134/.

Mehrabkhani, R. *Mullá Ḥusayn: Disciple at Dawn*. Los Angeles: Kalimát Press, 1987.

Modarres, Fath'u'lláh. *Tárík͟h-i Amr-i Bahá'í dar Najaf-Ábád* (History of the Bahá'í Faith in Najafabad). Ed. Vahid Rafati. Darmstadt: 'Asr-i-Jadíd, 2004.

Momen, Moojan (ed.). *The Bábí and Bahá'í Religions, 1844–1944*. Oxford: George Ronald, 1981.

— *The Baha'i Communities of Iran, 1851–1921*. Vol. 1: *The North of Iran*. Oxford: George Ronald, 2015.

— *Bahá'u'lláh: A Short Biography*. Oxford: OneWorld, 2007.

Montefiore, Simon Sebag. *Jerusalem: The Biography.* London: Weidenfeld & Nicholson, 2011.

Mount Carmel Projects. *Vineyard of the Lord.* Issues 1–46 (1994–2001). Newsletters, published in Haifa at the Bahá'í World Centre.

Mú'ayyad, Ḥabíb. *Khátirat-i-Ḥabíb* (Memoirs of Ḥabíb). Tehran, 1961. Vol. 1. Hofheim-Langenhain: Bahá'í Verlag, 1998. Trans. and ed. Ahang Rabbani: *Eight Years Near 'Abdu'l-Bahá: The Diary of Dr. Habíb Mú'ayyad.* Witnesses to Bábí and Bahá'í History, vol. 3. E-book, 2007. Available at: http://bahai-library.com/pdf/r/rabbani_diary_habib_muayyad_2013.pdf.

Muhajir, Iran Furutan. *The Mystery of God.* New Delhi: Bahá'í Publishing Trust, 1971.

Muhammad-Husayni, Nusrat'u'llah. *The Báb, His Life, His Writings, and the Disciples of the Báb's Dispensation* (in Persian). Dundas, ON: Institute for Bahá'í Studies in Persian, 1995.

— *Taíikh-i Amr-i Bahá'í dar Shahr-i-Qúm* (History of the Bahá'í Faith in the city of Qum). Darmstadt: 'Asr-i-Jadíd, 2005.

Nak͟hjávání, 'Alí. *Shoghi Effendi: The Range and Power of His Pen.* Rome: Casa Editrice Bahá'í, 2007.

National Spiritual Assembly of the Bahá'ís of the United States. *Be Yad-i Dust (In Memory of the Friend): A Tribute to Hand of the Cause of God Abu'l-Qásim Faizi, 1906–1980.*Wilmette, IL: 1988.

Núr, Izzátu'lláh. *K͟háṭirát-i-muhájirí az Iṣfahán dar zaman-i-s͟hahida-á Sulṭánu's͟h-S͟huhadá' va Maḥbúbu's͟h-S͟huhadá'* (A pioneer from Isfahan during the time of the martyrdom of the King of Martyrs and the Beloved of Martyrs).Tehran: National Spiritual Assembly of the Bahá'ís of Iran, 128 BE/1972 AD.

Ong, Rose. 'Myanmar: History of the Bahá'í Faith', online article, 2008. Available at: http://bahai-library.com/history_bahai_faith_myanmar.

Pajuheshnameh (A Persian Journal of Bahá'í Studies, supplement of *Payám-i-Bahá'í*). Published in Canada, 1998–2000.

Pappe, Illan. *The Rise and Fall of a Palestinian Dynasty: The Husaynis 1700–1948.* London: Saqi Books, 2010.

Payám-i-Bahá'í. Periodical. Beausoleil, France: Assemblée spirituelle nationale des Bahá'ís de France.

Phelps, Myron H. *The Master in 'Akká.* RP Los Angeles: Kalimat Press, 1985.

Porter, Yves, *Palaces and Gardens of Persia.* Paris: Flammarion, 2003

Preston, Lt.-Col. *The Desert Mounted Corps: An Account of the Cavalry Operations in Palestine and Syria, 1917–1918.* Boston/New York: Houghton Mifflin, 1921. Available at: https://archive.org/details/desertmountedcoroopres. *Map of Haifa available at:* http://1914-1918.invisionzone.com/forums/index.php?showtopic=166228.

Rabbani, Ahang. "Abdu'l-Bahá in Abu-Sinan: September 1914–May 1915', in *Bahá'í Studies Review,* vol. 13 (2005), pp. 75–103. Available at: http://bahai-library.com/rabbani_abdulbaha_abu_sinan.

— 'The Afnán family: Some biographical notes'. Online article, 2007. Available at: http://bahai-library.com/rabbani_afnan_family.

— 'Efforts to preserve the remains of the Báb: Four historical accounts', in *Bahá'í Studies Review,* vol. 11 (2003), pp. 83–95. Available at: http://bahai-library.com/pdf/r/rabbani_preserve_remains_bab.pdf.

Rabbaní, Ruḥíyyih. *The Priceless Pearl.* London: Bahá'í Publishing Trust, 1969.

Randall-Winckler, Bahiyyih. *My Pilgrimage to Haifa, November 1919.* Wilmette, IL: Bahá'í Publishing Trust, 1996.

— *William Henry Randall: Disciple of 'Abdu'l-Bahá.* With M. R. Garis. Oxford: OneWorld, 1996.

Rafati, Vahid. 'Az nāmahā-yi qudamā', in *'Andalíb,* vol. 23 (2007), no. 91.

— 'Bahá'u'lláh in Haifa', in *A Persian Journal of Bahá'í Studies: Supplement of Payám-i Bahá'í,* vol. 2, no. 1 (Autumn 1997).

— *Peyk-e Rástán (The Messenger of the True Ones: Bahá'í Sacred Writings, Biographies and Works of Jináb-i-Ismu'lláh-i-Aṣdaq and his family).* Darmstadt: 'Asr-i-Jadíd, 2005.

Redman, Earl. *Shoghi Effendi Through the Pilgrim's Eye.* Vol. 1: *Building the Administrative Order, 1922–1952.* Oxford: George Ronald, 2015.

Remey, Charles Mason. *Observations of a Bahá'í Traveller, 1908.* Washington DC: Carnahan Press, 1909.

— *Reminiscences and Letters.* Copy in the Bahá'í World Centre Library.

Rohani, Aziz. *Sweet and Enchanting Stories.* Incorporating in Section B: *Dr Zia Baghdadi's Memories.* Hong Kong: Juxta, 2005. Available at: http://juxta.com/wp-content/uploads/sweet_enchanting_electronic.pdf.

Ruhe, David S. *Door of Hope: The Bahá'í Faith in the Holy Land*. Oxford: George Ronald, 2nd rev. ed. 2001.

— *Robe of Light*. George Ronald, 1994.

Ruḥíyyih Kẖánum, Amatu'l-Bahá. 'Tribute to Shoghi Effendi', presentation at the Kampala International Conference, 26 January 1958, in *Bahá'í News,* May 1958. Available at: http://bahai-library.com/rkhanum_kampala_1958_jan.

Rutstein, Nathan. *Corinne True: Faithful Handmaid of 'Abdu'l-Bahá*. With the assistance of Edna M. True. Oxford: George Ronald, 1987.

— *He Loved and Served: The Story of Curtis Kelsey*. Oxford: George Ronald.1982.

Saiedi, Nader. *Gate of the Heart: Understanding the Writings of the Bab*. Waterloo, Canada: Wilfried Laurier University Press, 2013.

Safiníy-i Irfán: Studies in Principal Beliefs and Sacred Texts of the Bahá'í Faith. Book 6. Darmstadt: 'Asr-i-Jadíd, 2003.

Salmání, Ustád Muḥammad-'Alí. *My Memories of Bahá'u'lláh*. Trans. Marzieh Gail. Los Angeles: Kalimát Press, 1982.

Samuel, Edwin. *A Lifetime in Jerusalem: The Memoirs of the Second Viscount Samuel*. London: Vallentine, Mitchell, 1970.

Seikaly, May. *Haifa: Transformation of an Arab Society, 1918–1939*. London: Tauris, 1995, 2002.

Shahídí, Kẖalíl. *A Lifetime with 'Abdu'l-Bahá: Reminiscences of Kẖalíl Shahídí*. Trans. and annotated Ahang Rabbani. 2008. Available at: http://bahai-library.com/pdf/r/rabbani_reminiscences_khalil_shahidi.pdf.

Sheil, Mary. *Glimpses of Life and Manners in Persia*. London: John Murray, 1856 (Facsimile).

Shoghi Effendi. *The Bahá'í Faith 1844–1952: Information Statistical and Comparative*. Wilmette, IL: Bahá'í Publishing Trust, 1953.

— *Citadel of Faith: Messages to America, 1947–1957*. Wilmette, IL: Bahá'í Publishing Trust, 1965.

— *Directives from the Guardian*. Comp. Gertrude Garrida. New Delhi: Bahá'í Publishing Trust, 1973.

— *God Passes By* (1944). Wilmette, IL: Bahá'í Publishing Trust, rev. ed. 1994.

— *The Promised Day Is Come* (1941). Wilmette, IL: Bahá'í Publishing Trust, rev. ed. 1980.

— *The World Order of Bahá'u'lláh: Selected Letters by Shoghi Effendi* (1938). Wilmette, IL: Bahá'í Publishing Trust, 2nd rev. ed. 1974.

Shoghi Effendi and Lady Blomfield. *The Passing of Abdu'l-Baha*. Haifa: Rosenfeld Bros.,1922. Available at: http://bahai-library.com/shoghieffendi_blomfield_passing_abdulbaha.

Showers, Anita R. *Gardens of the Spirit. The History of the Gardens at the Bahá'í Holy Places in Haifa and 'Akká, Israel.* Sydney: Bahá'í Publications Australia, 2010.

Sohrab, Mirza Ahmad. *Abdul Bahá in Egypt.* New York: Sears, for the New History Foundation, 1929. Available at: http://bahai-library.com/pdf/s/sohrab_abdulbaha_egypt.pdf.

Sprague, Sydney. *A Year With the Bahá'ís in India and Burma* (1908). Los Angeles, Kalimát Press, 1986.

Star of the West: The Bahai Magazine. Periodical, 25 vols. 1910–1935. Vols. 1–14 RP Oxford: George Ronald, 1978. Complete CD-ROM version: Talisman Educational Software/Special Ideas, 2001. Available at: http://bahai.works/Star_of_the_West.

Stephens, E. S. 'Abbas Effendi: His personality, work & followers', in *Fortnightly Review*, vol. 95 (June 1911). See http://bahaitributes.wordpress.com/2008/12/18/ethel-stefana-stevens-1879-1972.

Stockman, Robert H. *'Abdu'l-Bahá in America.* Wilmette, IL: Bahá'í Publishing Trust, 2012.

Storrs, Sir Ronald. *The Memoirs of Sir Ronald Storrs.* New York: Arno Press, 1972.

Taherzadeh, Adib. *The Child of the Covenant.* Oxford: George Ronald, 2000.

— *The Covenant of Bahá'u'lláh.* Oxford: George Ronald, 1995.

— *The Revelation of Bahá'u'lláh.* Oxford: George Ronald, 1974–1987; vol. 1: *Baghdad 1853–1863*; vol. 2: *Adrianople 1863–1868*; vol. 3: *'Akká: The Early Years 1868–1877*; vol. 4: *Mazra'ih & Bahji 1877–92.*

True, Corinne; Mirza Hadí. *Table Talks and Notes Taken at Acca.* Chicago: Baha'i Publishing Society, 1907. Available at: http://bahai-library.com/true_hadi_table_talks.

Tudor Pole, Wellesley. *Writing on the Ground.* London: Neville Spearman, 1968.

Udasin, Sharon. 'Four Mount Carmel caves nominated to join UNESCO', in *The Jerusalem Post*, 29 June 2012.

United Nations Educational, Scientific and Cultural Organization (UNESCO). 'Sites of human evolution at Mount Carmel: The Nahal Me'arot/Wadi el-Mughara Caves'. Online article, available at: http://whc.unesco.org/en/list/1393.

The Universal House of Justice. *Bahá'í Holy Places at the World Centre.* Haifa: Bahá'í World Centre, 1968.

— *The Ministry of the Custodians, 1957–1963.* Haifa: Bahá'í World Centre, 1992.

— *A Synopsis and Codification of the Kitáb-i-Aqdas.* Haifa: Bahá'í World Centre, 1973.

Vernon, Kathy. *Bahá'u'lláh's Garden: Jacksonville Florida 1919–69.* Unpublished. Available at: http://bahai-library.com/vernon_bahaullahs_garden.

Walbridge, John. 'The Bahá'í Faith in Turkey'. Online article, available at: http://bahai-library.com/walbridge_bahai_faith_turkey.

Wavell, General Sir Archibald. *Allenby: A Study in Greatness. The biography of Field-Marshal Viscount Allenby of Megiddo and Felixstowe, G.C.B., G.C.M.* London: Harrap, 1944.

Weinberg, Robert. *Ethel Jenner Rosenberg*, Oxford: George Ronald, 1995.

— *Lady Blomfield: Her Life and Times.* George Ronald, 2012.

White, Roger. *Notes Postmarked the Mountain of God.* New Leaf Publishing, 1992.

Wilhelm, Roy. 'Two glimpses of 'Abdu'l-Bahá', in *The Bahá'í World*, vol. IX (1940–1944), pp. 802–7.

Wilhelm, Roy; Cobb, Stanwood; Coy, Genevieve. *In His Presence: Visits to 'Abdu'l-Bahá.* Los Angeles: Kalimát Press, 1989.

Woodcock, May; Bryant, A. M. Letter to Mrs A.M. Bryant, 1909. Available at: http://bahai-library.com/woodcock_bryant_letter.

Wortz, Cornelia. Unpublished recollections. Bahá'í World Centre library, Audio-Visual Department. AV CT141-335.

Yazbak, Mahmoud. *Haifa in the Late Ottoman Period, 1864–1914.* Leiden: Brill, 1998.

Yazdi, Ali M. *Blessings Beyond Measure.* Wilmette, IL: Bahá'í Publishing Trust, 1988.

Zarqání, Mírzá Maḥmúd. *Maḥmúds Diary.* Translated by Mohi Sobhani, with the assistance of Shirley Macias. Oxford: George Ronald, 1998.

Zayn, Moneer (Munír). 'The final burial of the Báb on Mt. Carmel: Extracts from Mirza Moneer's letters, Acca, Syria, March 22, 1909' in *Star of the West*, vol. 11, no. 19 (2 March 1921), pp. 316–17.

REFERENCES AND NOTES

Foreword

1 See www.bahai.org.
2 See http://news.bahai.org/story/642.
3 The author has received such personal feedback from VIPs and journalists he has accompanied to the Shrine.

1. The Retrieval

1 For the arrival date, see *The Dawn-Breakers*, p. 518; Taherzadeh, *The Revelation of Bahá'u'lláh*, vol. 3, p. 422.
2 Mírzá Táqí Khán, the Amír-Niẓám (equivalent to Prime Minister). See *The Dawn-Breakers*, p. 500.
3 An account by the scholar Faḍil-i-Mázindarání says he was 'accompanied by several other Bábís' (see Ahang Rabbani, 'Efforts to preserve the remains of the Báb'). In *Ḥaḍrat-i-Nuqtiy-i Úlá* (The Life of the Báb), pp. 352–4, the author M.-A. Faizi says Sulaymán Khán rushed to Tabriz 'with a group of Bábís'.
Sulaymán Khán was one of the first Bábís of Tabriz. He had become a Shaykhi and 'studied under Siyyid Kazim Rashti at Karbala. He became a Babi through his friends Mulla Yusif Ardabili and Mullá Mahmud Khu'i and began spreading the religion until the governor, Hamzih Mirza, arrested him. However, Sulayman Khan's redoubtable mother, Haji Khanum, demanded her son's freedom. Sulayman Khan eventually left for Tehran . . .' (Momen, *The Baha'i Communities of Iran*, vol. 1, p. 364).
4 The date is confirmed in Shoghi Effendi, *God Passes By*, p. 54. In *The Dawn-Breakers* the day is named as 'Sunday, the 28th of Sha'ban, in the year 1266 A.H', with the footnote saying July 9, 1850. However, 9 July 1850 was a Tuesday.
5 Ruhe, *Robe of Light*, p. 115. Anís was 'the step-son of a prominent Usuli cleric of the town, Aqa Sayyid 'Ali Zunuzi' (Momen, *The Baha'i Communities of Iran*, vol. 1, p. 363).
6 In his book *Mullá Ḥusayn: Disciple at Dawn,* Mehrabkhani writes that Sám Khán had been the chief of police of Mashhad and had become impressed with Mullá Ḥusayn, to whom the Báb had first proclaimed His mission in 1844, and, although he did not become a believer, had an affection for the Bábís (p. 158).
7 Ruhe, *Robe of Light*, p. 115.
8 Also known as Áqá Ján Big. 'His Nasiri regiment replaced the Armenians' (Balyuzi, *The Báb*, p. 158; see also *The Dawn-Breakers*, p. 514; Shoghi Effendi, *God Passes By*, p. 53). In *The Bahá'í Faith 1844–1952,* Shoghi Effendi writes that this commander 'lost his life, six years after the martyrdom of the Báb, during

the bombardment of Muhammarih by the British' and that the regiment lost in 1850 'two hundred and fifty of its officers and men in an earthquake near Ardibil', while the remaining five hundred were shot two years later, in Tabriz, 'for mutiny' (p. 23).

9 The killing of a prophet is called 'vaticide".

10 Faḍil-i-Mázindarání says the sacred remains were initially abandoned in the town square but this is not mentioned in *God Passes By*, the authoritative history by Shoghi Effendi. The alternative account can be found in Ahang Rabbani, 'Efforts to preserve the remains of the Báb'.

11 Balyuzi, *The Báb*, p. 159. See also note 20 below.

12 The description by Ḥájí 'Alí-'Askar, a Bábí who saw the illustration, appears in *The Dawn-Breakers*, p. 518: 'An official of the Russian consulate, to whom I was related, showed me that same sketch on the very day it was drawn. It was such a faithful portrait of the Báb that I looked upon! No bullet had struck His forehead, His cheeks, or His lips. I gazed upon a smile which seemed to be still lingering upon His countenance. His body, however, had been severely mutilated. I could recognize the arms and head of His companion, who seemed to be holding Him in his embrace. As I gazed horror-struck upon that haunting picture, and saw how those noble traits had been disfigured, my heart sank within me. I turned away my face in anguish and, regaining my house, locked myself with my room. For three days and three nights, I could neither sleep nor eat, so overwhelmed was I with emotion. That short and tumultuous life, with all its sorrows, its turmoils, its banishments, and eventually the awe-inspiring martyrdom with which it had been crowned, seemed again to be re-enacted before my eyes. I tossed upon my bed, writhing in agony and pain.'

Momen writes: 'The Russian consul in Astarabad in the 1870s, Feodor Bakulin, was much interested in collecting material on the Babi and Baha'i religions (while in Tabriz he appears to have discovered the sketch of the remains of the Bab made on the day of His execution)' (*The Baha'i Communities of Iran*, vol. 1, p. 325).

13 He was an officer in the service of the Shah's father. 'Abdu'l-Bahá called him 'one of the nobles of Adhirbáyján devoted to the Báb' (*A Traveler's Narrative*, p. 28).

14 *The Dawn-Breakers*, p. 519. Midhí Khán's title was 'Kalantar'.

15 See 'Abdu'l-Bahá, *A Traveler's Narrative*, p. 28. Described as 'one of the gang-leaders and fearless rogues of Tabriz' in the account by Faḍil-i-Mázindarání quoted by Ahang Rabbani, 'Efforts to preserve the remains of the Báb'.

16 Shoghi Effendi, *God Passes By*, p. 273; Cameron and Momen, *A Basic Bahá'í Chronology*, p. 51. Some of the accounts of the retrieval and surrounding events differ in certain details. This account attempts to be consistent with that by Shoghi Effendi, and draws on the most likely details in other accounts.

17 Faḍil-i-Mázindarání, in Rabbani, op. cit. The term 'believers' is used to mean followers of the Báb, also referred to as Bábís, and later to followers of Bahá'u'lláh, also known as Bahá'ís. Ḥusayn-i-Mílání was martyred in Tehran in 1852. A report said he was killed by a platoon of infantry with their bayonets (Momen, *The Bábí and Bahá'í Religions 1844–1944*, p. 142).

18 Another version of the story, which could be somewhat compatible, is that the guards were well-bribed and feigned sleep (Ruhe, *Robe of Light*, p. 117).

See also Hogenson, *Lighting the Western Sky*, p. 147: 'Even though a guard was set over them, greed overpowered any sense of duty, making it possible for the heartbroken followers of that young Herald of the Cause of God to steal away His remains after paying bribes.'

19 'Abdu'l-Bahá (*A Traveler's Narrative*, p. 27) confirms that the 'Bábís carried away the two bodies'. Taherzadeh (*The Revelation of Bahá'u'lláh*, vol. 3, p. 424) says the remains were placed in the cloak, or *aba*, by one of the other Bábís. Blomfield (*The Chosen Highway*, p. 30) says the bodies were 'wrapped in one aba and taken to the house of Rahim-i-Kalantar'.

20 Accounts by 'Abdu'l-Bahá in *A Traveler's Narrative*, p. 28; Shoghi Effendi in *God Passes By*, p. 54; Nabíl-i-Zarandí in *The Dawn-Breakers*, p. 519; Balyuzi in *The Báb*, p. 160; and Taherzadeh in *The Revelation of Bahá'u'lláh*, vol. 3, p. 424, as well as the account by Hand of the Cause Mírzá Ḥasan Adíb Taliqání in Ahang Rabbani, 'Efforts to preserve the remains of the Báb', do not identify the location of the silk factory. However, Muhammad-Husayni in his book *The Báb*, p. 576, indicates that the silk factory was in Tabriz. It would appear, then, that it was likely to be in Tabriz, given that there has been no mention in the works of these texts that it was elsewhere. Other historians also do not mention a transfer to any other city or village.

There is a different view, however. A descendant of Ḥájí Aḥmad, Samandar Milani of Perth, Western Australia, in personal correspondence to the author, 22 August 2016, said it was his understanding, based on what he was told by family members, that it was in the village of Milan, which is about 25 kilometres from Tabriz. The Bahá'í author Guy Murchie reported that during his visit in 1964 the grandson of Ḥájí Aḥmad Mílání, who was his guide in Tabriz, told him that the sacred remains were taken to the village of Milan 15 miles away (*Bahá'í News*, no. 424 (1966), p. 5).

In earlier correspondence on 22 November 2014, Mr Milani provided information about his family. Ḥájí Aḥmad's family had been Shaykhis (followers of Shaykh Aḥmad Al-Aḥsá'í (1753–1826)) and had been waiting for the Promised One. Mr Milani's great-great-grandfather and all bar one of his seven sons became Bábís after a visit to the local mosque by a 'Letter of the Living', one of the first disciples of the Báb. The family was instrumental in protecting the sacred remains of the Báb (and those of Anís). The Milani sons disguised themselves as 'crazy and poor people' and kept an eye on the remains, keeping the dogs away. Mr Milani said his great-grandfather's silk factory was later destroyed by religious enemies of the Faith when they learned that the remains had been concealed there. He said his grandfather, Inayatollah, born when his father was 82, visited 'Abdu'l-Bahá while on pilgrimage in Haifa. The Master pointed to Mount Carmel and asked if he saw the path of the kings. Initially he saw nothing, but on a subsequent and last visit with the Master, during that pilgrimage, he had a vision of the Terraces. Samandar Milani was an irrigation engineer on the Terraces project in the 1990s.

21 Ruhe, *Robe of Light*, pp. 117–18. Dr Ruhe indicates his view that before Sulaymán Khán arrived at the silk factory he had secretly shrouded the bodies in white silk and placed them in a chest.

22 *The Dawn-Breakers,* p. 519; Shoghi Effendi, *God Passes By,* p. 54: Balyuzi, *The Báb,* p. 160.

23 Also known as Mírzá Áqāy-i-Kalím.

24 According to Taliqání's account (Rabbani, op. cit.), Bahá'u'lláh's letter was addressed to one of the followers of the Báb, Áqá Siyyid Ibrahim Khalíl. See also *The Dawn-Breakers*, pp. 519–21.

25 Faḍil-i-Mázindarání, in Rabbani, op. cit. This account indicates that Ḥasan Áqá Tafríshí also travelled with the casket. M. A. Faizi indicates this, too, in *Ḥaḍrat-i-Nuqtiy-i Úlá*, pp. 352–4. In 1850 Tabriz was more populous than Tehran and most of Iran's imports and exports passed through it. That would help explain the customs houses on the road to Tehran. For more on Tabriz, see Momen, *The Bahai Communities of Iran*, vol. 1, p. 362. Tribal reasons were also probably a reason for the customs houses. Travellers would need to explain the reason for their journey (email from Fuad Izadinia to the author, 5 November 2016).

26 The involvement of Sulaymán Khán is clear from Shoghi Effendi, *God Passes By*, p. 54. The presence of the courier is indicated in Taherzadeh, *The Revelation of Bahá'u'lláh*, vol. 3, p. 424. It is not clear how many, if any at all, of the original group returned with Sulaymán Khán and his party.

27 Ruhe, *Robe of Light*, p. 118.

28 A week is a calculation based on estimates of the speed of a horse, care taken with the casket, the need to rest the horses, and the terrain. See also Taherzadeh, *The Revelation of Bahá'u'lláh*, vol. 3, p. 424.

29 There are two accounts of where Bahá'u'lláh was. The account by Hand of the Cause Ḥájí Mírzá Ḥasan Adíb of Talaqan states that he was at Shimiran, near Tehran. Nábil (*The Dawn-Breakers*, p. 520) writes that he was in Karbila on the instructions of the Prime Minister (Amír-Niẓám). Karbila is also identified as His location in Taherzadeh, *The Revelation of Bahá'u'lláh*, vol. 3, p. 424.

30 Shoghi Effendi, *God Passes By*, p. 273. An outline of the successive stages in the transfer of the sacred remains of the Báb can be found on pp. 20–21 of *The Bahá'í Faith 1844–1952: Information Statistical and Comparative*, compiled by Shoghi Effendi.

31 Also known as Mírzá 'Abdu'l-Karím-i-Qazvíní. See Taherzadeh, *The Revelation of Bahá'u'lláh*, vol. 3, p. 424. Mírzá Aḥmad was martyred in 1852. *The Dawn-Breakers*, p. 521, describes this time.

32 The author is grateful to Mr Khosro Vahdat of Brisbane, Australia, formerly of Tehran, for this information. He visited this place as a child with his late mother. The shrine is also known as Ibn Babuyyih; see Rabbani, op. cit.

33 Also spelled Rayy, Rey is a district south of Tehran but now absorbed by the city.

34 *The Dawn-Breakers*, p. 521. In *Robe of Light*, p. 117, Ruhe refers to a purported sealed letter by the Báb predicting His martyrdom and giving instructions about His remains. Dr Ruhe's account, p. 118, of the order in which the casket was placed in hiding places in Tehran seems at variance with that in Shoghi Effendi, *God Passes By*, pp. 273–4, and a map provided in Balyuzi, *Eminent Bahá'ís in the Time of Bahá'u'lláh*, p. 327.

2. Momentous Events

1 'Abdu'l-Bahá (1844–1921), the eldest son of Bahá'u'lláh, is one of the central figures of the Bahá'í Faith. He was Head of the Bahá'í Faith from 1892 to 1921 and was also known as the 'Master'. In His last Will and Testament, Bahá'u'lláh

appointed 'Abdu'l-Bahá (known to the general public as Abbás Effendi) His successor as Head of the Bahá'í Faith, instructing all Bahá'ís to turn to Him as the authorized interpreter of the Bahá'í Writings and as the perfect exemplar of the Faith's spirit and teachings. 'Abdu'l-Bahá emphasized He was not of the same station as His Father; He had taken the name 'Abdu'l-Bahá (servant of Bahá'u'lláh) thereby underlining that point.

2 'More than four thousand souls were slain, and a great multitude of women and children, left without protector or helper, distracted and confounded, were trodden down and destroyed ('Abdu'l-Bahá, *A Traveler's Narrative*, p. 28).

3 Balyuzi, *Bahá'u'lláh, The King of Glory*, pp. 86–7.

4 Shoghi Effendi, *God Passes By*, p. 77.

5 Balyuzi, *Bahá'u'lláh, The King of Glory*, p. 86.

6 For Bahá'u'lláh's description of that experience, see Shoghi Effendi, *God Passes By*, pp. 101–2.

3. Looking for a Safe Place

1 Ḥájí Ákhund (1842–1910) also known as 'Alí-Akbar-i-Shahmírzádí, was later elevated to the rank of Hand of the Cause of God, one of the four so appointed by Bahá'u'lláh. He was buried in the Shrine of Imám-Zádih Ma'ṣúm, once the resting place of the sacred remains of the Báb. For accounts of his life, see Taherzadeh, *The Revelation of Bahá'u'lláh*, vol. 4, pp. 294–301; Harper, *Lights of Fortitude*, pp. 3–7, and http://bahai-library.com/momen_encyclopedia_akhund_haji.

2 To be called Jamál in this text. He was a great teacher of the Faith who later became a Covenant-breaker (one who claimed to be a Bahá'í but opposed the Head of the Faith). See Taherzadeh, *The Revelation of Bahá'u'lláh*, vol. 3, p. 425; vol. 2, p. 290.

3 *The Dawn-Breakers*, p. 521.

4 Mírzá Áqá of Kashan (known as Munib).

5 *The Dawn-Breakers*, p. 521; see also the account by Fáḍil-i-Mázindarání, in Ahang Rabbani, 'Efforts to preserve the remains of the Báb'.

6 Fáḍil-i-Mázindarání says it was two other men who removed the casket, Haṣan Áqá and his brother, and that it was their wives who had pretended to be pilgrims (Ahang Rabbani, 'Efforts to preserve the remains of the Báb'). However, it is clear that Bahá'u'lláh's Tablet was addressed specifically to Ḥájí Ákhund and Jamál; see Shoghi Effendi, *God Passes By*, p. 274, although he does not specifically identify who removed the casket. See also Taherzadeh, *The Revelation of Bahá'u'lláh*, vol. 3, pp. 425–6.

7 Shoghi Effendi, *God Passes By*, p. 274.

8 Taherzadeh, *The Revelation of Bahá'u'lláh*, vol. 3, p. 426.

9 Identified as 'farmers' in an account by 'Abdu'l-Ḥusayn Avárih, based on the recollections of Ḥájí Ákhund, in Manuchehri, 'Further extracts concerning the remains of the Báb in Tehran'.

10 It was a custom to place valuables in a coffin.

4. The Holy Land

1 'It seems, in retrospect, the keenest irony that the selection of the Holy Land as the place of Bahá'u'lláh's forced confinement should have been the result of pressure from ecclesiastical and civil enemies whose aim was to extinguish

His religious influence. Palestine, revered by three of the great monotheistic religions as the point where the worlds of God and of man intersect, held then, as it had for thousands of years, a unique place in human expectations' (Bahá'í International Community, *Bahá'u'lláh*, p. 23).

2 Taherzadeh, *The Revelation of Bahá'u'lláh*, vol. 3, p. 11.
3 Translation by Dr Vahid Rafati, quoted in Izadinia, *The Major Opus.*
4 Not to be confused with the Knights Templar, the Crusader Order of the 11th century who were in Acre and other parts of the Holy Land.
5 Izadinia, *The Major Opus.*
6 ibid., quoting from Gollmer, *Mein Herz ist bei Euch,* pp. 44–5.
7 Izadinia in *The Major Opus* compares translations and refers to an unpublished article by Faruq Izadinia who analyses the misunderstandings created by the person who translated the Tablet.

5. The Casket on the Move

1 Surnamed Amínu'l-Bayán, the First Trustee of the Ḥuqúqu'lláh. See Shoghi Effendi, *God Passes By*, p. 274; Taherzadeh, *The Revelation of Bahá'u'lláh*, vol. 3, pp. 73–6.
2 Mullá Ṣadiq had met Bahá'u'lláh in Baghdad in 1861. He was the father of Hand of the Cause Ibn-i-Aṣdaq, and passed away in 1874. The date of his involvement in changing the hiding place of the sacred remains is arrived at via calculations using the dates in Balyuzi, *Eminent Bahá'ís in the Time of Bahá'u'lláh*, pp. 18–21, where his role is briefly mentioned. It is also mentioned in Rafati, *Peyk-e Rástán*, p. 335.
3 Taherzadeh (*The Revelation of Bahá'u'lláh*, vol. 3, p. 427) says 1884–5. The Islamic year 1301 which he quotes began on 2 November 1883 and finished on 20 October 1884, so it is more likely to be 1884.
4 Mírzá Asadu'lláh-i-Iṣfáhání married the sister of Munírih Khánum, the wife of 'Abdu'l-Bahá, but later became a Covenant-breaker.
5 'several other localities': see Shoghi Effendi, *God Passes By*, p. 274. For the second location identified, see Chapter 7 in this book.
6 Taherzadeh, *The Revelation of Bahá'u'lláh*, vol. 3, p. p. 428. However, Ahang Rabbani in 'Efforts to preserve the remains of the Báb' refers to the same year 1269 (AH) as 1890. The solar year crossed the Gregorian years so it is not clear which year it was.
7 The bestowal of this surname thrilled him, says Ahang Rabbani in 'Efforts to preserve the remains of the Báb'. In the same publication, an account by Hand of the Cause Mírzá Ḥasan Adíb Taliqání says the house was in the Sar Qabr Aqa district.
8 It was common to keep such items in a box.

6. The Site for the Shrine

1 The first being His arrival as a prisoner in strict confinement in 1868.
2 The 'Temple' here is Bahá'u'lláh Himself. See an example of this terminology in Taherzadeh, *The Revelation of Bahá'u'lláh*. vol. 3, p. 133.
3 Translation by Dr Vahid Rafati, 'Bahá'u'lláh in Haifa', also quoted in Izadinia, *The Major Opus.*

4 Now the Haifa Museum.

5 Now the corner of Allenby Street and the Italian lane.

6 The vacant land has now been made into a beautiful small garden and is regularly visited by Bahá'í pilgrims. The house next door still exists: it was a Templer House whose owners, the Pfander family, inscribed 'Der Herr ist Nahe 1871' (The Lord is Nigh 1871) over the door. The door is now a window and the inscription remains. Bahá'u'lláh visited that house for medical treatment, and was seen in the room at the north-west corner at ground level, as was recounted in Australia in 1977 by an eyewitness (Ruhe, *Door of Hope*, p. 229, note 5).

7 Deiss later sold his vineyard on the mountain to 'Abdu'l-Bahá and became his gardener (Ruhe, *Door of Hope*, p. 193).

8 'Abdu'l-Bahá, Tablet to Áqá Mírzá 'Abdu'l-Ḥusayn Afnán of Yazd, in A.-Q. Afnan, *Ahd-i-A'lá*, p. 414.

9 See photograph in *The Dawn-Breakers*, p. 598; also in Balyuzi, *Eminent Bahá'ís*, p. 323.

10 Zikrullah Khadem, 'Carmel: The Mountain of God and the Tablet of Carmel', in Javidukht Khadem, *Zikrullah Khadem*, p. 281). The size of the trees indicates that they would have been about five years old. Taherzadeh says Bahá'u'lláh's tent was pitched in the centre (*The Revelation of Bahá'u'lláh*, vol. 4, p. 358).

11 Shoghi Effendi, *God Passes By*, p. 194. Balyuzi, *Bahá'u'lláh, The King of Glory*, p. 374. The 'terrace' behind the Shrine of the Báb is natural – caused by one or more of the geological fault lines that run almost directly up Hatzionut Avenue. The Templers did not build any significant terraces in this area. The land which 'Abdu'l-Bahá was finally able to purchase was the only relatively flat land in the area. The area below the circle of cypress trees, where the Shrine was developed, was a barren, rocky slope.

Hand of the Cause 'Alí-Akbar Furútan writes that the Guardian spoke to him of Bahá'u'lláh's visit to the cypress trees with 'Abdu'l-Bahá and how Bahá'u'lláh had said (Mr Furútan takes care to say that the words attributed to the Guardian are as he recalled them later and are not his exact words): 'Áqá [Master], in future thou must purchase this land, which is very pleasant and has a good view, and transfer the remains of the Báb from Iran to here' (*The Story of My Heart*, pp. 111–12).

Hand of the Cause Zikrullah Khadem ('Carmel . . .', op. cit. p. 282) writes that the Guardian told him on 7 April 1937 that Bahá'u'lláh had told 'Abdu'l-Bahá to inter the sacred remains of the Báb in a structure with nine rooms, additional storeys and a dome.

These remains were not to be regarded as magic talismans or fetish objects with magical properties as are found in some traditions. As 'Abdu'l-Bahá would later explain: 'Holy places are undoubtedly centres of the outpouring of Divine grace, because on entering the illumined sites associated with martyrs and holy souls, and by observing reverence, both physical and spiritual, one's heart is moved with great tenderness'(quoted in the Universal House of Justice, *Synopsis and Codification of the Kitáb-i-Aqdas*, note 26, p. 61).

12 For the text, see Annex 4.

13 Shoghi Effendi, *Citadel of Faith*, p. 96. Bahá'u'lláh was there for three days, according to the memoirs of Dr Habíb Mu'ayyad, vol. 2, p. 258, as quoted in Zikrullah Khadem, 'Carmel . . .', op. cit. p. 280.

14 Momen, *The Bábí and Bahá'í Religions*, p. 235; Taherzadeh, *The Revelation of Bahá'u'lláh*, vol. 4, p. 352; Ruhe, *Door of Hope*, pp. 186–7.
15 Zikrullah Khadem, 'Carmel . . .', op. cit. p. 292.
16 Taherzadeh, *The Revelation of Bahá'u'lláh*, vol. 4, pp. 251–67. Adib Taherzadeh (1921–2000) was a member of the Universal House of Justice from 1988 to 2000. Among his books was the four-volume work (1973–1988) on the life and spiritual Revelation of Bahá'u'lláh.
17 'Alí Nakhjavání, in a speech to the Bahá'ís of the United States in 1995. Available at: https://www.youtube.com/watch?v=gZGoZprpgpo. See also Taherzadeh, *The Revelation of Bahá'u'lláh*, vol. 4, p. 358.
18 Bahá'u'lláh, Tablet of Carmel, in *Gleanings from the Writings of Bahá'u'lláh*, XI, p. 16.
19 Giachery, *Shoghi Effendi: Recollections*, p. 83: 'Shoghi Effendi further mentioned that 'Abdu'l-Bahá, on completing the initial six rooms, had named each of the five doors after one of the followers of the Faith, including those who had been associated with the construction of the Shrine, and that He always referred to the Shrine as the 'Throne of the Lord', and to the Casket of the Báb also as the 'Throne'. Even the Holy Dust was called by Him the 'Throne'.
20 Bahá'u'lláh, Tablet of Carmel, in *Gleanings from the Writings of Bahá'u'lláh*, XI, p. 15.
21 ibid. p. 16.
22 Shoghi Effendi, *God Passes By*, p. 345.
23 Known as the Kitáb-i-'Ahd.

7. Setting His Strategy

1 The Universal House of Justice has written on this matter: http://bahai-library.com/uhj_wives_bahaullah.
2 The sons were Muḥammad-'Alí, Badí'u'lláh and Ḍíyá'u'lláh (alternate spelling: Ziya'u'llah). The name of the second wife of Bahá'u'lláh was Fáṭimih. She and her daughter Ṣamadíyyih also came to oppose 'Abdu'l-Bahá.
3 His wife, Munírih Khánum, said that she and her brother used to stand at a window of Mírzá Músá's house in Acre where she was staying prior to her marriage and watch Him swimming –'such a strong and graceful swimmer' (Blomfield, *The Chosen Highway*, p. 87).
4 Blomfield, *The Chosen Highway*, p. 89.
5 The author heard this in Haifa in 1980 from Aziz Yazdi, who had spent time with 'Abdu'l-Bahá. Mr Yazdi (1909–2004) was an inaugural Counsellor member of the International Teaching Centre; see http://news.bahai.org/story/297. 'Abdu'l-Bahá's secretary Dr Youness Afroukhteh also describes this; see Afroukhteh, *Memories of Nine Years in 'Akká*, p. 195, and another translation in Taherzadeh, *The Covenant of Bahá'u'lláh*, pp. 205–6. 'Abdu'l-Bahá's sister, Bahíyyih Khánum, the Greatest Holy Leaf, was also fluent in these languages (*Bahá'í World*, vol. XVIII, p. 60).
6 Quoted in Riaz Khadem, *Prelude to the Guardianship*, p. 44. In Acre, His hands sometimes bled as people scrambled for what He had to offer them.
7 ibid. p. 46.
8 Ma'ani, *Leaves of the Twin Divine Trees*, p. 321–2.

9 Shoghi Effendi, *God Passes By*, p. 268.
10 Caliph: meaning a *successor*, i.e. a successor to the Prophet Muhammad. He was the supreme religious and political leader of Sunni Islam.
11 See Momen, *The Baha'i Communities of Iran*, vol. 1, pp. 53–5; also Núr, *Kháṭirát-i-muhájirí az Iṣfahán*, pp. 68–75, quoted in Ahang Rabbani, 'Efforts to preserve the remains of the Báb'.
12 Shoghi Effendi listed this house where the sacred remains were concealed on a list of 'principal Bahá'í historic sites in Persia owned by the Bahá'í Community' (Shoghi Effendi, *The Bahá'í Faith 1844–1952: Information Statistical & Comparative*, p. 18).
13 '*sanduq-e-ihani*' (Núr, *Kháṭirát-i-muhájirí az Iṣfahán*).
14 ibid.
15 Javidukht Khadem, *Zikrullah Khadem*, p. 283.
16 Balyuzi, *'Abdu'l-Bahá*, p. 127.
17 A.-Q. Afnán, *Ahd-i-A'lá*, p. 415; Ḥaydar-'Alí, *Stories from the Delight of Hearts*, p. 149. 'Abdu'l-Bahá had purchased other tracts of the land in the area earlier (Afroukhteh, *Memories of Nine Years in 'Akká*, p. 118). His Tablet to Mírzá Áqá Afnán in Port Said indicates the date. The price is described in M.-A. Faizi, *Malakíy-i-Karmil*: '. . . therefore the Master, with many difficulties and obstacles caused by the Covenant-breakers, purchased the land from its owner Elias Modavvar, the son-in-law of Jubran Sa'ad, who had previously wanted 1,000 pounds for it, for a reasonable price . . .' (p. 44, translated). A reasonable price was 60 pounds. A map of the area dated about 1872 indicates that at that date the land was owned by a Mr Pfander, a German Templer.
18 Ruhe, *Door of Hope*, p. 193. The map of the area dated about 1872 shows land owned by Deiss to the east of the future Shrine site but does not show the site above and behind the Shrine.
19 Transcript by Gerhard and Gertrude Bubeck of interview of Maria Diess, later Maria Vonberg, conducted by their daughter Gisela Schmelzle in Adelaide, Australia (Bahá'í World Centre Library, AV CT 141–335). Photographic evidence shows that the vines were still there in 1905, and 'Abdu'l-Bahá was not released until 1908. More finance was available for the purchase after that date. After He came back from His travels in 1913 He established closer friendships with the Templers.
20 A term used for members of the Bahá'í Faith.
21 'Abdu'l-Bahá, *Muntakhabátí az Makátib-i-Ḥaḍrat-i-'Abdu'l-Bahá*, vol. 4, no. 60, pp. 68–9.

8 Concealment and Transfer

1 Mírzá Asadu'lláh's wife was a sister of Munírih Khánum, making him the Master's brother-in-law. He received his directions from 'Abdu'l-Bahá in about late May 1898. He was on pilgrimage in the year 1316 AH, which began on 22 May 1898 and came to an end on 11 May 1899. 'In the year 1316 A.H., Mírzá Asadu'lláh was on pilgrimage. The Master commissioned him to go to Iran and get the box containing the Holy Remains and bring it to Haifa. In accordance with this instruction, Mírzá left the Holy Land immediately to go to Tehran' (A.-Q. Afnán, *Ahd-i-A'lá*, p. 408). To get across the mountains between Persia

and Iraq (then part of the Ottoman Empire) ahead of the winter, he would have had to travel to Persia and get underway promptly, thus fixing the date of the instruction from the Master as late spring, 1898.

2 In Persian, *takht-i-raván*. 'Abdu'l-Bahá was not referring to the type of *takht-i-raván* in which a horse pulls and the others push. To carry an object with the utmost reverence and respect, as required by Him, could not involve the use of beasts of burden. Lady Blomfield misunderstood when she writes in *The Chosen Highway* (p. 31) that those charged with the transportation 'hired mules and riding in a "Takht-i-Raván" (similar to a howdah), with the box they brought it all the way by land from Tihrán through Baghdád, and at length arrived safely at Haifa.' Given the Master's instructions, the use of the howdahs on mules was not appropriate for the casket containing the sacred remains. Unfortunately some dictionaries do not distinguish between howdahs and running thrones carried by people. A howdah would be *kajaveh* or *hoodaj* and these were not terms used by the Master. The casket did not go all the way by land.

3 Tablet of 'Abdu'l-Bahá to Áqá Mírzá 'Abdu'l-Ḥusayn Afnán of Yazd (A.-Q. Afnán, *Ahd-i-A'lá*, pp. 414–15) says that He had dispatched Mírzá Asadu'lláh with some others and that with the utmost care, reverence and grandeur, without anyone except Mírzá Asadu'lláh knowing what was being transported but suspecting it was Holy Writings, they carried the Great Throne, the Pure Body and Sanctified Temple with utmost lowliness and humility on the running throne to the Land of Sham – Beirut – and from there by ship brought it to the Holy Land. The Master specifically referred to 'some believers' (paraphrase from a provisional translation by Fuad Izadinia). It is unclear why Charles Mason Remey refers to only two believers in his description of the mission to bring the sacred remains to the Holy Land: 'A few years ago, arrangements having been made for the entombment of The Báb's remains on Mount Carmel, two of the Bahá'ís set out for Persia . . .' (Remey, *Observations of a Baha'i Traveller*, p. 37).

4 In Jewish tradition, the Shekhinah came to refer to the box and its contents and was called the 'Ark of the Covenant'. It was prepared by the early Jews as ordered by God, so that He could always be there protecting His people. The Jews took the Shekhinah with them everywhere and it was seen as the cause of their triumph. Finally it was laid in the Temple of Solomon but was later on lost to enemies. For more information see Johnson, *The History of the Jews*, pp. 63–4.

5 Al-Baqarah 2: 248: 'And their prophet said to them, "Indeed, a sign of his kingship is that the chest will come to you in which is assurance from your Lord and a remnant of what the family of Moses and the family of Aaron had left, carried by the angels. Indeed in that is a sign for you, if you are believers."' Ishráq Khávarí (*Qámús-i-Tawqí'-i 108 (BE),* p. 57) under the heading Sarcophagus-Sakinatullah, refers in Persian to this verse: 'we have sent down from heaven a sarcophagus in whose heart was the *Sakinatu'lláh* (where the Lord resides)' and says this is an allusion to the Book of the Covenant – the Tablets of the Ten Commandments which God sent down to Moses. Moses put them in a sarcophagus, which was named *Sakinatu'lláh* (in Hebrew *Shekhinah*), meaning a box which contained the divine trust and glory. Ishráq Khávarí writes that 'Abdu'l-Bahá said that the meaning of this Quranic verse is an allusion to the sarcophagus which contains the illumined body of His Holiness, the Most

Great Lord (*Rabb-i-'Alá*, referring to the Báb) and that body, that throne, is the 'Sakinatu'lláh'. Due to the references of Sakinatu'lláh in the Qur'án, Imám Ḥusayn named His daughter Sakinah, the place of peace. In a Tablet to Áqá Siyyid Ismá'íl of Rangoon, 'Abdu'l-Bahá refers to the service this Bahá'í rendered in providing the sarcophagus for the remains of the Báb, and says it is the sarcophagus referred to in the Qur'án (Baqarah 2:248) and that the Sakinah (Sakinatu'lláh) is the illumined Temple, the shining robe of the Most Pure countenance, referring to the Báb (ibid.).

6 I rely here on Balyuzi, *'Abdu'l-Bahá* (p. 87) for information on this companion of Mírzá Asadu'lláh: 'Mírzá Asadu'lláh was the emissary, who at the bidding of 'Abdu'l-Bahá, had safely taken the remains of the Báb from Iran to the Holy Land. Mírzá Asadu'lláh was assisted by Ḥusayn Rúhí, the capable and devoted son of a Bahá'í of Tabriz.' Mr Balyuzi (ibid. p. 527) refers to that Bahá'í of Tabriz as 'Ḥájí 'Ali-'Askar, who had perforce abandoned home and taken the road to exile'. Further confirmation has not yet been uncovered.

For the Master's tribute to Ḥájí 'Ali-'Askar see 'Abdu'l-Bahá, *Memorials of the Faithful*, pp. 161–4, as well as His mention of Ḥusayn as a boy in the Most Great Prison, where he suffered from scarlet fever. 'Abdu'l-Bahá says that to be in prison with the Blessed Beauty was the 'greatest of all distinctions' (ibid. p. 25). For more information on Ḥájí 'Ali-'Askar's meetings with the Báb, see *The Dawn-Breakers*, pp. 239–40; see also Salmání, *My Memories of Bahá'u'lláh*, pp. 54, 57.

According to information provided to Fuad Izadinia by eminent Bahá'í historian Dr Vahid Rafati, Ḥusayn Rúhí was still active in Bahá'í activities in the time of Shoghi Effendi and passed away in Jordan (email to author from Fuad Izadinia, 2 June 2016).

Ḥaydar-'Alí (*Bihjatuṣ-Ṣudúr*, p. 376), says that Áqá Muḥammad-Ḥusayn, son of Vákil Rúhí, joined Mírzá Asadu'lláh in Baghdad. See also note 25 below. I surmise here that the differences in his own name and the name of his father tend to indicate that these were different people.

7 Qom and Kashan are between Tehran and Isfahan. This stop is not mentioned by Shoghi Effendi in *God Passes By*, p. 274: 'Mírzá Asadu'lláh, together with a number of other believers, transported them by way of Isfahan, Kermanshah, Baghdad . . .' However, he does mention it in *The Bahá'í Faith 1844–1952: Information Statistical and Comparative*, p. 18, where he listed the Qom house where the sacred remains were concealed on a list of 'principal Bahá'í historic sites in Persia owned by the Bahá'í Community'.

8 A.-Q. Afnán, *Ahd-i-A'lá*, p. 414 citing Tablet of 'Abdu'l-Bahá to Áqá Mírzá 'Abdu'l-Ḥusayn Afnán of Yazd. See also Taherzadeh, *Revelation of Bahá'u'lláh*, vol.3, p. 430 : 'As directed, by 'Abdu'l-Bahá, Mírzá Asadu'lláh, together with a number of other believers who did not know what the case contained, transported the sacred remains to the Holy Land via Baghdad, Damascus and Beirut.'

9 A.-Q. Afnán, *Ahd-i-A'lá*, p. 409.

10 'The story of Ustád Ismá'íl Úbudíyyát' in National Spiritual Assembly of the United States, *Bi Yad-i Dust* (In Memory of the Friend), pp. 80–93 (translation by Fuad Izadinia). Ustád Ismá'íl Úbudíyyát was later involved in transporting the sacred remains in the Holy Land. He was one of eight who carried the

box containing the casket from a house in Haifa to the site of the Shrine, and probably down into the vault.

11 See A.-Q. Afnán, *Ahd-i-A'lá*, pp. 407–10. Distances covered on the transfer of the sacred remains are approximate, using those cited today between cities. They would have varied somewhat in the past according to routes taken.

12 Ḥájí Mírzá Ḥaydar-'Alí, *Bihjatuṣ-Ṣudúr*, p. 272.

13 Ḥájí Mírzá Ḥaydar-'Alí writes: 'The casket was well hidden in the house' (*Stories from the Delight of Hearts*, p. 148). And further: 'After the passing of Bahá'u'lláh, the beloved Master sent Mírzá Asadu'lláh to bring the box containing the Holy Remains. He went to Tehran and from there he went to Isfahan and met with Mírzá Asadu'lláh who was the Vizier of Isfahan and he was a very dedicated soul to the Covenant. The sister of Mírzá Asadu'lláh, who in servitude, steadfastness and love was way ahead of every man or woman, was the respected wife of the Vizier' (*Bihjatuṣ-Ṣudúr*, p. 375). A photograph of the Vizier can be seen on p. 136 of Balyuzi, *Eminent Bahá'ís in the Time of Bahá'u'lláh*.

14 This was told to the father of A.-Q. Afnán by Mírzá 'Aṭá'u'lláh himself; see A.-Q. Afnán, *Ahd-i-A'lá*, pp. 408–10.

15 Ḥaydar-'Alí, *Bihjatuṣ-Ṣudúr*, p. 375.

16 Camels, which were slower, were used to cart heavier loads but would not have been used on this journey.

17 A.-Q. Afnán, *Ahd-i-A'lá*, p. 409. This is the most likely route, taking into account a range of references. Due to the secrecy of the mission, the sequence from Qom to Arak cannot be absolutely confirmed, but all places named were visited.

18 ibid.

19 Zaynu'l-Muqarrabín (Mullá Zaynu'l-'Abidín) was one of the 19 Apostles of Bahá'u'lláh as designated by Shoghi Effendi. He was a mujtahid, a doctor of Islamic law. He submitted questions to Bahá'u'lláh regarding the Kitáb-i-Aqdas (see the Appendix to that book).

20 Modarres, *Táríkh-i Amr-i Bahá'í dar Najaf-Ábád* (History of the Bahá'í Faith in Najafabad), pp. 78–80. According to Faizi-Moore (*Faizi*, p. 113), Ḥájí Báqir left part of his property to the Bahá'í community and was buried there, behind a library named after Zaynu'l-Muqarrabín, opposite the room where the sacred remains were kept. Modarres says that the library itself was that room and that the whole property was later owned by the Bahá'ís and was a meeting place for them. To read more about Najafabad, see Faizi-Moore, *Faizi,* Chapter 5, pp. 78–119, which deals mainly with the experiences of the Hand of the Cause Abu'l-Qásim Faizi in that place.

21 Shoghi Effendi listed the Kermanshah house where the sacred remains were concealed on the list of 'principal Bahá'í historic sites in Persia owned by the Bahá'í Community' (*The Bahá'í Faith 1844–1952: Information Statistical and Comparative,* p. 18). This house later on became the possession of Prince 'Abdu'l-Ḥusayn Mírzá, the Farmanfarma. During his governorship of Shiraz he learnt the importance of that house to the Bahá'í community, and offered it to the Faith (A.-Q. Afnán, *Ahd-i-A'lá*, pp. 409 and 432, fn. 5; historian Dr Vahid Rafati pointed to this information in an email to Fuad Izadina, 12 May 2016). In the Tablet to the Bahá'ís of Shiraz praising the Farmanfarma for this donation, 'Abdu'l-Bahá expressed the importance of his generous gift, stating that whatever else

the Prince did in his life would be forgotten, but this act would be the cause of his glory in both worlds. The Master wrote that He had met the son of the Prince in Paris and that the donation had become a cause of much happiness. 'Abdu'l-Bahá said the 'fragrant body' (the sacred remains of the Báb) had not been able to rest in one place for 50 years (after the Báb's martyrdom) for fear of the enemies (Haifa, 10 Rajab, 1338 (c. 1919), in *Majmú'iy-i-Makatib-i Haḍrat-i-'Abdu'l-Bahá* (Collected Tablets of 'Abdu'l-Bahá), no. 52, p. 380).

22 Ḥaydar-'Alí, *Bihjatuṣ-Ṣudúr*, p. 376. It could be reasonably speculated that it had been signed by the Vizier.

23 Balyuzi, *Bahá'u'lláh, The King of Glory*, pp. 105–6. For another description of that journey, see Ruhe, *Robe of Light*, pp. 166–73.

24 A.-Q. Afnán, *Ahd-i-A'lá*, pp. 407–10, relating the story of the photograph as told by 'Aṭá'u'lláh Núrbakhsh. In a letter to the present author dated 6 May 2015, Mr 'Ali Nakhjavání wrote: 'The early believers often commented that Mírzá Asadu'lláh and seven other believers – making a total of eight – had been involved in the project in the course of its long trail to Akka. And this, they believed, was the fulfilment of the verse in the Qur'án, "The Inevitable'", Verse 69:17, where it is stated: "on that day eight shall bear up the throne of thy Lord".' In another letter of the same date Mr Nakhjavání refers to an excerpt from Vernon, *Bahá'u'lláh's Garden* (p. 13): 'What Vernon describes as "an escort of Baha'is" was a group of eight believers, headed by Mírzá Asadu'lláh Iṣfáhání, who under the direction of the Master were to transport the sacred remains from Iran to the Holy Land.'

25 According to an account in Ḥaydar-'Alí, *Stories from the Delight of Hearts*, p. 148, when Mírzá Asadu'lláh and his party arrived in Baghdad, they handed the casket to some trusted Bahá'ís and after visiting Shi'ah shrines returned home. It says that Ḥusayn-i-Vákil, a cousin of the author of that book, acted as custodian there. The English language *Stories from the Delight of Hearts* is an abridged version of the Persian original. In the complete Persian edition, *Bihjatuṣ-Ṣudúr*, p. 375, Ḥaydar-'Alí writes that Ḥusayn-i-Vákil, named in that book Áqá Muḥammad-Ḥusayn, son of Vákil Rúhí, joined the party carrying the casket to the Holy Land. We know from other sources, including a Tablet of 'Abdu'l-Bahá, that Mírzá Asadu'lláh and others from the original party also continued on (A.-Q. Afnán, *Ahd-i-A'lá*, pp. 414 –15). See also note 7 above.

26 'Wherever they passed, as per the government's decree, there was utmost respect and reverence' (Ḥaydar-'Alí, *Bihjatuṣ-Ṣudúr*, p. 376). It could again be speculated that the document was signed by the Vizier.

27 Rabbani, *The Priceless Pearl*, p. 235.

28 Ḥaydar-'Alí, *Bihjatuṣ-Ṣudúr*, p. 375. A report by Charles Mason Remey that it was disguised as a bale of merchandise would not be accurate.

29 Such was the secret nature of this part of the sacred mission that the only description yet uncovered is that it was 'eventful' (Remey, *Observations of a Bahá'í Traveller*, p. 38). The memoirs of Mírzá Asadu'lláh-i-Iṣfahání are still in manuscript form (information provided to the author by the Bahá'í World Centre, 29 June 2014).

30 *The Bahá'í World*, vol. III, p. 81. The house still exists today (letter from Mr 'Alí Nakhjavání to the author, 6 May 2015). 'Abdu'l-Bahá was later to write a

stirring tribute to this hero of the Faith in which he said that while still a child Muḥammad Muṣṭafá (1837–1910) had 'lit the light of faith in the chapel of his heart' and that as a man he was physically strong, afraid of nobody, and 'with all his heart, he assisted the travellers to the Holy Land, those who had come to circumambulate that place which is ringed around by the Company on high' (Abdu'l-Bahá, *Memorials of the Faithful*, pp. 131–4). His father, Shaykh Muḥammad-i-Shibl ('Shibl' meaning 'lion cub' in Arabic, denoting his courage) had become a believer after meeting Mullá 'Alíy-i- Basṭámí, a Letter of the Living, in Baghdad. He had hosted in his house in Baghdad the Bábí heroine Ṭáhirih (also named as a Letter of the Living), and then with his son escorted her to the Persian city of Qazvin where she lived. Father and son then went to Tehran where they met Mullá Ḥusayn, the first Letter of the Living (*The Dawn-Breakers*, pp. 272–3). Shaykh Muḥammad-Shibl was later murdered, presumably for his faith, and his body never recovered. He was placed upon horseback, forced to ride in front of his escort and, upon reaching the desert, was shot (information from Dr Zia Bagdadi, in Vernon, *Bahá'u'lláh's Garden*, p. 13).] Muḥammad Muṣṭafá, a merchant, was only 16 when Bahá'u'lláh arrived in Baghdad. He became devoted to Him even before His declaration, and later was arrested for his faith. He travelled to Acre to be near Bahá'u'lláh and it was then that he was instructed to establish his home in Beirut. He provided 'invaluable' service not only to Eastern Bahá'ís but also to many American pilgrims, who bore 'testimony to the nobility of his spirit and the strength of his character'. A tribute to him said: 'In him the Cause has lost a great and useful servant. All loved and revered him and looked up to him as one of the spiritual souls of the earlier days. His winsome manner and gentleness of heart attracted all those who came in contact with him and carried away the sweet fragrance of his life' (*Star of the West*, vol. 1, no. 17 (1911), p. 10). For further information about Muḥammad Muṣṭafá, see Balyuzi, *Eminent Bahá'ís*, p. 270, and photograph, p. 271.

The Apostles of Bahá'u'lláh were 19 eminent early followers of Bahá'u'lláh designated as such by Shoghi Effendi; the listing is included in *The Bahá'í World*, vol. III (pp. 80–81). They consolidated the followers of the Faith, and helped spread its teachings. They filled a similar role to the sons of Jacob, the Apostles of Jesus, the companions of Prophet Muhammad and the Báb's Letters of the Living.

31 He was married to 'Alí Nakhjavání's maternal aunt, Zeenat Khánum. Mr Nakhjavání, though, never met him because Dr Bagdadi moved to the United States. Upon his passing in 1937, Shoghi Effendi sent a message which included these words: 'Distressed sudden passing dearly beloved Dr. Bagdádí. Loss inflicted (upon) national interests (of) Faith irreparable. His exemplary faith, audacity, unquestioning loyalty, indefatigable exertions unforgettable' (*The Bahá'í World*, vol. III, pp. 535–9). Dr Bagdadi had the privilege of spending time as a child in the presence of Bahá'u'lláh. He also spent time in the presence of the Master. He studied medicine in Chicago, played an important role in the establishment of the Bahá'í Temple in Wilmette and rendered many other services to the Faith.

32 Vernon, *Bahá'u'lláh's Garden*, p. 13.

33 Memoirs held in the Archives at the World Centre. Excerpt provided to the author by the Department of the Secretariat of the Universal House of Justice, 29 June 2014.

34 Spies in the employ of the Covenant-breakers from Bahá'u'lláh's own family could be found in the telegraph offices and ports throughout the region; see Afroukhteh, *Memories of Nine Years in 'Akká*; Hogenson, *Lighting the Western Sky*, p. 147.

35 According to Hogenson, *Lighting the Western Sky*, p. 147, the Master had given Mírzá Asadu'lláh a code and if told to send the sacred remains by land they were to come by sea, and vice versa, and that this deception worked.

36 A.-Q. Afnán, *Ahd-i-A'lá*, p. 410. That author quotes Núri'd-Din Zayn, and also says that the enemies of 'Abdu'l-Bahá travelled to Beirut but by the time they got there the object of their quest had gone.

37 Perhaps Charles Mason Remey had heard of how the casket was concealed and mistakenly thought that it was carried as a bale of merchandise between Baghdad and Beirut. See note 28 above.

38 Shoghi Effendi, *God Passes By*, p. 274.

39 Known as Shaykh of Tariqat-e Shadeliyyih. When ill, he had been visited by 'Abdu'l-Bahá two or three times (Layla Ábádih'í, unpublished memoirs).

40 Known as the House of 'Abdu'lláh Páshá.

41 Much later, a report in the *Bahá'í News (Star of the West)* in 1910 by Joseph Hannen (p. 16) said that in Washington DC on the anniversary of the Declaration of the Báb, the son of Mírzá Asadu'lláh, Dr Amin Fareed (later a notorious Covenant-breaker) 'gave details of the transfer of the body of the blessed Báb from its temporary resting place in Persia to the tomb on Mount Carmel'. However, there are no details in the report of what Dr Fareed said.

42 Shahídí, *A Lifetime with 'Abdu'l-Bahá*, p. 35.

43 Tablet of 'Abdu'l-Bahá to Áqá Mírzá 'Abdu'l-Ḥusayn Afnán of Yazd, in A.-Q. Afnán, *Ahd-i-A'lá*, p. 414 (provisional translation by Fuad Izadinia). During the following week, 'Abdu'l-Bahá said: 'The good news that I had promised is this: the sacred remains of the Exalted Báb have safely left the soil of Iran and just arrived in the Ottoman land. They are now completely out of danger. Truly, there is such an ecstasy and happiness that I cannot describe . . .' (Shahídí, *A Lifetime with 'Abdu'l-Bahá*. p. 35).

44 Excerpts from an address presented by 'Alí Nakhjavání during the World Centre seminar commemorating the fiftieth anniversary of the passing of the Greatest Holy Leaf, held in the reception concourse of the permanent Seat of the Universal House of Justice, 17 July 1982, published in *The Bahá'í World*, vol. XVIII (1979–1983), pp. 59–67. There is a mention in that address that the casket stayed in that house for a decade but subsequent research indicates otherwise.

A story heard by the author that the Greatest Holy Leaf prostrated herself at the entrance of her room due to the presence inside of the sacred remains of the Báb is likely to be false. In personal correspondence with the author on 4 April 2015, Mr Nakhjavání wrote: 'My aunt (Zeenat Bagdadi) never ever said anything about prostrations . . . It is true that the existence of the remains of the Báb in that room was certainly not generally known, and the Greatest Holy Leaf was very discreet and circumspect . . . never ostentatious and loud.'

9. The Sarcophagus

1 Siyyid Muṣṭafá Rúmí, born in Baghdad, was one of the first Bahá'ís in Burma. He was declared a martyr after he was murdered by a mob in 1942 during World War II, aged about 99, and was posthumously named a Hand of the Cause by Shoghi Effendi; see Butt, 'An account of the services of Siyyid Muṣṭafá Rúmí', in *The Bahá'í World*, vol. X, pp. 117–120; Harper, *Lights of Fortitude*, pp. 109–14; Balyuzi, *'Abdu'l-Bahá*, p. 529. Shoghi Effendi later said that his resting place should be regarded as the 'foremost shrine (in the) community of Burmese believers' (Butt, op. cit., pp. 519–20). His memorial building and grave are in Burma, now Myanmar.

2 According to a Tablet to Mírzá Áqá Afnán in Port Said, in A.-Q. Afnán, *'Ahd-i-A'lá*, p. 415.

3 *sang-e-marmar*, marble stone. Several accounts describe it as alabaster (*Ministry of the Custodians*, p. 155; Giachery, *Shoghi Effendi*, p. 54).

4 Ḥaydar-'Alí, *Stories from the Delight of Hearts*, p. 150.

5 'Abdu'l-Bahá made his request to the Bahá'ís of Rangoon, in Tablets to Mírzá 'Abdu'l-Ḥusayn Afnán and Mírzá Mihdí Shírází; see also Balyuzi, *'Abdu'l-Bahá*, pp. 92, 129; Giachery, *Shoghi Effendi*, p. 54; M.-A. Faizi, *Malakíy-i-Karmil*, p. 45; A.-Q. Afnán, *Ahd-i-A'lá*, pp. 414–16; Ishráq Khávarí, *Qámús-i-Tawqí'-i 108 (BE)*, pp. 38, 43. 47, 49, 50. The Master referred to Rangoon in many Tablets, and not Mandalay. There are, however, references to the sarcophagus being made by the Bahá'ís of Mandalay; see *Ministry of the Custodians*, p. 155, describing 'the honour of conferred on the Mandalay Bahá'ís of being permitted to construct the alabaster sarcophagus'; Butt, 'An account of the services of Siyyid Muṣṭafá Rúmí'; and Counsellor Rose Ong in her account of the history of the Bahá'í Faith in Myanmar (http://bahai-library.com/history_bahai_faith_myanmar). At the time, Mandalay, 700 kilometres north of Rangoon, was the capital and the Burmese king lived there. Could these discrepancies indicate that the Mandalay Bahá'ís attended to the construction in Rangoon?

Ḥájí Mírzá Ḥaydar-'Alí wrote that there was a well-known mine of the finest marble in Rangoon (*Bihjatuṣ-Ṣudúr,* p. 381). In an email to Fuad Izadinia on 2 August 2016, Mr 'Alí Nakhjavání wrote that he would assume that the marble of the sarcophagus could well have originated from deposits in Mandalay.

6 Ishráq Khávarí, *Qámús-i-Tawqí'-i 108 (BE),* p. 42; Ḥaydar-'Alí, *Stories from the Delight of Hearts*, p. 151. A report by Zayn said it was gilded three times, while another report quotes 'Abdu'l-Bahá as saying: 'I ordered a marble casket with The Greatest Name inlaid in gold from Bombay' (Rohani, *Sweet and Enchanting Stories*, p. 80).

7 The banner also carries the calligraphic representation by Mishkín-Qalam of the name of Bahá'u'lláh, known as the 'Greatest Name'.

8 Ḥabíbu'lláh Afnán, *Memories of the Báb, Bahá'u'lláh and 'Abdu'l-Bahá*, p. 155.

9 Ḥaydar-'Alí, *Bihjatuṣ-Ṣudúr*, pp. 381–2. There is also an account minus a little detail in the English abridgement of that book, *Stories from the Delight of Hearts*, p. 151.

10 Ishráq Khávarí, *Qámús-i-Tawqí'-i 108 (BE),* p. 84 (translation by Fuad Izadinia).

11 'Abdu'l-Bahá, Tablet to Áqá Mírzá 'Abdu'l-Ḥusayn Afnán, in A.-Q. Afnán, *'Ahd-i-A'lá*, p. 414.

12 Layla Ábádih'i, unpublished memoirs.

13 Rohani, *Sweet and Enchanting Stories*, p. 80. Dr Zia Bagdadi here summarizes what he recalled 'Abdu'l-Bahá had said: 'When it arrived, I did not wish it to be opened at customs and it was not opened.' Ishráq Khávarí, in *Qámús-i-Tawqí'-i 108 (BE),* reports that 'Abdu'l-Bahá said: 'From Bombay, a marble box on which the Greatest Names were written by golden letters arrived. As it landed, I didn't want this to be opened at the Custom Office, and it was not opened' (p. 69).

14 'In 1899 he carried to the Holy Land with other Bahá'ís, the marble casket made by the Bahá'ís of Mandalay for the Holy Remains of the Báb. He was received by 'Abdu'l-Bahá most graciously and was the recipient of special favours' (Butt, 'An account of the services of Siyyid Muṣṭafá Rúmí', p. 517). One of the other Bahá'is who made the journey may have been Abbás-'Alí Kazeruni, who was known as Ghulam Ḥusayn. He received a Tablet from 'Abdu'l-Bahá referring to him as a carrier, or one in charge. He was one of the three who made the preparations for the crate containing the sarcophagus to reach Haifa in good condition. However, there is no clear indication yet found that he accompanied the sarcophagus to Haifa (Ishráq Khávarí, *Qámús-i-Tawqí'-i 108 (BE),* p. 84).

15 Taherzadeh, *The Revelation of Bahá'u'lláh*, vol. 3, p. 431.

16 M.-A. Faizi, *Malakíy-i-Karmil*, p. 49.

17 In personal correspondence, Mr 'Alí Nakhjavání told the author in 2012 that the casket was transferred 'to a house in Haifa, which 'Abdu'l-Bahá had rented, to serve as a temporary facility to accommodate Western pilgrims. Reference to this house is made in one of the Persian letters of Shoghi Effendi to the friends in the East. (This is the letter quoted in Ishráq Khávarí, *Qámús-i-Tawqí'-i 108 (BE).*) Then it was from this house that the empty casket was transferred to the already built Shrine, and placed in its empty vault.'

18 Arabic, meaning 'sacred fold', a name often given to Bahá'í centres. The word 'Hazira' or 'Haḍira' means the place where sheep are kept, but by adding the word 'Quds' – 'sacred, holy' – the meaning changes to 'the place where the sheep of God - the believers – meet; in other words a divine and safe shelter where the friends gather for the remembrance of God. See also note 19 in Chapter 13.

19 Information from Fuad Izadinia; see also Gail, *Summon Up Remembrance*, pp. 110–11. Paris Square is now also known as Taxi Square.

20 Gail, *Summon Up Remembrance*, p. 111.

21 'Abdu'l-Bahá, Tablet to Áqá Mírzá 'Abdu'l-Ḥusayn Afnán, in A.-Q. Afnán, *'Ahd-i-A'lá*, p. 414. The Bahá'ís of Rangoon shipped another alabaster sarcophagus to be used in the Shrine of Bahá'u'lláh, and it 'reached the shores of the Mediterranean but, because of the unsettled situation in the Near East area, it could never be brought to its destination'. Bahá'u'lláh's sacred remains had been interred seven years earlier but the Bahá'ís may have thought a special coffin had been prepared. The Guardian asked Dr Ugo Giachery in the late 1940s, 'to arrange for its transportation to the Holy Land, but the worsening political situation did not permit the consummation of the plan'. Dr Giachery wrote that the sarcophagus was now 'in good hands waiting for the opportunity to be sent to its rightful destination and thus fulfil another wish of the Guardian, as part of his plan to beautify that Holy Shrine' (Giachery, *Shoghi Effendi*, p. 137).

10. The Foundation

1 Egypt's Ibrahim Pasha ruled Acre for 10 years from 1831 but it was then restored to the Ottomans. There were occasional skirmishes between the Ottomans and Egyptians.

2 Seikaly, *Haifa: Transformation of an Arab Society, 1918–1939*, p. 20. The town at that time was close to the bay to the east of the Templer colony, to the north-east of Wadi Nisnas. In pre-18th century times, the town had been to the west, near where the hospital is today. See map in Balyuzi, *Bahá'u'lláh, The King of Glory*, p. 375.

3 Afroukhteh, *Memories of Nine Years in 'Akká*, pp. 122–3.

4 ibid. p. 125.

5 ibid. p. 113.

6 Ben-Artzi, *The Case of the German Templers in Eretz-Israel*, p. 26.

7 It was called the Musterhaus (model house). It served as a school initially and was enlarged in 1890. See Ben-Artzi, *The Case of the German Templers in Eretz-Israel*, p. 27.

8 Among the characteristics of Templer architecture in Haifa were the use of local limestone, a boxy appearance, and a simple symmetrical facade design (Goldman, *The Architecture of the Templers in their Colonies in Eretz-Israel, 1868–1948*, p. 496). Interestingly, in light of the use of a Templer style design for the exterior of the Shrine: 'The most influential determinants on the built form of the Templers' houses was their social and spiritual motivation; their architecture became a tool to promote their mission for creating a new and better society' (ibid. pp. 510–11). The Templer designs were unique: 'The knowledge and intelligence embedded in the Templer buildings were imported . . . which the Germans maintained when they immigrated, and made the necessary adjustments to local conditions. This, combined with the input of local conditions, materials, and economy, created a new type of structure unprecedented in Eretz-Israel; in this sense, these houses were genuinely original; a synthesis between a building construction tradition, imported from Württemberg, some elements which were common in Württemberg such as the symmetrical plan, the chimneys, the basement, or the hip-on-gable roof, and local materials like limestone, later steel rails, and concrete. Some were created in Palestine as part of their adaptability: the prefab elements, wooden shutters, iron hardware. Other imported elements did not catch on, and remained isolated cases such as the latticework copied from Lochgau, or the fishscale wooden shingles in Walhalla . . . Some elements were imported from other countries, but the tradition of their use was German, like the clay tiles and the dimensional lumber. The integration of all these created a new type of house in Eretz-Israel' (ibid. p. 487).

9 'Abdu'l-Bahá had written to the Afnáns, relatives of the Báb, in Port Said because he wanted them to physically work on the project but there is no record of the response.

10 There is a sweet story about 'Abdu'l-Bahá teasing Áqá Bálá in a rather self-deprecating way but also with a little lesson about human nature. Since Áqá Bálá was 'one of the pure of heart' – he was on pilgrimage at the time – the Master agreed to his request to build Him a bath in His residence. Áqá Bálá ordered some metal parts for a shower from Beirut, and began building the bath. After only three

days' work, and before the materials had arrived, the Master asked if the bath was ready. When told the reason for the delay, He then asked when it would be ready. What Áqá Bálá replied is unknown, but 'Abdu'l-Bahá smiled broadly and said 'the story of you and I resembles the story of an Arab who did not have a hat for three years to protect his head from the elements. A generous donor took him to a cloth merchant to get the material for a turban and have it measured. The salesman brought out a roll to measure the right length but the Arab did not wait. He grabbed the uncut material and began wrapping it around his head. When the salesman asked him to wait so the cloth could be measured the Arab said: 'How long am I supposed to wait. If I wait any longer I will catch my death of cold!' The insight about the lack of patience of one with raised expectations remains both humorous and accurate to this day. The full story is told in Afroukhteh, *Memories of Nine Years in 'Akká*, pp. 272–3.

11 See the Bahá'í magazine *Áhang-i-Badí'*, vols. 17 & 18, year 8, pp. 356 onwards. Other references include Fáḍil-i-Mázindarání, *Ẓuhúru'l-Ḥaqq*, vol. 8, section 2, p. 1056; Giachery, *Shoghi Effendi: Recollections*, pp. 214–15; and the Bahá'í magazine *Payam-i-Bahá'í*, vol. 267, p. 15. Mullá Abú-Ṭálib-i-Karimoff was an Azerbaijani citizen living in Baku who had accepted the Faith in the days of Bahá'u'lláh. He was rich and a staunch believer. He attained the presence of Bahá'u'lláh in Acre towards the last years of Bahá'u'lláh's life.

12 Ruhe, *Door of Hope*, p. 100; see the aerial photo of the area, p. 99. However, unless Mullá Abú-Ṭálib's sons came twice to Acre, a reference in Ruhe, *Door of Hope*, p. 100, to their arriving in the time of Bahá'u'lláh seems incorrect (personal correspondence from Mr 'Alí Nakhjavání, 6 May 2015).

13 Giachery, *Shoghi Effendi*, p. 215; *Áhang-i-Badí'*, vols. 17 & 18, year 8, pp. 356 onwards.

14 Shoghi Effendi, *God Passes By*, pp. 274–5; Balyuzi, *'Abdu'l-Bahá*, p. 92. Shoghi Effendi did not give the foundation stone any special mention or identify its location. Khayru'lláh later rebelled against 'Abdu'l-Bahá; for an excellent description of him and his activities, see Hogenson, *Lighting the Western Sky*.

15 Hogenson, *Lighting the Western Sky*, p. 307.

16 A drawing by Mason Remey in the 1920s indicates there are vaulted ceilings. The drawing is on the wall in the Mansion of Mazra'ih.

17 Shoghi Effendi writes (*God Passes By*, p. 275) that construction began about the time the sarcophagus arrived. Balyuzi (*'Abdu'l-Bahá*, p. 92) says construction began 'as the new century dawned'; see also Taherzadeh, *The Covenant of Bahá'u'lláh*, p. 223.

11. Crisis and Construction

1 Monahan, Quarterly report of Haifa V. Consulate for quarter ending 31 Dec. 1900, FO 195 2097, quoted in Momen, *The Bábí and Bahá'í Religions*, p. 319.

2 Balyuzi, *'Abdu'l-Bahá*, pp. 127–8.

3 Monahan, op. cit. p. 319. Few knew that the holy remains of the Báb were intended to be brought to be interred on Mount Carmel. It was not until 1909 that 'Abdu'l-Bahá's intentions became clear.

4 Esslemont, *Bahá'u'lláh and the New Era*, p. 55. The northern rooms (now the Shrine of 'Abdu'l-Bahá) were initially used for gatherings of the Bahá'ís.

5 Afroukhteh, *Memories of Nine Years in 'Akká,* p. 134.
6 Balyuzi, *'Abdu'l-Bahá,* pp. 127–8, for information about the following paragraphs. According to a 'summary of 'Abdu'l-Bahá's statements' in another report, 'the governor (Mutasarif) of 'Akká, though not a believer, was friendly towards us and appointed a three-man team to investigate the matter. The team was comprised of Amín Effendi, a believer, Ṣálih Effendi, who was associated with us, and a parliamentarian of the 'Akká governorate' (Memoirs of Dr Zia Bagdadi, in Rohani, *Sweet and Enchanting Stories,* p. 79).
7 Memoirs of Dr Zia Bagdadi, in Rohani, *Sweet and Enchanting Stories,* p. 79; Balyuzi, *'Abdu'l-Bahá,* p. 128.
8 From a road across the face of the slope. It was known by various names in following years, such as Mountain Road and UNO Avenue. It is now called Hatzionut (Zionism) Avenue.
9 Afroukhteh, *Memories of Nine Years in 'Akká,* p. 120.
10 Memoirs of Dr Zia Bagdadi, in Rohani, *Sweet and Enchanting Stories,* p. 79. See also Mú'ayyad, *Eight Years Near 'Abdu'l-Bahá,* p. 451.
11 Quoted in Shoghi Effendi, *God Passes By,* pp. 275–6.
12 Afroukhteh, *Memories of Nine Years in 'Akká,* p. 120. Áqá Riḍáy-i-Qannad looked after 'Abdu'l-Bahá's financial affairs.
13 See Mú'ayyad, *Eight Years Near 'Abdu'l-Bahá,* p. 453 (p. 315 in the original Persian); memoirs of Dr Zia Bagdadi, in Rohani, *Sweet and Enchanting Stories,* p. 80; Badi Bushrui, 'Kúh-i-muqaddas Karmil va isṭiqrar-i arsh-i-Mubárak dar Maqám-i-A'lá' (The Holy Mountain of Carmel and Burying the Blessed Remains in the Shrine of the Most High) in *Áhang-i-Badí',* year 28, vols 3 & 4, p. 10.
14 Quoted in Shoghi Effendi, *God Passes By,* p. 275.
15 See *Maḥmúd's Diary,* p. 24; Hogenson, *Lighting the Western Sky,* p. 247 and photo between pp. 236–7. Phoebe Hearst had inherited great wealth on the death of her husband and used it for many philanthropic purposes. She was the mother of William Randolph Hearst, the US publisher. In 1898, she had led the first pilgrimage by Western Bahá'ís to the Holy Land. In her later years, having been the victim of repeated demands for money on the part of unscrupulous individuals she became somewhat withdrawn from Bahá'ís, but 'Abdu'l-Bahá called her 'Mother of the Faithful' and on her passing in 1919 revealed Tablets in praise of her (see Hogenson, op. cit., pp. 247, 265–6, 271).
16 Ḥuqúq'u'lláh, 'The right of God', a law instituted by Bahá'u'lláh in the *Kitáb-i-Aqdas.* It involves Bahá'ís making a 19% voluntary payment on any wealth in excess of what is necessary to live comfortably, after the remittance of any outstanding debt, to the Head of the Faith. 'Abdu'l-Bahá also showed his generosity to the local community by spending large amounts of money to maintain Mountain Road (see Afroukhteh, *Memories of Nine Years in 'Akká,* pp. 120–21).
17 Modarres, *Táríkh-i Amr-i Bahá'í dar Najaf-Ábád* (History of the Baha'i Faith in Najafabad), pp. 160–73. This would appear to refer to Phoebe Hearst because the account also says that when 'Abdu'l-Bahá went to the West, He visited that lady in her house and gave handsome tips to her servant(s); also that she became withdrawn from the Faith. Both details are consistent with the identification of Mrs Hearst.
18 Information from Fuad Izadinia, in personal correspondence to the author: 'This is the reported saying of the beloved Guardian to the pilgrims when my

grandfather and grandmother in 1953 were in his presence.'
19 Afroukhteh, *Memories of Nine Years in 'Akká*, p. 120.

12. Enemies Step Up Attacks

1 Afroukhteh, *Memories of Nine Years in 'Akká*, p. 119.
2 The 'Sakinatu'lláh' (Abode of God) had been stolen in earlier historic times. Shoghi Effendi, in a message to Mihraban Bihjat on 10 February 1934, wrote: 'What is understood of the coffin (the Ark of the Covenant) is a certain container which contained the laws of the religion of Moses and it had been the point of attraction of the Sons of Israel (Jews) during the days of Moses, and the enemies of the Sons of Israel stole the coffin for a while. This means that the enemies conquered the House of God' (Ishráq Khávarí, *Qámús-i-Tawqí'-i 108 (BE)*, p. 58).
3 'Extracts from Mírzá Moneer's letters, Acca, Syria, March 22, 1909', in *Star of the West*, vol. 11, no. 19 (2 March 1921), p. 316: 'few of the believers knew that nine years ago the remains of His Holiness, The Bab had been quietly placed in the (place of) Hazerat-o-Ikoods [Ḥaziratu'l-Quds] on Mount Carmel.' This was the name given to one of the houses rented by 'Abdu'l-Bahá (see Chapter 9, note 18). According to Rafati, the casket had been removed to that house in Haifa before the arrival of the government inspectors.
4 Letter from Ali-Kuli Khan, 15 March 1955, in Gail, *Summon up Remembrance*, p. 285. A.-Q. Afnan, in *Ahd-i-A'lá*, confirms the supposition, writing that the remains of the Báb had been transferred to Haifa nine years before their entombment (1900) and that the casket was kept in the sarcophagus for all those years.
5 Photographs taken as the time show these methods.
6 Alkan, *Dissent and Heterodoxy*, pp. 154–7, citing official Ottoman documents.
7 Momen, *The Bábí and Bahá'í Religions*, 1844–1944, p. 319. Shoghi Effendi described Majdi'd-Dín (also spelt Majdu'd-Dín), the son of Bahá'u'lláh's faithful brother Mírzá Músá, as the most redoubtable adversary of 'Abdu'l-Bahá. He played a predominant part in kindling the hostility of Sultan 'Abdu'l-Hamid and Jamal Pasha, and was the chief instigator of Muḥammad-'Alí, archbreaker of Bahá'u'lláh's Covenant.
8 Balyuzi, *'Abdu'l-Bahá*, p. 92. The treacherous half-brothers of 'Abdu'l-Bahá could sell valuable gifts sent to Acre by Bahá'ís but which had not been accepted by Bahá'u'lláh or 'Abdu'l-Bahá, both of whom lived abstemious lives. There is a report that these half-brothers also sold a third share of the Mansion of Bahji to Acre police chief Yaḥyá Ṭábúr Áqásí (Taherzadeh, *The Covenant of Bahá'u'lláh*, p. 227). This police chief is also referred to in H. Afnán, *Memories of the Báb, Bahá'u'lláh and 'Abdu'l-Bahá*.
9 This was later confirmed by Badí'u'lláh; see Momen, *The Bábí and Bahá'í Religions, 1844–1944*, p. 319.
10 Taherzadeh, *The Covenant of Bahá'u'lláh*, p. 227.
11 A reduced number of Eastern pilgrims still visited Haifa, however (Afroukhteh, *Memories of Nine Years in 'Akká*, pp. 116, 122).
12 Lampooned by the British press as 'Abdul the Damned' (see Balyuzi, *'Abdu'l-Bahá*, p. 96).
13 A cipher telegram of 20 August 1901 came from Istanbul with orders to imprison 'Abdu'l-Bahá and other family members (Alkan, *Dissent and Heterodoxy*, pp. 154–7).

14 Shoghi Effendi, *The Bahá'í Faith 1844–1952: Information Statistical and Comparative*, p. 5.

15 In his report for the quarter ending 30 September 1901 (Momen, *The Bábí and Bahá'í Religions, 1844–1944*, p. 319), Monahan wrote: 'It is supposed that the Ottoman Government took alarm at Abbas Effendi's increasing wealth and influence especially his influence of Americans and other foreigners. His disciples are however at large in and around Haifa and Acre, except the one or two surviving original exiles who accompanied his father here from Adrianople in 1868. These are kept in Acre with the three brothers.'

16 Balyuzi, *'Abdu'l-Bahá*, p. 94.

17 Momen, *The Bábí and Bahá'í Religions, 1844–1944*, pp. 319–20.

18 Shoghi Effendi, *God Passes By*, p. 275.

19 Afroukhteh, *Memories of Nine Years in 'Akká*, pp. 209–10. Misunderstandings were rife. An American journalist working for the *Chicago Record-Herald*, William E. Curtis, who visited the Holy Land in 1900–01, got it wrong about the purpose of the building – thinking it was a Shrine for Bahá'u'lláh – and how it was funded. He said that every year Americans visited 'Abdu'l-Bahá and brought him gifts of money, most of which was used 'in the construction of a shrine and temple upon Mount Carmel, above the town of Haifa, where Abbas Effendi intended to bury the remains of his father and establish the center of his church. As the movement is supposed to be secret the Turkish authorities became alarmed at the number of American visitors and their liberal contributions, so Abbas Effendi was prohibited from leaving Acre, and has not been able to complete the shrine. The walls are up, the roof is laid and part of the interior finished' (quoted in Momen, *The Bábí and Bahá'í Religions, 1844–1944*, p. 320). His claim about 'Abdu'l-Bahá appealing for funds was not only untrue but was contradicted by many others who met Him.

20 Alkan, *Dissent and Heterodoxy*, pp. 154–7.

21 Shoghi Effendi, *God Passes By*, p. 266.

22 See Shoghi Effendi, *God Passes By*, pp. 269–71; Balyuzi, *'Abdu'l-Bahá*, pp. 111–23. Shoghi Effendi was seven and ten years old in the years 1904 and 1907 respectively so is likely to have remembered such occasions. Moojan Momen realized several decades ago that there is a problem concerning the dates of the Commissions, based on Ottoman records and correspondence by British consular officials (*The Bábí and Bahá'í Religions*, 1844–1944, pp. 322–3). More recent research published by Vahid Rafati and Necati Alkan would suggest that the second Commission took place in 1905; indeed, Alkan has concluded that there was only one Commission, since the accounts of the second visit by the commissioners refer to a particular bombing in Istanbul, and that occurred in 1905. A letter from Muḥammad-Taqí Man<u>sh</u>ádí, a Bahá'í who was in Acre with 'Abdu'l-Bahá in 1905, says the Commission arrived on 25 May 1905 and left on 23 July 1905 (Alkan, *Dissent and Heterodoxy*, pp. 154–7, citing Rafati, 'Az nāmahā-yi qudamā', in *'Andalíb*, vol. 23, no. 91, pp. 46–50).

23 Balyuzi, *'Abdu'l-Bahá*, pp. 112–13.

24 ibid. p. 113.

25 Bahá'u'lláh's burial place at Bahjí outside Acre.

26 'Abdu'l-Bahá, *Selections from the Writings of 'Abdu'l-Bahá*, no. 188, pp. 217–18.

27 Balyuzi, *'Abdu'l-Bahá*, p. 114.
28 Taherzadeh, *The Child of the Covenant*, p. 217.
29 ibid. p. 218.
30 Afroukhteh, *Memories of Nine Years in 'Akká*, p. 380.
31 Balyuzi, *'Abdu'l-Bahá*, p. 119. The report of the commissioners noted that since the Commission arrived, Abbas Effendi had not left his house (Alkan, *Dissent and Heterodoxy*, pp. 154–7).
32 'Abdu'l-Bahá, *Selections of the Writings of 'Abdu'l-Bahá*, p. 218.
33 Afroukhteh, *Memories of Nine Years in 'Akká*, p. 362.
34 Official documents, in Alkan, *Dissent and Heterodoxy*, pp. 154–7. Dr Alkan also notes that 'Abdu'l-Bahá referred to possible exile to Fizan in one of his Turkish poems (http:// reference.bahai.org/fa/t/ab/MAS9).
35 Afroukhteh, *Memories of Nine Years in 'Akká*, pp. 363–4. The offer came from an Italian named Escobino who was the acting consul for Spain and whose family had an agency for the Italian Steamship Company.
36 Afroukhteh, *Memories of Nine Years in 'Akká*, p. 362. One source says this is what was said in Turkish: '*Chukh matin dur*/Çok *metindir*' – it is very strong (Javidukht Khadem, in *Zikrullah Khadem*, p. 283).
37 Afroukhteh, *Memories of Nine Years in 'Akká*, p. 387.
38 Alkan, *Dissent and Heterodoxy*, pp. 154–7.
39 'Abdu'l-Bahá, *Selections from the Writings of 'Abdu'l-Bahá*, no. 188, p. 222.
40 *Memories of Nine Years in 'Akká*, p. 363. This was the former home of 'Abdu'lláh Páshá, now a place visited by Bahá'í pilgrims.
41 'Abdu'l-Bahá, *Selections from the Writings of 'Abdu'l-Bahá*, no. 188, p. 218.
42 See Afroukhteh, *Memories of Nine Years in 'Akká*, p. 364; Alkan, *Dissent and Heterodoxy*, pp. 154–7, citing Rafati, 'Az nāmahā-yi qudamā', in *'Andalíb*, vol. 23, no. 9, pp. 46–50. A report appeared in the *Times* of London in August 1905, included a patently wrong allegation against 'Abdu'l-Bahá about Him building a palace – the Shrine building had only six rooms, was similar to other Templer buildings and in no way resembled a palace. It mentioned that He had been exiled, which was also incorrect. 'A sort of peripatetic inquisition composed of five Turkish Pashas from Constantinople, is reported by the *Echo de Paris* to be now visiting the Syrian towns to inquire into the present movement . . .The Babi's chief Abbas Effendi has been exiled because he was building a palace on Mount Carmel which commands the fortress of St Jean d'Acre [Acre]. He was accused of erecting a fortress for the Egyptians or Arabs.' This report, headlined 'The Arab Revolt', seems to be reporting events in July (see Alkan, op. cit.).
43 Afroukhteh, *Memories of Nine Years in 'Akká*, p. 379.
44 There were four commissioners, under the chairmanship of 'Arif Bey, who was later ignominiously shot dead by a sentry in Istanbul. He was of the Court of Appeal. Other members were General Sukru Pasha, the brigadier Rasim Pasha and Colonel Edhem Pasha (Alkan, *Dissent and Heterodoxy*, citing official Ottoman papers, pp. 154–7). The commissioners were to suffer 'an ignominious fate'; in addition to 'Arif Bey, the second was robbed of all his possessions, the third was exiled and the fourth sank into abject poverty (Shoghi Effendi, *The Bahá'í Faith 1844–1952: Information Statistical and Comparative*, p. 24).

13. The Building

1 The site of an ancient Templar hospice of the Knights Templar, a completely different organization of a much earlier era than the German Templers. This was the only source of hard stone. Some had been used for the ramparts in Acre. This kind of stone was used for the aqueduct between Nahariya and Acre, and probably the mosque in Acre. The same strong stone was probably used in the foundations as well.

2 See Chase, *In Galilee*, photo of camels carrying stone, p. 19. This may be just a generic image and not connected with the actual construction of the Shrine.

3 Irwin, 'Shrines and gardens', p. 353.

4 Photographs that show the uncompleted walls and the barrel-like formwork were taken by Edward Getsinger.

5 The loose material in the roof was totally removed in 2010 during the restoration project. Heavy reinforced concrete was poured into the gap when the two buildings (old and the superstructure) were attached together.

6 Researcher Fuad Izadinia speculates that it is a municipal reference number from the time of 'Abdu'l-Bahá or even of Shoghi Effendi.

7 'Abdu'l-Bahá, Tablet to Mírzá Muḥammad-Báqir Afnán, dated 28 Sha'ban 1321 AH, in Rafati, 'Bahá'u'lláh in Haifa'. Muḥammad-Báqir Afnán was the grandson of the younger uncle of the Báb, Mírzá Ḥasan-'Alí; see 'Mount Carmel Projects update', in *Vineyard of the Lord*, no. 23, p. 7.

8 See Chapter 10 for more information about these masons.

9 Ḥájí Abu'l-Ḥasan-i-Ardikání (c.1831–1928), known as Amín-i-Iláhi (trustee of God) or Ḥájí Amín. For further information about his life see Balyuzi, *Eminent Bahá'ís in the Time of Bahá'u'lláh*, p. 263; Taherzadeh *The Revelation of Bahá'u'lláh*, vol. 3, pp. 77–86; Harper, *Lights of Fortitude*, pp. 47–9. He was an Apostle of Bahá'u'lláh and was posthumously named a Hand of the Cause by Shoghi Effendi.

10 See Chapter 11, note 16.

11 For details of his life see Taherzadeh, *The Revelation of Bahá'u'lláh*, vol. 3, pp. 73–6. He was shot in Azerbaijan during a quasi-rebellion there. Ḥájí Amín was injured.

12 See Chapter 3, note 1. A photograph of the two in the prison, their feet in stocks and chains around their necks, can be seen in Taherzadeh, *The Revelation of Bahá'u'lláh*, vol. 3, p. 60.

13 Known as Amín-i-Amín – Trustee of the Trustee.

14 Cole, 'Foreword to facsimile edition', in Abu'l-Faḍl, *The Bahá'í Proofs*, p. xiii. For a biographical summary of his life see Balyuzi, *Eminent Bahá'ís in the Time of Bahá'u'lláh*, pp. 263–5.

15 Cole, op. cit., p. ix.

16 'Tributes and eulogies by Abdul-Baha Abbas (Extracts from the Diary of Mirza Ahmad Sohrab)' in Abu'l-Faḍl, *The Bahá'í Proofs*, p. 23.

17 ibid. 23–5. There are other tributes by the Master in that section: pp. 19–27.

18 Shoghi Effendi, *Citadel of Faith*, p. 171.

19 Arabic for "sacred fold", a term used for a Bahá'í Centre. Lit. paradise, it has a numerical value of 1327, which is the year that the remains of the Báb were interred in His permanent Shrine. The term Ḥáẓíratu'l-Quds is translated

in *Epistle to the Son of the Wolf*, p. 7, as the habitations of holiness. Fáḍil-i-Mázindarání (*Asráru'l-Á͟thár*, vol. 3, pp. 116–17) notes that this phrase was used in the writings of Bahá'u'lláh to refer to the innermost Sanctuary of Paradise, and that 'Abdu'l-Bahá in the Tablet of Visitation of the Vakílu'd-Dawlih used this expression as a reference to the Shrine of the Báb on Mount Carmel. This term has been employed by the Prince S͟hayk͟hu'r-Ra'ís in a poem marking the occasion of the interment of the Báb at Naw-Rúz 1909.

20 Mú'ayyad, *Eight Years Near 'Abdu'l-Bahá*, p. 465.

21 See Gail, *Summon Up Remembrance*, p. 223. There had been no interments at that time. Very few people outside the Bahá'í community would have called the building a tomb then because they did not know its purpose. In 1906, Florence Khan was in Haifa with her husband, Ali-Kuli Khan, who was the first to translate into English some important Bahá'í scripture. Florence (née Breed) was a former Boston society young woman. They were the first Persian-American Bahá'í family to come on pilgrimage.

22 As it was then called. Haifa, as Gail notes, grew in size and the name changed to the Bay of Haifa.

23 Bahíyyih K͟hánum, the Greatest Holy Leaf.

24 The Báb is believed to be the 'return' of Elijah.

25 Gail, *Summon Up Remembrance*, pp. 274–5. Perhaps Florence's husband, Ali-Kuli Khan, had yet to learn that the sacred remains had been in the room he had worked in years earlier, or he had not told his wife about this fact due to the necessity to keep this information secret. A colourized photograph of the cypress grove, taken some time between 1903 and 1911, shows it in a state quite different to how it was described in 1891 when Bahá'u'lláh was there, when the cypress trees were small, and also different from how that circle appears today. Some of the trees in the colourized photograph tower above others and the grove is quite densely populated with vegetation. Dr Getsinger later published an album of the photographs.

26 For a biography of her life, see Rutstein, *Corinne True*. In 1952 when she was 90 years old, Shoghi Effendi elevated her to the rank of Hand of the Cause. She died in 1961 aged 99.

27 The third row was not added until after the death of 'Abdu'l-Bahá.

28 True, *Table Talks and Notes Taken at Acca*, pp. 14–15.

29 Chase, *In Galilee*, p. 10.

30 The entrance from Mountain Road, later UNO Avenue, now Hatzionut Street. 'Abdu'l-Bahá had bought this access route with great difficulty (see Chapter 11). He built the path and it remains, though different in appearance today.

31 House of the custodian 'Abbás-Qulí of Qom, which was demolished in the 1930s.

32 The name of 'Abdu'l-Bahá, used by people who were not in the Bahá'í community, and by Bahá'ís in public.

33 Raḥmatu'lláh Najaf-Ábádí was the caretaker, 'Abbás-Qulí was the custodian.

34 'Alláh-u-Abhá', a greeting still used today among Bahá'ís. It means 'God is Most Glorious'.

35 When Bahá'u'lláh sat in the grove, there were 15 finger-thin cypress trees, as noted by Zikrullah Khadem in his article on Mount Carmel. Later, fighting for

space, some of the 15 died. An historian of the Bahá'í gardens in Haifa, Andrew Blake, who was a senior horticulturalist at the Bahá'í World Centre from 1998 to 2005, says that analyses of photographs show that seven trees remain from the time of Bahá'u'lláh. Two new ones were planted in 2000.

36 Chase, *In Galilee*, pp. 14–18.

37 ibid. p. 14.

38 For details of his life (1875–1951) see Harper, *Lights of Fortitude*, pp. 115–28. In 1951, Roy Wilhelm was appointed posthumously a Hand of the Cause by Shoghi Effendi. During his lifetime, all 'Abdu'l-Bahá's letters to America were sent care of him, to be forwarded to the intended recipients. He also handled the financial affairs of 'Abdu'l-Bahá in the United States.

39 Wearing rings with a designated Bahá'í symbol is common among Bahá'ís but not compulsory.

40 Alláh-u-Abhá (God is Most Glorious.)

41 Wilhelm, 'Two glimpses of 'Abdu'l-Bahá', pp. 804–5.

42 Mu'ayyad, *Eight Years Near 'Abdu'l-Bahá*, pp. 31–2.

43 Haifa and Acre are now connected. Haifa-born Aaron Ceichanover, based at Technion-Israel Institute of Technology in Haifa, won the Nobel Prize for chemistry in 2004, and there are other examples of local excellence in the sciences and arts.

44 Translation from Mu'ayyad, *Kh͟áṭirát-i-Ḥabíb*, vol. 1, pp. 19, 21, 22, 53, in Zikrullah Khadem, 'Carmel: The Mountain of God and the Tablet of Carmel', p. 280.

45 Translation by Fuad Izadinia from Mu'ayyad, *Kh͟áṭirát-i-Ḥabíb* vol. 1, p. 81. Similar translations are provided by Adib Taherzadeh in *The Covenant of Bahá'u'lláh*, pp. 225–6, and by Ahang Rabbani in Mu'ayyad, *Eight Years Near 'Abdu'l-Bahá*, p. 98–9, which notes: 'This Tablet was recorded (in Arabic) in the diary of Dr Zia Bagdadi'.

46 Translated by Adib Taherzadeh from Mu'ayyad, *Kh͟áṭirát-i-Ḥabíb*, vol. 1, p. 449, in Taherzadeh, *The Covenant of Bahá'u'lláh*, p. 226.

14. Release and Aftermath

1 Shoghi Effendi, *The Bahá'í Faith 1844–1952: Information Statistical and Comparative*, p. 5.

2 'Abdu'l-Bahá, in *Star of the West*, vol. 24, no. 11, p. 350.

3 'Abdu'l-Bahá, *Selections from the Writings of 'Abdu'l-Bahá*, pp. 225–7.

4 Information about the custodians is from an interview with Mr 'Alí Nak͟hjavání by Andrew Blake, a senior horticulturalist at the Shrine, on 15 July 2003. The first person to look after the Shrine was Raḥmatu'lláh Najaf-Ábádí, but he was a 'keeper', or caretaker, not a custodian.

5 Letter from Genevieve Coy, 'On Mount Carmel', 1 June 1922, in *Star of the West*, vol. 13, no.10 (January 1923), pp. 283–4.

6 See Muhajir, *The Mystery of God*, photographs on pp. 98, 174 and 153. In 1919, the Master sent Shoghi Effendi, who had been suffering from bouts of malaria, to spend a few nights there (see Riaz Khadem, *Prelude to the Guardianship*, p. 68).

7 He married Nazireh Khanum and had five sons and two daughters, and later served Shoghi Effendi for about a decade. In about 1932 he returned with his

family to Najafabad in Iran, where in 1952 at the request of Shoghi Effendi he wrote his memoirs which provided important historical details. Four years later he died in Isfahan and was buried in the Bahá'í cemetery there (Modarres, *Táríkh-i Amr-i Bahá'í dar Najaf-Ábád*, pp. 160–73).

8 Rabbani, *The Priceless Pearl*, p. 85.

9 The Templer children used to climb Mount Carmel and harvest carob to make jam for winter. Carob, olive, almond and fig trees had long grown there (email to the author from Fuad Izadinia, 28 July 2016).

10 Information from Andrew Blake, email to the author, September 2013. He cites one source as 'Abbas Effendi: His personality, work & followers', by Ethel Stefana Stevens in the *Fortnightly Review*, vol. 95 (June 1911). E. S. Stephens, later Lady Drower, stayed in 'Abdu'l-Bahá's house and wrote about Him and the Bahá'í Faith, notably in her novel *The Mountain of God* (1911). See http://bahaitributes.wordpress.com/2008/12/18/ethel-stefana-stevens-1879–1972.

11 The exact purchase date of the land behind the Shrine has not yet been firmly established, according to Andrew Blake, an historian of the Bahá'í gardens in Haifa and who was a senior horticulturalist at the Bahá'í World Centre, 1998–2005. Old photographs, Mr Blake says, confirm that fruit trees were planted amongst the grape vines surrounding the circle of cypress trees during 'Abdu'l-Bahá's time, and that these trees were retained until they died of old age – even after Shoghi Effendi had developed the area into a formal ornamental garden. Fruit trees remaining from the Master's time include two olive trees behind the Shrine – they are close together 'almost like they are twining or dancing around each other' (email from Andrew Blake to the author, 3 August 2012). Also from that time, Blake says, are the three sour orange trees immediately to the north of and on the same level as the Shrine. Two are on one side of the steps leading down to the lower terraces, and one remains on the other side.

15. Interment of the Sacred Remains

1 See Zayn, 'The final burial of the Bab on Mt. Carmel' in *Star of the West*, vol. 11, no. 19 (2 March 1921), p. 316. Mirza Moneer (Munír) was one of the two sons of Zaynu'l-Muqarrabín, an Apostle of Bahá'u'lláh.

2 In later years this was confirmed. To enter what was then room #2 (then the middle eastern room), there was a 32 cm step. The floor of the room was 8 cm lower than the inner shrine floor (room #9), as opposed to room #6 (then the middle western room, which was 40 cm lower. All the Shrine's rooms were covered with red tiles except for room#9 and room #2, which were covered with thick gypsum. In the floor of room #2 there was an area 2.5m x 2.5m, marked clearly with a white lime plaster, indicating where the steps had been. The floor was made of rubble, different from the natural formation of the mountain. This indicates that the steps were made provisionally for the occasion and then the opening to the vault was sealed. Then fill was added after the passing of 'Abdu'l-Bahá, who may well have kept His Will and Testament and perhaps Tablets of the Divine Plan on the top steps of the entrance for protection. It is known He kept them in the Shrine vicinity. Mr Nakhjavání has confirmed to the author that the entrance to the lower areas was in room #2, later filled in by the Guardian. After the restoration (2008–11), the floor of room #2 was lowered 40 cm to be at the

same level as rooms #4 and #6, thus making #9, the inner Shrine, 40 cm higher than all the other rooms.

According to Mírzá Munír Zayn (op. cit.), a week before the feast of Naw-Rúz 'Abdu'l-Bahá sent two Bahá'ís from Acre to Haifa to make preparations for the interment ceremony. The Canadian pilgrim May Woodcock may have been referring to this work when she wrote: 'One believer had given up business and came and camped with his family near the Tomb for some weeks, during which time he had worked with pick and shovel to dig a hole in the foundation of the Tomb through which the sarcophagus had been passed. They could not employ skilled labourers for fear of drawing the attention of the Nakazeen [Covenant-breaking enemies of the Faith]' (Letter to Mrs A.M. Bryant by May Woodcock and A.M. Bryant, 1909). It is more likely that the entrance was already in place but just needed to be made functional, and stairs installed.

3 I<u>sh</u>ráq <u>Kh</u>ávarí, *Qámús-i-Tawqí'-i 108 (BE).* This probably took place in the second week of March when the box could have been stored securely in the vault. For security reasons, the box containing the casket needed to be taken up separately, because hauling the sarcophagus was an event that many would witness due to the effort required to haul it up the mountain.

4 In his memoirs, Raḥmatu'lláh Najaf-Ábádí mentions the arrangement with the three boxes, one being the casket with the sacred remains inside, see Modarres, *Táríkh-i Amr-i Bahá'í dar Najaf-Ábád*, pp. 160–173.

5 See Chapter 8, note 24, for the significance of the number of men carrying the casket. The Qur'án has a reference to eight: 'on that day eight shall bear up the throne of thy Lord' or 'And the angels will be on its sides, and eight will, that Day, bear the Throne of thy Lord above them' (trans. Yusuf Ali).

6 The custodian would have had a long key to the metal door of the vault.

7 It was about 60 years.

8 In 'The story of Ustád Ismá'íl Úbudíyyát', Mr Úbudíyyát mentions a Tablet from the Master called 'I wish you would count Us as one of you' (see National Spiritual Assembly of the United States, *Bi Yad-i-Dust*, pp. 80–93). In his introduction to Mr Úbudíyyát's story, Mr Faizi writes: 'By the will of 'Abdu'l-Bahá, it was that eight of the friends become the bearers of the Holy Remains of the Most Great Lord . . .' The Tablet of the Master, as recorded in *Bi Yad-i Dust* (p. 87), was revealed in honour of the eight believers Ustád Muḥammad-'Alí; Áqá Mihdí; Áqá Muḥammad-Ibráhím; Áqá Abu'l-Qásim; Áqá Najaf-'Alí; Áqá Qanbar-'Alí; Áqá Raḥmatu'lláh and Ustád Ismá'íl (next to the last-named is written 'Abdu'l-Bahá). The Tablet praises God for having enabled those believers to have gone to the Ḥaẓíratu'l-Quds the name of the Shrine building before the interment), and having planted fragrant flowers (roses), and where 'Abdu'l-Bahá was with them in heart and soul. The Tablet said that those believers should be very thankful that they could become the gardeners of such a holy spot and especially being the carrier of such a gift from one place to the next. According to Ustád Ismá'íl, the 9th name ('Abdu'l-Bahá) is there because He said: 'I wish you would count Us as one of you'. This was a revelation to them, because the night before they had written the eight names and one of them had suggested to write 'Abdu'l-Bahá's name as the ninth one; that is what they did.

9 See Zayn, 'The final burial of the Bab on Mt. Carmel', p. 316.

10 Modarres, *Táríkh-i Amr-i Bahá'í dar Najaf-Ábád*, pp. 160–173.

11 This is not Ustád 'Abdu'l-Karím who helped build the Shrine and after whom a door to the Shrine is named. 'Abdu'l-Karím *gush borideh* means 'cut off ear 'Abdu'l-Karím' – he had one of his ears cut off.

12 M.-A. Faizi, *Malakíy-i-Karmil*, p. 49; see also Zayn, 'The final burial of the Bab on Mt. Carmel', p. 316. Raḥmatu'llah's list differs a little from another list provided by Ustád Ismá'íl Úbudíyyát; see Modarres, *Táríkh-i Amr-i Bahá'í dar Najaf-Ábád*, pp. 160–173.

13 Layla Ábádih-i (unpublished memoirs) also describes the incident but she is recalling what somebody else said. Raḥmatu'lláh was an eye witness.

14 Known as the *sardabe* (cool room).

15 Zayn, 'The final burial of the Bab on Mt. Carmel', p. 317. In *God Passes By*, Shoghi Effendi writes: 'On the 28th of the month of Ṣafar 1327 A.H., the day of the first Naw-Rúz (1909), which He celebrated after His release from His confinement, 'Abdu'l-Bahá had the marble sarcophagus transported with great labour to the vault prepared for it . . .' (p. 276). See also the memoirs of Raḥmatu'lláh in Modarres, *Táríkh-i Amr-i Bahá'í dar Najaf-Ábád*.

16 Giachery, *Shoghi Effendi: Recollections*, p. 54: 'Shoghi Effendi as a youth of thirteen [he was 12], had been an eye-witness to this historical and moving event.' Mr Giachery, a Hand of the Cause of the God, writes that Shoghi Effendi 'related to him the whole episode of the placing of the Báb's luminous remains in the alabaster sarcophagus that had been donated and sent by the Bahá'ís of Rangoon, Burma'.

17 From the unpublished memoirs of Layla Ábádih-i: 'On that special day, the beloved Master asked the Greatest Holy Leaf and the Household to go to the Shrine and be prepared for the ceremony of delivering the Blessed Remains from the wooden box into the marble sarcophagus. Mr Scott from the United States accompanied the Master and they reached the Shrine before the rest' (translation by Fuad Izadinia; a similar translation can be found in Ma'ani, *Leaves of the Twin Divine Trees*).

18 This list has been compiled from an analysis of those loyal Bahá'ís involved with the preparation of the event as well as through pilgrims' notes and other material.

19 Ḥájí Mírzá Muḥammad-Taqí, Afnán-i-Yazdi. He was from Yazd and had used most of his fortune to build the Ishqabad Bahá'í Temple. In *Memorials of the Faithful*, 'Abdu'l-Bahá writes that after this Bahá'í had 'expended everything he possessed' to rear the Temple, bar 'a trifling sum', he journeyed to the Holy Land 'and there beside that place where the chosen angels circle, in the shelter of the Shrine of the Báb, he passed his days, holy and pure, supplicating and entreating the Lord'. The Master called him 'an uncommonly happy man. Whenever I was saddened, I would meet with him, and on the instant, joy would return again. Praise be to God, at the last, close by the Shrine of the Báb, he hastened away in light to the Abhá Realm; but the loss of him deeply grieved 'Abdu'l-Bahá. His bright grave is in Haifa, beside the Ḥazíratu'l-Quds, near Elijah's Cave' (pp. 128–9). He passed away in Haifa on 30 August 1911 at the age of 81 and was the first to be buried in the Haifa Bahá'í cemetery. 'Abdu'l-Bahá ranked him as one of the 24 elders mentioned in the Book of Revelation, and revealed two Tablets of Visitation in his honour (Ahang Rabbani, 'The Afnán family: Some biographical notes').

20 'Abdu'l-Karím *gush borideh* had been fired by the Master, so would not have been present.

21 Memoirs of Raḥmatu'lláh, in Modarres, *Táríkh-i Amr-i Bahá'í dar Najaf-Ábád.*

22 May Woodcock wrote: 'The believers who were with Him, as well as the ladies who were standing or kneeling about the entrance to the Tomb, wept with Him, and for Him too who made such a pathetic figure beside the Tomb of the One Who had proclaimed His Glorious Advent' (http://bahai-library.com/woodcock_bryant_letter). This indicates that May did not see, or clearly see, the events she was describing.

23 Shoghi Effendi, *God Passes By*, p. 276. In addition to his own observations, Shoghi Effendi also seems to have given literary treatment to the description in the letter dated 22 March 1909 from Mírzá Munír Zayn: 'Our Beloved, with his hair waving around his beautiful head, his face shining with light, looking inspired, tragic and majestic, rushed down and threw himself on his knees. He placed the remains of The Bab in the large coffin (in the marble-casket) and leaning his blessed head on the border of the coffin, he wept, wept, wept – and all wept with him. That night the Master did not sleep' (Zayn, 'The final burial of the Bab on Mt. Carmel', p. 317).

24 Blomfield, *The Chosen Highway*, pp. 31–2.

25 Quoted in Shoghi Effendi, *God Passes By*, p. 276. He also wrote: 'By a strange coincidence, on that same day of Naw-Rúz, a cablegram was received from Chicago, announcing that the believers in each of the American centres had elected a delegate and sent to that city . . . and definitely decided on the site and construction of the Mashriqu'l-Adhkár.'

26 'Tablet from 'Abdu'l-Bahá for the 18 Martyrs of the Third Nayríz upheaval', provisional translation available at: http://www.nayriz.org/template.php?pageName=tablet202. This website is an extension to Ahdieh and Chapman, *Awakening: A History of the Bábi and Bahá'í Faiths in Nayríz.* There were numerous Tablets with the same contents to different individuals and the Tehran Assembly; see M.-A. Faizi, *Malakíy-i-Karmil*, p. 65. The Tablet quoted here is found in a different translation, by Ahmad Sohrab, in *Bahá'í News*, vol. 1, no. 3 (28 April 1910), p. 4 (This publication became *Star of the West*); but Sohrab writes 'Tabriz' instead of 'Nayríz'.

27 Memoirs of Raḥmatu'lláh, in Modarres, *Táríkh-i Amr-i Bahá'í dar Najaf-Ábád.*

28 Layla Ábádih-i, unpublished memoirs, quoting from 'Abbás-Qulí, in Ma'ani, *Leaves of the Twin Divine Trees*, p. 183.

29 'Abdu'l-Bahá was given the title 'Most Great Branch' by Bahá'u'lláh.

30 'Tablet from 'Abdu'l-Bahá for the 18 Martyrs of the Third Nayríz upheaval', provisional translation available at: http://www.nayriz.org/template.php?pageName=tablet202. In the same Tablet He wrote:

'O heavenly Friends! Nayríz became the place of bloodshed in these days; Holy Ones from amongst the celestial friends gave up their lives and went to the Altar of Love in the Path of the Lucid Light. Consequently, eyes are crying and hearts are burning. Sighs and moans are reaching the Pinnacle of Heaven. The severe sorrow began a renewed time of mourning.'

These horrific persecutions, which continued for several days, are described in Ahdieh and Chapman, *Awakening: A History of the Bábi and Bahá'í Faiths in*

Nayríz, pp. 207ff. 'Abdu'l-Bahá revealed one Tablet to the family of every martyr of Nayríz – as well as a collective Tablet of Visitation for the martyrs. See also Ishráq Khávarí, *Qámús-i-Tawqí'-i 108 (BE)*, pp. 45–6.

31 Shoghi Effendi, *God Passes By*, p. 273. The other two 'principal objectives' were the establishment of the Faith in America, and the construction of the Bahá'í Temple in 'Ishqábád (letter written on behalf of the Guardian to the National Spiritual Assembly of the United States and Canada, 14 December 1933, in *Bahá'í News*, no. 51 (February 1934), p. 5).

32 Shoghi Effendi, *God Passes By*, p. 273.

33 ibid. pp. 295, 314.

34 Point to which people turn in prayer.

35 Research is currently under way about the date or dates of arrival of the German Templers, including their purpose in coming to the Holy Land and whether they came all at one time or in successive journeys. An 1868 arrival is recorded in Momen, *The Bábí and Bahá'í Religions 1844–1944*, p. 216.

36 Shoghi Effendi, *God Passes By*, p. 277.

16. Gatherings at the Oriental Pilgrim House

1 Shoghi Effendi (*God Passes By*, p. 307) refers to the approximate date of completion and calls it the Oriental Pilgrim House.

2 Account by a son of Mírzá Ja'far Raḥmání, Mr Abu'l-Faḍl Raḥmání, in Rohani, *Sweet and Enchanting Stories*, pp. 43–7.

3 Áqá Mírzá Ja'far said: 'Perchance, no trace of me and my name will remain, but the name of Thy blessed personage shall last in the world at least five hundred thousand years' (ibid. p. 46).

4 It is not yet known who constructed the building. However, it could well have been those men who built the Shrine: Áqá Ashraf, Áqá Bálá and Ustád 'Abdu'l-Karím. The architecture does not appear very similar to Templer designs. Perhaps the builders were the architects.

5 M.-A. Faizi, *Malakíy-i-Karmil*, pp. 170–79. Mr Faizi says that an account by Mírzá Ja'far was published in *Najm-Bakhtar* (Star of the East), no. 88, 8 Sha'aban 1331 AH (about 1909).

6 Rohani, *Sweet and Enchanting Stories*, p. 46. These are 'Abdu'l-Bahá's words as reported by one of Mírzá Ja'far's sons, Abu'l-Faḍl Raḥmání, and should not be taken as exact. For more on 'Abdu'l-Bahá's sense of humour, see Yazdi, *Blessings Beyond Measure*, pp. 35–7; Ballenger, 'The Master Humorist'; see also http://bahai-library.com/compilation_humor_laughter.

7 In Persian: 'Een Mehmankhaneh-ye rouhanist va bani-ye an Mírzá Ja'far-i-Raḥmáníy-i Shírází 1327 AH (1909) AD'. The words can be seen there to this day.

8 Mírzá 'Alí-Ashraf Láhijání.

9 M.-A. Faizi, *Malakíy-i-Karmil*, pp. 170–79. Mírzá Ja'far kept on serving the Faith during the time of Shoghi Effendi, who wrote to him on 18 May 1927 assuring him that remembrance of his services would continue throughout history. He was exiled from Russian territory, arriving in Persia with almost no possessions. He obtained a job in the public service in the province of Fars and passed away in 1931 in his home town, Jahrum. One of his sons, Mr Hádí Raḥmání, who

was a Bahá'í pioneer to Afghanistan, visited Haifa and was told by the Guardian that the fact that his father had been the builder of the Pilgrim House, one of the very first Bahá'í buildings on Mount Carmel, was a great bounty. In reality, the Guardian said, the builder of the Shrine of the Báb was Bahá'u'lláh, and that the one who carried it out was 'Abdu'l-Bahá (ibid.).

10 In later years, Western pilgrims stayed elsewhere, though they met and heard talks in the Eastern Pilgrim House, then referred to simply as the Pilgrim House. A pilgrim reception centre operated elsewhere for a number of years but has now closed. Pilgrims now hear talks in the Seat of the International Teaching Centre, but meet in the Pilgrim House and use newly built kitchen facilities below, where once lived the gardener, 'Abdu'l-Raouf Rowhani, who served Shoghi Effendi, and his wife, Bahereh Khánum.

11 The day the Báb proclaimed His spiritual station. The date was calculated by the lunar calendar. Later Bahá'ís throughout the world celebrated it on 23 May, but now it is observed again according to the lunar calendar.

12 See Chapter 15, note 19.

13 Howard Struven (1882–1977) married Ruby (Hebe) Moore, the sister of Lua Getsinger, one of the Disciples of 'Abdu'l-Báha. In 1912 'Abdu'l-Bahá visited their house in Baltimore, a city where he told the Bahá'ís :

'When I reach the Holy Land, I shall lay my head on the threshold of the Blessed Shrine and, weeping, I shall supplicate on your behalf for assistance and heavenly favors, eternal honor and everlasting joy' (Zarqání, *Maḥmúd's Diary*, p. 385). For further information on Howard Struven, see: http://worcesterbahais.org/content/howard-c-struven.

14 *Star of the West*, vol. 1, no.8 (1 August 1910), pp. 1–2.

15 Probably inside the Pilgrim House and nearby.

16 *Star of the West*, vol. 1, no. 8 (1 August 1910), p. 7.

17 Messrs Remey and Struven were on a travel teaching trip, begun in 1909, in which they circled the globe, visiting Hawaii, Japan, China, Singapore, Burma and India, arriving in the Holy Land in 1910. They then returned to the United States of America.

18 Mú'ayyad, *Eight Years Near 'Abdu'l-Bahá*, p. 104.

19 After a month in Egypt, He embarked for Europe but turned back to Alexandria due to his health and stayed there until August 1911. Then He visited France, Switzerland and England before returning to Egypt for the winter, arriving on 2 December 1911. On 25 March 1912, 'Abdu'l-Bahá boarded the *Cedric* – which regularly travelled between Alexandria and New York City, stopping in Naples. It had been suggested that He might prefer to travel on the maiden voyage of the ill-fated *Titanic* but, He reportedly said, he preferred a longer sea journey. He arrived in the United States on 11 April 1912. He travelled extensively in North America, including a visit to Canada. He left on 5 December that year and visited England, Scotland, France, Germany, Hungary, and Austria, arriving back in Egypt in June 1913.

20 See http://rsmd.net/research/brittingham-isabella. In September 1901 Isabella Brittingham went on pilgrimage, visiting 'Abdu'l-Bahá for several days. The knowledge of the Faith she gained helped her complete a book, *The Revelation of Bah-Ullh in a Sequence of Four Lessons*, published by the Bahai Publishing

Society of Chicago in 1902 and subsequently issued in at least nine editions through 1920. It offered the American Bahá'ís one of the first accurate summaries of the life of Bahá'u'lláh available in English.

21 Mú'ayyad, *Eight Years Near 'Abdu'l-Bahá*, pp. 128–9.

22 Khan, *Prophet's Daughter*, pp. 78–9.

23 ibid.

17. War, Tyranny and Liberation

1 Hogenson, *Lighting the Western Sky*, p. 260.

2 Newark, 27 June 1912, while sitting in a gazebo in a park (Zarqání, *Maḥmúd's Diary*, p. 147). The Committee of Union and Progress was the ruling political party. See also Yazdi, *Blessings Beyond Measure*, p. 31; Walbridge, 'The Bahá'í Faith in Turkey'.

3 Stockman, *'Abdu'l-Bahá in America*, p. 213.

4 Balyuzi, *'Abdu'l-Bahá*, pp. 399, 400, 402.

5 Sohrab, *Abdul Baha in Egypt*, p. 141.

6 Letter from Shoghi Effendi to the Bahá'ís of the West, 17 July 1932, *in Bahíyyih Khánum: The Greatest Holy Leaf*, p. 40.

7 Khan, *Prophet's Daughter*, p. 85.

8 Balyuzi, *'Abdu'l-Bahá*, p. 403.

9 See Shoghi Effendi, *Directives from the Guardian*, no. 1: 'As to the three aims which Shoghi Effendi has stated in his 'America and the Most Great Peace' to have been the chief objectives of 'Abdu'l-Bahá's ministry, it should be pointed out that the first was: The establishment of the Cause in America; the erection of the Bahá'í Temple in 'Ishqábád, and the building on Mt. Carmel of a mausoleum marking the resting-place of the Báb were the two remaining ones' (Letter written on behalf of Shoghi Effendi to the National Spiritual Assembly of the United States and Canada, 14 December 1933, in *Bahá'í News*, no. 51 (February 1934), p. 5).

10 Bahá'í invocation: 'O Thou Glory of Glories!', see Bahá'u'lláh, *The Kitáb-i-Aqdas*, p. 180.

11 Mírzá Aḥmad Sohrab recorded in his diary these words by 'Abdu'l-Bahá, quoted in Esslemont, *Bahá'u'lláh and the New Era*, p. 228.

12 'Abdu'l-Bahá wrote: 'Some have asserted that 'Abdu'l-Bahá is on the eve of bidding his last farewell to the world, that his physical energies are depleted and drained and that before long these complications will put an end to his life. This is far from the truth. Although in the outward estimation of the Covenant-breakers and defective-minded the body is weak on account of ordeals in the Blessed Path, yet, Praise be to God! through the providence of the Blessed Perfection the spiritual forces are in the utmost rejuvenation and strength. Thanks be to God that now, through the blessing and benediction of Bahá'u'lláh, even the physical energies are fully restored, divine joy is obtained, the supreme glad-tidings are resplendent and ideal happiness overflowing' (Esslemont, *Bahá'u'lláh and New Era*, p. 59, from *Star of the West*, vol. V, no. 14, p. 213).

13 His predictions were clear and recorded in the newspapers. For example: 'the continent of Europe is one vast arsenal, which only requires one spark at its foundations and the whole of Europe will become a wasted wilderness', in

Buffalo New York Courier, 11 September 1912, available at: http://centenary.bahai.us/news/persian-peace-apostle-predicts-war-europe.

14 At that time, some were permitted to stay longer than the current nine-day period.

15 Balyuzi, *'Abdu'l-Bahá*, p. 411.

16 Mú'ayyad, *Eight Years Near 'Abdu'l-Bahá*, p. 203.

17 Two Bahá'ís from the United States were with them: Lua Getsinger and Edith Sanderson, see Weinberg, *Lady Blomfield*, pp. 177–8.

18 See Mú'ayyad, *Eight Years Near 'Abdu'l-Bahá*, p. 203. As a pilgrim, Ḥájí Mírzá Ḥaydar-'Áli had met Bahá'u'lláh. He passed away in 1920. For extracts in English from his memoirs see *Stories from the Delight of Hearts*.

19 Maude and Maude, *The Servant, The General and Armageddon*, pp. 41–2. This book is a comprehensive account of the period.

20 Mú'ayyad, *Eight Years Near 'Abdu'l-Bahá*, p. 201: 'As one of the highest army generals, [Jamal Pasha] had assembled an enormous force to attack and reduce Egypt and [capture] the Suez Canal. Tens of thousands of camels were arrayed solely for the transportation of the army's water rations. His agents had confiscated whatever food, clothing, weapons, money, surplus and stored grains they could find. Thoroughly desolate, the citizens were left without the most basic provisions as the realm was cleansed of everything useful for the needs of the military. If anyone protested, hanging was the immediate response. They would perpetrate whatever act of tyranny, oppression, injury, calumny, murder, treachery and sedition that was needed to achieve their end under the umbrella of the Committee for National Defense.'

21 See http://www.loc.gov/exhibits/americancolony/amcolony-locust.html.

22 Rabbani, *The Priceless Pearl*, p. 235. This is from Shoghi Effendi's Message to the Bahá'ís of the East, Naw-Rúz 1952; an alternative translation is given by Zikrullah Khadem, in 'Carmel: The Mountain of God and the Tablet of Carmel' (p. 284): 'The Guardian relates that as 'Abdu'l-Bahá was "sitting, facing the holy Shrine and gazing upon that holy structure, a phrase issued from His pure tongue: 'It did not come to pass that the Shrine of the Báb be completed. God willing, it will be done. We have brought it thus far.'"'

23 Rabbani, *The Priceless Pearl*, p. 235.

24 Bahá'u'lláh had addressed the leaders of West and East in a series of Tablets He revealed in Adrianople before his exile to the prison city of Acre in the Holy Land. See Bahá'u'lláh, *The Summons of the Lord of Hosts*.

25 *Star of the West*, vol. VII, no. 10 (8 September 1916).

26 'Abdu'l-Bahá, *Tablets of the Divine Plan*, Foreword by Amin Banani, p. xi. The documents were hidden there in 1917.

27 Spelled in various places Djamal, Djemal Jamal, Jemal Pasha. Pasha is not a person's name, but a high rank given to governors, generals and dignitaries in the Ottoman Empire. Jamal Pasha was also known as Biyuk Djemal Pasha. His mission was to attack the Suez Canal area to ensure the British kept big troop numbers in Egypt rather than deploying them to fight in the war (or attack Turkey). See Djemal Pasha, *Memoirs of a Turkish Statesman, (1913–1919)*; and also extracts from his memoirs published in New York in 1922 by George Doran Co., at http://www.armeniangenocidedebate.com/files/books/MemoriesDjemalPasha.pdf.

28 Montefiore, *Jerusalem: The Biography*, pp. 395–6.

29 To read his later description of his attitudes towards punishment, see Djemal Pasha, *Memoirs of a Turkish Statesman*, for example p. 219. 'I am certain that to the executions in April 1916, alone, do we owe the fact that there was no rising in Syria during the two and half years following Sherif Hussein's declaration of independence.'

30 Yazdi, *Blessings Beyond Measure*, pp. 24–5. Jamal Pasha claimed the opposite: 'As I knew that one of the most effective ways of pleasing the Arabs was to avoid requisitioning anything from them and pay for what we wanted cash down, the first order I issued on my arrival was that nothing should be taken by way of requisition from the civil population of Syria and Palestine in the 4th Army area. Prompt cash was to be paid for everything of any description whatever food, equipment or clothing' (*Memoirs of a Turkish Statesman*, p. 202).

31 Mú'ayyad, *Eight Years Near 'Abdu'l-Bahá*, pp. 199–200.

32 Balyuzi, *'Abdu'l-Bahá*, p. 412.

33 ibid. p. 413. See also Blomfield, *The Chosen Highway*, pp. 204–5, where an editor's footnote records that the description of this episode is translated from the Persian of Mírzá Jalál Iṣfahání (son-in-law of 'Abdu'l-Bahá, and son of the King of Martyrs).

34 Balyuzi, *'Abdu'l-Bahá*, p. 414. See also Shoghi Effendi (*God Passes By*, p. 304), who describes Jamal Pasha as 'the brutal, the all-powerful and unscrupulous Jamál Pá<u>sh</u>á, an inveterate enemy of the Faith through his own ill-founded suspicions and the instigation of its enemies'.

35 'Abdu'l-Bahá would spend some time visiting Tiberias in the Galilee where He would check the grain crops that had been planted by the Bahá'ís there under his supervision. He ensured that grain was stored in ancient pits the Romans had made centuries earlier. This foresight protected the people from famine and even was to feed some of the liberating troops.

36 Yazdi, *Blessings Beyond Measure*, p. 32. Bahá'í students at the Syrian Protestant College in Beirut, attended by Ali Yazdi and Shoghi Effendi, would spend their summer vacations in Haifa. 'There was an anteroom to the Shrine of the Báb that was assigned to them, and we spent very happy summers there. When I was in Haifa, I greatly enjoyed being with Shoghi Effendi and with them' (p. 55). Describing walking back from the business section he writes that all the streets were winding there, and the roads were dirt roads, not macadam: 'I remember it being very quiet in Haifa' (p. 25).

37 ibid, p. 32. It is yet unclear which particular commissioners were involved or what they were investigating.

38 Shoghi Effendi, *God Passes By*, p. 306.

39 See Tudor Pole, *Writing on the Ground*, p. 142. He writes he had first heard of the Bahá'í Faith in 1908 and had met 'Abdu'l-Bahá in 'Palestine, Egypt, Paris, London and Bristol' (pp. 140, 142). Tudor Pole served in intelligence first in Cairo, and later at Ludd (Lod), Jaffa and Jerusalem. He had obtained the information from the British espionage service (p. 152).

40 Yazdi, *Blessings Beyond Measure*, p. 40. For an account of Tudor Pole's final views on the Bahá'í Faith, see Weinberg, *Lady Blomfield*, p. 252.

41 Weinberg, *Lady Blomfield*, p. 187. This book has a comprehensive section on this topic, pp. 185–9.

42 See historic film footage of General Edmund Allenby entering Jerusalem on foot and reading the Jerusalem proclamation, 11 December 1917, available at: http://www.criticalpast.com/video/65675050558_Sir-Edmund-Allenby_World-War-I_Jerusalem-proclamation_Jaffa-Gate.
43 Weinberg, *Lady Blomfield*, pp. 187–9.
44 For a comprehensive account, see Maude and Maude, *The Servant, The General and Armageddon*, pp. 101–24.
45 See Preston, *The Desert Mounted Corps in Palestine and Syria 1917–1918.* A map is available at: http://1914-1918.invisionzone.com/forums/index.php?showtopic=166228. A plaque marking this site is at the top of Mount Carmel, just behind the Yefe Nof entrance to the Top Terrace. It is near the memorial commemorating the visit of the Kaiser in 1898.
46 Balyuzi, *'Abdu'l-Bahá,* p. 430. A photograph of the Jodhpur and Mysore Lancers entering Haifa is available at: http://1914-1918.invisionzone.com/forums/index.php?showtopic=83044, quoting Wavell, *Allenby: A Study in Greatness.* The Indian Army now marks 23 September (1918) as Haifa Day. A memorial in Delhi commemorates those who died on that day.
47 Blomfield, *The Chosen Highway* p. 220.
48 Storrs, *The Memoirs of Sir Ronald Storrs,* p. 337. He had formerly been oriental secretary to Lord Kitchener.
49 ibid. p. 70.
50 From Shoghi Effendi's diary, quoted in Khadem, *Prelude to the Guardianship*, pp. 50–51.
51 The German Consul was a Templer.
52 Latimer, *The Light of the World*, 'The Evening Meal, 24 November 1919'.
53 In Tiflis, Armenia, on 21 July 1922, while returning from another diplomatic mission to Moscow, Jamal Pasha was assassinated by Armenians, part of a campaign to avenge the Armenian massacres of World War I.
54 See Balyuzi, *'Abdu'l-Bahá*, p. 443.
55 Shoghi Effendi, Diary Letter, in *Star of the West,* vol. 9, no. 17 (19 January 1919), p. 195.

18. Post-war Gatherings at the Shrine of the Báb

1 The Master had given a 'short but thrilling' talk that morning to pilgrims and others at His residence in celebration of the Declaration of the Báb (according to the lunar calendar). Shoghi Effendi 'was privileged to chant some of the prayers revealed by Bahá'u'lláh in memory of the Supreme Declaration' (Shoghi Effendi's Diary, 6 January 1919, quoted in Khadem, *Prelude to the Guardianship,* pp. 34–5).
2 He did not know he would be appointed Guardian.
3 Shoghi Effendi's Diary, 6 January 1919, quoted in Khadem, *Prelude to the Guardianship*, p. 35.
4 ibid. 12 January 1919, quoted ibid. p. 40.
5 ibid, 15 January 1919, quoted ibid. p. 42.
6 Yazdi, *Blessings Beyond Measure*, p. 71.
7 They had met in Boston during 'Abdu'l-Bahá's visit there in 1912. For more on this remarkable Bahá'í, see Randall-Winckler, *William Henry Randall: Disciple of*

'Abdu'l-Bahá: see also Chapter 19 of this book.

8 The decorations on the door can still be seen today.

9 Ḥají Mírzá Ḥaydar-'Alí, known as the Angel of Carmel, the subject of *Stories from the Delight of Hearts.*

10 Anointing with rose water is not a ritual associated with the Shrine but was a pleasant custom of those days.

11 Referring to the threshold of the prayer room, not the inner Shrine.

12 See Annex 5.

13 Latimer, *The Light of the World.*

14 Genevieve Coy (1886–1963) was Director of the Tarbíyát Bahá'í school in Persia, and later served at Green Acre and as a Bahá'í pioneer to Rhodesia, now Zimbabwe.

15 This path was not particularly steep.

16 Now known as the Pilgrim House, which is to the east of the Shrine.

17 H. Emogene Hoagg was an early American Bahá'í. During 1900, 1913, 1914 and 1920 she lived and served in the household of 'Abdu'l-Bahá, sometimes for months at a time,

18 Rúḥí Afnán, grandson of 'Abdu'l-Bahá and cousin to Shoghi Effendi. He later broke the Covenant. See Taherzadeh, *The Covenant of Bahá'u'lláh*, pp. 358–60.

19 Lotfullah Hakim, member of the first Universal House of Justice, from 1963 to 1968.

20 Before Shoghi Effendi widened it into an arch.

21 Coy, 'A week in Abdul-Baha's home', in *Star of the West*, vol. 12, no. 10 (8 September 1921), p. 167; no. 11 (27 September 1921), pp. 179–81.

22 ibid. pp. 181–2.

23 ibid. no. 12 (16 October 1921), p. 198, describing the evening of 5 September 1920. The light was a lamp, not an electric light

24 ibid. no. 11 (27 September 1921), p. 188; no. 12 (16 October 1921), pp. 195–6.

25 To a gathering at the Shrine on Sunday, 4 January 1920, in *Star of the West*, vol. 13, no. 8 (November 1922), pp. 220–21. For previous recorded statements, see Chapter 13, p. 71, and Chapter 17, pp. 91–2.

26 Shoghi Effendi's Diary, 30 June 1919, quoted in Nakhjávání, *Shoghi Effendi: The Range and Power of His Pen*, pp. 21–2.

27 ibid. 4 March 1919, quoted ibid. pp. 23–4.

19. The Western Pilgrim House

1 See Bahá'í International Community, *Bahá'í Holy Places in Haifa and the Western Galilee.*

2 'Abdu'l-Bahá would often stay overnight in his room on the roof of the house of 'Abbás-Qulí next to the Shrine.

3 Coy, 'A week in Abdul-Baha's home', in *Star of the West*, vol. 12, no. 10 (8 September 1921), p. 166.

4 ibid. p. 165.

5 ibid. no. 12, p. 197.

6 ibid.

7 Ruhe, *Door of Hope*, p. 180.

8 Randall-Winckler, *William Henry Randall: Disciple of 'Abdu'l-Bahá*, p. 138.

9 ibid. pp. 54–5.
10 ibid. p. 163.
11 ibid. p. 172.
12 ibid. p. 188, Tablet of 'Abdu'l-Bahá to Harry Randall, 17 September 1920. Shoghi Effendi was later to name Harry as one of 19 Disciples of 'Abdu'l-Bahá (ibid. p. 258).
13 Izadinia, *The Major Opus*, p. 37.
14 ibid.
15 Cornelia Wortz, unpublished recollections, in Bahá'í World Centre Library.
16 In a conversation with the author on 17 May 2016, Bizhan Vahdat of Brisbane, Australia recalled Gerhard Bubeck's brother telling him this.
17 Peter Lange, archivist to the Templer Society, email to Fuad Izadinia, 5 May 2016.
18 Clara Klingeman (née Struve) in *Some Childhood Stories Remembered.*

20. Terraces and Lights

1 'Abdu'l-Bahá, *Muntakhabátí az Makátib-i-Ḥaḍrat-i-'Abdu'l-Bahá*, vol. 4, p. 15.
2 He was chair of Botany at Bombay University and planned a Bahá'í House of Worship in India; see Balyuzi, *'Abdu'l-Bahá*, p. 446.
3 'Abdu'l-Bahá also supported the similar Pro-Jerusalem Society, founded by Sir Ronald Storrs (Storrs, *Memoirs*, p. 328).
4 Dr Ciffrin may have worked on this project with Gottlieb Schumacher (1857–1925), the son of Templer Jacob Schumacher (email to author from Fuad Izadinia, 29 April 2016).
5 Geddes, 'Notes after a visit to Sir Abdul-Baha (Abbas Effendi)', in *Star of the West*, Vol. 12, No. 7 (13 July 1921), pp. 136–7, reprinted from *Bahai News* (Bombay); also quoted in Balyuzi, *'Abdu'l-Bahá*, pp. 446–8. The location of the school mentioned by Geddes is uncertain.
6 Here Sir Patrick acknowledges Abdu'l-Bahá's knighthood awarded by the British on 27 April 1920.
7 ibid.
8 Rabbani, *The Priceless Pearl*, p. 236.
9 Rutstein, *He Loved and Served*, p. 67.
10 Roy Wilhelm (1875–1951), was posthumously elevated to the rank of Hand of the Cause of God by Shoghi Effendi.
11 The Báb, *Selections from the Writings of the Báb*, p. 87. This verse was later to inspire Shoghi Effendi.
12 Known as 'Husayn the electrician', he had come from India. See Rutstein, *He Loved and Served*, p. 40.
13 1894–1970.
14 Rutstein, *He Loved and Served*, p. 47.
15 Audio interview with his daughter Carol Rutstein (née Kelsey) 2007. Available at: http://www.bahaipodcast.com/archives.asp?pYrID=2007.
16 Rutstein, *He Loved and Served*, p. 53.
17 ibid., photographs between pp. 64 and 65.
18 ibid. p. 85. For a photograph of Valeria Kelsey, see ibid. between pp. 17 and 18.
19 Words of 'Abdu'l-Bahá as recollected by Dr Zia Bagdadi, in Rohani, *Sweet and Enchanting Stories*, p. 115.

21. The Shrine Becomes the Tomb of 'Abdu'l-Bahá

1 However, the Templer children could sometimes be found there, seeking shelter from the summer sun while playing in the vicinity.

2 Where the first Bahá'í Temple had been erected. *Star of the West* reported: 'Jináb-i-Fádil tells of how the friends in Russia invited 'Abdu'l-Bahá to visit their city, how 'Abdu'l-Bahá accepted the invitation and then, before the journey was accomplished, departed from this world' (vol. 14, no. 9 (1923), p. 264). Shoghi Effendi's Diary for 17 July 1919 mentions the possibility of these journeys (quoted in Nakhjavání, *Shoghi Effendi: The Range and Power of His Pen*, pp. 22–3). China is not named in that list but is mentioned in *Star of the West*: 'One day on Mount Carmel Abdul Baha told of his plans to go to China in the days of his imprisonment and exile, of how he longed to travel to all nations in the service of the Kingdom . . . "Then I thought I might go to Kashgar, one of the provinces of China and a place not visited up to that time by any Bahai teacher. I was going to travel alone and with no baggage – only a handbag containing a number of tablets and books and papers and pens. I secured even my passport; the old Mofti stood as my guarantor . . ."' (vol. 13, no. 7 (October 1922), pp. 185–6). But He realized the Governor would have prevented Him from leaving on that journey, and so did not attempt it. Kashgar is a city in the Xinjiang Uyghur Autonomous Region, in China's far west.

3 Even though Bahá'ís are consoled by their belief in the afterlife, they see grief at the passing of loved ones as natural. With the passing of the Master, so loved and so loving, the grief was especially intense. A book that helps convey the loving nature of 'Abdu'l-Bahá, and His emphasis on the importance of loving one another, is Hogenson, *Lighting the Western Sky*.

4 Shoghi Effendi and Lady Blomfield, *The Passing of 'Abdu'l-Baha*, pp. 2–5. This account includes a range of indications that 'Abdu'l-Bahá was aware of His impending death. For example, in October 1921 He spoke to a Turkish friend, Dr Sulayman Rafat Bey, a guest, who had been told by cablegram of the sudden death of his brother. 'Abdu'l-Bahá comforted him: 'Sorrow not, for he is only transferred from this plane to a higher one. I too shall soon be transferred, for my days are numbered . . . And it will be in the days that are shortly to come' (p. 4). A daughter of the Master, Munavvar Khánum, wrote to Ruth Randall: 'The beloved Master knew exactly beforehand when he would leave us. The reason I know this so certainly is on account of a dream which he had about two weeks before the end (the dream was that BAHA'ULLAH appeared to him and said: "Destroy this room in which you are" the "room" being his blessed body), and also because he requested us to send for Shoghi Effendi to come back from Oxford, England, "for a very great and important reason," as he said. He also gave us many hints of his approaching departure' (*Star of the West*, vol. 12, no. 18 (7 February 1922), p. 275). See also Rabbani, *The Priceless Pearl*, p. 45, who relates that a few weeks before 'Abdu'l-Bahá died, He had directed that a cable be sent to Shoghi Effendi for him to return at once. A letter was written instead, and it arrived in England after the Master had passed away. A contrasting report comes from the pilgrim Louise Bosch, who wrote that the family had asked 'Abdu'l-Bahá 'if they should cable Shoghi Effendi to come, but Abdul-Baha said no, a letter would do' (*Star of the West*, vol. 12, no. 18 (7 February 1922), p. 279).

5 Quoted in Balyuzi, *'Abdu'l-Bahá*, p. 452.

6 *Star of the West*, vol. 13, no. 1 (21 March 1922), p. 22.
7 Shoghi Effendi and Lady Blomfield, *The Passing of 'Abdu'l-Baha*, p. 2; see also Shoghi Effendi, *God Passes By*, p. 311. For further information on Lady Blomfield at the time of the death of 'Abdu'l-Bahá, see Weinberg, *Lady Blomfield*, pp. 215–27.
8 Balyuzi, *'Abdu'l-Bahá*, p. 461.
9 Shoghi Effendi and Lady Blomfield, *The Passing of 'Abdu'l-Baha*, p. 7; see also letter from Munavvar Khánum to Ruth Wales Randall, 22 December 1921, in *Star of the West*, vol. 12, no. 18 (7 February 1922), p. 275.
10 Shoghi Effendi and Lady Blomfield, *The Passing of 'Abdu'l-Baha*, pp. 7–8.
11 See Ioas, 'Interview of Sachiro Fujita'. This doctor is not Dr Ḥabíb Mú'ayyad, the Bahá'í who had been sent by 'Abdu'l-Bahá to Beirut to study medicine, and who later became the Master's personal doctor, as well as attending the sick on His behalf. Louise Bosch wrote that He had malarial fever several days previously as well, and that at her urging, He had taken a homeopathic remedy she had provided (*Star of the West,* vol. 12, no. 18, (7 February 1922), p. 277. In his memoirs, Dr Mú'ayyad mentions that in earlier years the Master used quinine sulphate (Mú'ayyad, *Eight Years Near 'Abdu'l-Bahá*, p. 396).
12 Letter from Mohammed Said Adham, who writes that the bronchitis attack had lasted about three days (*Star of the West*, vol. 12, no. 19 (2 March 1922), p. 292).
13 Shoghi Effendi and Lady Blomfield, *The Passing of 'Abdu'l-Baha*, pp. 7–8; see also letters from Ethel Rosenberg, 8 December 1921, in *Star of the West*, vol. 12, no. 19, pp. 300-301. Weinberg, *Ethel Jenner Rosenberg*, p. 185, notes there are some small discrepancies between these two accounts.
14 Ethel Rosenberg quoted the Krugs as saying 8.30 p.m.
15 Dr Krug, once hostile to the Faith that had been adopted by his wife, became a Bahá'í after meeting 'Abdu'l-Bahá in New York in 1912. For an excellent profile, see Gail, *Arches of the Years*, pp. 106–7. Mohammed Said Adham's report in *Star of the West*, vol. 12, no. 19, p. 292 says that Dr Krug, who closed the Master's eyes following His passing, was so severely affected by grief that he 'did not speak, but sat by himself meditating and sobbing', and went to the Shrine where he would 'kneel and sob, bowing his forehead to the ground' and had to be helped to his feet.
16 Quoted in Weinberg, *Ethel Jenner Rosenberg*, p. 185.
17 *Star of the West*, vol. 12, no.18, p. 281.
18 Account by Louise Bosch, ibid. p. 277. Presumably Dr Habíb, the Christian Arab doctor, and perhaps Dr Florian Krug, the pilgrim from New York, had left those medicines. Louise Bosch also writes that Rúhá Khánum said that half an hour before His passing,'Abdu'l-Bahá said to her: 'I am dying' (ibid. p. 276).
19 Louise Bosch said that the daughters woke the Master's wife, Munírih Khánum, but it does not appear she reached his bedside before His passing (ibid. p. 277). See also Esslemont, *Bahá'u'lláh and the New Era*, p. 65.
20 Balyuzi, *'Abdu'l-Bahá*, p. 452.
21 Balyuzi, ibid. pp. 462–3 lists seven Westerners present, but Ethel Rosenberg was not there. She arrived on 2 December (Weinberg, *Ethel Jenner Rosenberg*, p. 182).
22 *Star of the West*, vol. 12, no. 19 (2 March 1922), p. 297. Johanna Hauff, a young

woman from a Bahá'í family in Stuttgart, later translated the writings and delivered Bahá'í talks in factories and workshops in Germany. She had received a Tablet from the Master (see 'Abdu'l-Bahá, *Selections from the Writings of 'Abdu'l-Bahá*, no. 28, p. 57).

23 *Star of the West*, vol. 12, no. 18, p. 277.

24 John and Louise Bosch in Gail, "Abdu'l-Bahá: Portrayals from East and West', in *World Order* (1971), vol. 6, no. 1, pp. 29–41; reprinted in Gail, *Dawn Over Mount Hira*, p. 211. Louise's account in *Star of the West*, vol. 12, no. 18, p. 278 differs slightly from her husband's. She wrote that Munírih Khánum held John's hand and Bahíyyih Khánum held hers. For some glimpses of the closeness of the Master and His wife, see Ma'ani, *Leaves of the Twin Divine Trees*, Chapter 12.

25 Gail, *Dawn Over Mount Hira*, pp. 211–12.

26 For a gripping account of the night of the passing and the drive to and from Bahjí, see Rutstein, *He Loved and Served*, pp. 94–7.

27 Rabbaní, *The Priceless Pearl*, p. 42; Weinberg, *Ethel Jenner Rosenberg*, p. 193.

28 Layla Ábádih'i, unpublished memoirs, quoting from 'Abbás-Qulí, in Ma'ani, *Leaves of The Twin Divine Trees*, p. 183.

29 There were the ordinary donations from believers in addition to those that arrived in response to the law of Ḥuqúq'u'lláh, and contributions from affluent Bahá'ís. In an email to the author on 30 April 2016, Fuad Izadinia comments: 'He was so generous that He could not keep money if He knew there were those who needed it. He commissioned Ḥájí Amín to give some of the funds on His behalf to those who he felt were needy, and there were so many orphans, so many wives of the martyrs who remained destitute, one being my own great-grandmother, who after the martyrdom of her husband, Ustád 'Abdu'r-Rahím Meshkibaf, in Yazd, used to receive five pounds each month and there were many similar.'

30 Ma'ani, *Leaves of Twin Divine Trees*, p. 339.

31 See Ruhe, *Door of Hope*. p. 149.

32 Recollections of John and Louise Bosch in Gail, "Abdu'l-Bahá: Portrayals from East and West'; reprinted in Gail, *Dawn Over Mount Hira*, p. 213.

33 *Star of the West*, vol. 12, no. 19, p. 297.

34 There is a report that a second ebony coffin, which accompanied the second sarcophagus, came to Haifa and was used for the Master (Ishráq Khávarí, *Qámús-i-Tawqí'-i 108 (BE)*, p. 84).

35 Remey, *Reminiscences and Letters*. p. 15. Mr Remey was not present at the funeral, but says he was given a sketch of the casket and attached a copy to his *Reminiscences and Letters*. It is not yet known if the coffin was especially built for 'Abdu'l-Bahá but Balyuzi writes that 'so hurriedly had the coffin been made that the lid could not be properly secured' (*'Abdu'l-Bahá*, p. 464).

36 *Star of the West*, vol. 12, no. 19, p. 297.

37 Momen, *The Bábí and Bahá'í Religions 1844–1944*, p. 348. See also Shoghi Effendi, *God Passes By*, p. 312. In his letter to Churchill, Lamington wrote, 'In his death I lose a cherished friend' (ibid.). Herbert Louis Samuel, 1st Viscount Samuel (1870–1963) was High Commissioner to Palestine 1920–1925. See http://www.jewishvirtuallibrary.org/jsource/biography/samuel.html.

38 *Star of the West*, vol. 12, no. 19, p. 292; Momen, *The Bábí and Bahá'í Religions*, p. 340. A fluent speaker of Arabic who had learned the language from Professor E.

G. Browne, the English orientalist who had met Bahá'u'lláh, Sir Ronald Storrs had met 'Abdu'l-Bahá in Acre, and in Egypt introduced him to Lord Kitchener; he was also among the first to visit the Master in Haifa when British troops entered it during World War I (see Balyuzi, *'Abdu'l-Bahá*, p. 139). He delivered a speech at the opening of the Bahá'í Centenary Exhibition in London on 20 May 1944 (*Bahá'í World*, vol. X, pp. 188–195). Sir Ronald said 'Abdu'l-Bahá visited him in Jerusalem, but it appears he was mistaken; see Rabbani, *The Priceless Pearl*: 'from 1868, when He arrived in 'Akká, until His death in 1921, 'Abdu'l-Bahá never set foot in Jerusalem' (p. 275).

39 Recollections of John and Louise Bosch in Gail,"Abdu'l-Bahá: Portrayals from East and West'; see Gail, *Dawn Over Mount Hira*, p. 213.

40 *Star of the West*, vol. 12, no. 19, p. 297. Louise Bosch, wrote: 'The sons-in–law and the grandsons and the six Persian pilgrims from Persia, and all the other Persians who had been like courtiers at the court of Abdul-Baha, were all busy and engaged with preparations for the interment . . .' (ibid. vol. 18, no. 12, p. 278).

41 Recollections of John and Louise Bosch in Gail,"Abdu'l-Bahá: Portrayals from East and West'; reprinted in Gail, *Dawn Over Mount Hira*, p. 213.

42 Email to the author, 27 January 2014.

43 *Star of the West*, vol. 12, no. 19, p. 297.

44 Mohammed Said Adham, in *Star of the West*, vol. 12, no. 19, p. 293; Rutstein, *He Loved and Served*, p. 99.

45 Johanna Hautz, in *Star of the West*, vol. 12, no. 19, p. 297.

46 Shoghi Effendi, *God Passes By*, p. 312. The staggering figure of 10,000 is also cited by Clara Klingeman in *Some Childhood Stories Remembered*. The official census undertaken in 1922 found the population of Haifa to be 24,634. See Seikaly, *Haifa: Transformation of an Arab Society 1918–1939*. 'Participated' does not necessarily mean that all 10,000 actually visited the Bahá'í property surrounding the Shrine.

47 Mohammad Said Adham, in *Star of the West*, vol. 12, no. 19, p. 292.

48 Shoghi Effendi, *God Passes By*, p. 313; Shoghi Effendi and Lady Blomfield, *The Passing of 'Abdu'l-Baha*, p. 10.

49 Redman, *Shoghi Effendi Through the Pilgrim's Eye*, vol. 1, p. 9, quoting materials from John and Louise Bosch in the US Bahá'í National Archives.

50 Lieutenant Colonel Sir George Stewart Symes (1882–1962) was a British Army officer who served as Governor of the Palestine North District from 1920 to 1925 (Governor of Phoenicia), and Chief Secretary to the Government of Palestine from 1925 to 1928. He was later Governor-General of the Sudan.

51 Shoghi Effendi, *God Passes By*, p. 313; Shoghi Effendi and Lady Blomfield, *The Passing of 'Abdu'l-Baha*, p. 10.

52 Email from Templer archivist Peter Lange, the great-grandson of Friedrich Lange, the head of the Templer community in 1921, to Fuad Izadinia, 5 May 2016. 'In the . . . report of Clara Klingeman it says that the heads of all religious associations participated in this cortège. There is no mention of a Templer name, but I am pretty sure that the Community Head of the German Colony was among them (in 1921 my great-grandfather Friedrich Lange was Community Head). Clara's report clearly shows that all Haifa was on their feet to participate in the funeral. For me it is obvious that the Templers of Haifa were among the

crowd, because they had seen 'Abdu'l-Bahá so many times walking through their Colony and had revered him.'

The first encounter of the Templers with the Master had been on 2 June 1871 when the leader of the Templers, Georg David Hardegg, met the Master in Acre. Mr Hardegg wrote: 'At the beginning, I told Abbas Effendi, if meeting me would cause inconvenience on the part of the authorities, I would leave it up to him to cancel the meeting. Upon which, he said there was a proverb in Persian: there is nothing beyond the colour black. In other words, after so much suffering, nothing could get any worse.' Mr Hardegg said he hoped and expected the German Kaiser would exert his influence in favour of spreading justice and freedom of conscience in the Orient (presumably, a hope that he would help free 'Abdu'l-Bahá). Mr Hardegg said that in Haifa there were several Persians who made their living as metal and wood workers: 'They are conspicuous by their open and friendly faces and their Persian attire.' He mentioned they were followers of 'Baha Allah' and that about 80 followers were confined by the Ottoman Government in Acre (Hardegg, in *Suddeutsche Warte*, weekly magazine of the Templers, 20 July 1871, translated by Martha Otto; report provided by Peter Lange, Templer society archivist).

'Abdu'l-Bahá is recorded as having said: 'Mr Hardegg is a friend of mine. When I was imprisoned, he visited me. At that time I was not allowed to leave Acre. Mr Hardegg always showed me a lot of love. He was the link between me and the Germans.' The Master is also reported to have smiled and nodded at a German coachman who went between Haifa and Acre, and would stand in the street opposite 'Abdu'l-Bahá's house and gave Him a smile as a greeting. The coachman's superiors at that time would not let Him visit the Master, and the rules for prisoners were such that he could not speak with Him (Gollmer, *Mein Herz ist bei Euch)*.

53 Persian Street was called by the Templers Persestrasse, now Haparsim. Weinstrasse (Vine Street), is now Hagefen, which means 'grapevine' in Hebrew. Some Templers had their homes and vineyards along Weinstrasse. Information on the names the German Templers gave to streets was graciously provided by Templer archivist, Peter Lange, who also advised that what is now Ben Gurion Avenue had been called by the Templers 'Koloniestrasse' (Colony Street) and was later changed by the British to Carmel Avenue (email from Peter Lange to Fuad Izadinia, 17 May 2016).

The cortège would not have crossed Hagefen and gone on to Abbas Street and then turned left to Mountain Road. As Mr 'Alí Nakhjavání wrote in an email to Fuad Izadinia on 16 May 2016: 'The stretch of road [up] from Hagefen . . . was and still is very, very steep. In my early years in Haifa, this stretch was rough and deeply dusty. It was tarmacked very much later. I rather doubt that the cortège would have taken that route. I had never heard of this.'

54 Named at some stage after 'Abbás Effendi ('Abdu'l-Bahá). "Abbás' means 'lion' in Arabic.

55 Klingeman, *Some Childhood Stories Remembered.*

56 One anecdote that records His contribution: 'In the afternoon some friends had tea in the company of 'Abdu'l-Bahá. He said, "Bring my overcoat so we can walk to the Shrine of the Báb." A number of friends accompanied him. His carriage

followed behind. En route, he rested in two places . . . Upon reaching a bend in the road, he spoke of the benefits of paved roads, noting, "This is indeed an amazing mountain and now it has good roads as well." (He meant that the large boulders had been removed.) . . . The group reached a particular spot, and 'Abdu'l-Bahá said, "I purchased this parcel of land in order to make the road wider. The wretched Matran [the Metropolitan of the Assyrian Church, a fierce enemy of 'Abdu'l-Bahá] seized it and fenced it with a wall; but now he has lost that as well."' (Ahang Rabbani (trans.), 'Abdu'l-Bahá in Abú-Sinan', from Mú'ayyad, *Eight Years Near 'Abdu'l-Bahá*, pp. 247–8, where the same translator has provided a slightly different version).

57 Shoghi Effendi and Lady Blomfield, *The Passing of 'Abdu'l-Baha*, p. 10.

58 Rutstein, *He Loved and Served*, p. 98.

59 See photographs in *Star of the West*, vol. 12, no. 19, pp. 200–298.

60 Shoghi Effendi and Lady Blomfield, *The Passing of 'Abdu'l-Baha*, p. 10; Mohammed Said Adham, in *Star of the West*, vol. 12, no. 19, p. 293, says one hour and twenty-five minutes.

61 A photograph graciously provided to the author by the US Bahá'í National Archives shows the stone wall about a metre higher than the roof top so the viewers had to lean on the wall.

62 See Balyuzi, *'Abdu'l-Bahá*, pp. 466–72.

63 ibid. p. 469.

64 ibid. p. 470. Louise Bosch seems to identify him as a newspaper correspondent (*Star of the West*, vol. 12, no. 18, p. 282). The translation given here is not the resumé in Balyuzi, *'Abdu'l-Bahá*, pp. 471–2, but a more literal translation of M. Bouzaglo's eulogy, published in *World Order*, vol. 6, no. 1 (Fall 1971), pp. 6–18; available at http://bahai-library.com/shoghieffendi_blomfield_passing_abdulbaha.

65 Rabbaní, *The Priceless Pearl*, p. 276.

66 Johanna Hauff described the eulogies as 'all by non-Baha'is who knew little of his teachings' (*Star of the West*, vol. 12, no. 19 p. 298). Mohammed Said Adham wrote: 'The speakers were all strangers – not Bahais, as the Bahais could only weep on this occasion' (ibid. p. 293).

67 Described as 'the first Jewish ruler of Palestine since Hyrcanus II, that last degenerate Maccabean, stepped ashore'. Bowle, *Viscount Samuel: A Biography*, p. 195.

68 Mohammed Said Adham, in *Star of the West*, vol. 12, no. 19, p. 293.

69 Samuel, *A Lifetime in Jerusalem*, pp. 18–19. In this book, Edwin, a son of Sir Herbert, and himself the second Viscount Samuel, writes: 'After the termination of his five years of office, he dreamed of establishing himself on Mount Carmel as a private citizen, and to concentrate on his philosophical writings.' He was prevailed upon to abandon his plan; 'Mount Carmel was, however, to form part of his title when he became a peer.' On pp. 4–6, Edwin Samuel writes that his father had a temperament 'more equable than that of anybody else I have ever known . . . rational in his thinking and well-balanced . . . a gentleman of the old school . . . his chuckle was infectious, his laughter hearty'. He was 'proud of being Jewish' and maintained 'the basic rules of Kashrut'. He attended the synagogue and did not work or travel on the Sabbath.

70 Shoghi Effendi, *God Passes By*, p. 312.

71 Shoghi Effendi refers only to 'one of the chambers of the Shrine' (ibid. p. 313). A photograph obtained by the author shows the coffin being carried into the north-east chamber.
72 This photograph has yet to be found.
73 Curtis Kelsey, audiotape, number 18317, recorded in Denver, Colorado, United States on 24 February 1962. Letter 18 April 1980 to Audio Visual Department, Bahá'í World Centre from William Richter, Ansar Associates, 1640 Holcomb Road, Victor, New York 14564.
74 See Modarres, *Táríkh-i Amr-i Bahá'í dar Najaf-Ábád.*
75 Rutstein, *He Loved and Served*, p. 100. In that book it is said the question was asked on the day before 'Abdu'l-Bahá died, but Raḥmatu'lláh, 31 years after the event, recalled that it happened eight days before the passing of the Master.
76 'In Mason Remey's diaries it is mentioned that the Shrine of the Master will be moved. Shoghi Effendi one day asked Mason Remey, as he was going around the Bay to 'Akká, to find a suitable spot between Haifa and 'Akká. This he did, following his instructions to look for an elevated spot in that sandy area' (interview with Mr 'Alí Nakhjavání by Andrew Blake, 15 July 2003). The present author recalls seeing, but has yet to relocate, a photograph of the site marked with a circle and a star on the ground.
77 Remey, *Reminiscences and Letters*, p. 12. It remains unclear as to which floor is being referred to. There remained an entrance in the south-east room of the Shrine, used in 1909, so major work was not needed to be done on the floor to take the casket down.
78 Ibid.
79 Balyuzi, *'Abdu'l-Bahá*, p. 464.
80 Letter from Ethel Rosenberg, 8 December 1921, in *Star of the West,* vol. 12, no. 19, p. 301. For more on her at the time of the death of 'Abdu'l-Bahá, see Weinberg, *Ethel Jenner Rosenberg*, pp. 181–200.
81 Weinberg, *Ethel Jenner Rosenberg*, p. 183.
82 Khadem, *Prelude to the Guardianship*, p. 202.
83 Rabbaní, *The Priceless Pearl*, p. 39.
84 ibid, p. 44.
85 ibid. p. 43.
86 Madame Ruḥíyyih Rabbání (1910–2000) was how she was known publicly, but to Bahá'ís as Amatu'l-Bahá Ruḥíyyih Khánum, a title given her by Shoghi Effendi. Born Mary Maxwell, she was a toddler when 'Abdu'l-Bahá stayed in her parents' home on His visit to Canada.
87 Amatu'l-Bahá Ruḥíyyih Khánum, 'Tribute to Shoghi Effendi', in *Bahá'í News,* May 1958.
88 Rabbaní, *The Priceless Pearl*, p. 46.
89 Quoted in Shoghi Effendi, *God Passes By*, pp. 313–14.
90 Perhaps the beautiful Tablet of Visitation for 'Abdu'l-Bahá, a prayer by the Master Himself; see Appendix 5.
91 Redman, *Shoghi Effendi Through the Pilgrim's Eye*, vol. 1, p. 16. 'Abdu'l-Bahá had much appreciated this hymn when sung by Lua Getsinger. She 'sang well, and whenever she sang the famous hymn, "Nearer my God to Thee", her gaze directed towards the Shrine of Bahá'u'lláh, it brought tears to the eyes of 'Abdu'l-Bahá'

(Balyuzi, *'Abdu'l-Bahá*, p. 97). Among the lyrics: 'Though like the wanderer, the sun gone down, Darkness be over me, my rest a stone; Yet in my dreams I'd be nearer, my God, to Thee . . .'

92 Shoghi Effendi, *God Passes By*, p. 314. He was later to pen this exquisite portrait of the Master: 'He is, and should for all time be regarded, first and foremost, as the Center and Pivot of Bahá'u'lláh's peerless and all-enfolding Covenant, His most exalted handiwork, the stainless Mirror of His light, the perfect Exemplar of His teachings, the unerring Interpreter of His Word, the embodiment of every Bahá'í ideal, the incarnation of every Bahá'í virtue, the Most Mighty Branch sprung from the Ancient Root, the Limb of the Law of God, the Being "round Whom all names revolve," the Mainspring of the Oneness of Humanity, the Ensign of the Most Great Peace, the Moon of the Central Orb of this most holy Dispensation – styles and titles that are implicit and find their truest, their highest and fairest expression in the magic name 'Abdu'l-Bahá. He is, above and beyond these appellations, the "Mystery of God" – an expression by which Bahá'u'lláh Himself has chosen to designate Him, and which, while it does not by any means justify us to assign to Him the station of Prophethood, indicates how in the person of 'Abdu'l-Bahá the incompatible characteristics of a human nature and superhuman knowledge and perfection have been blended and are completely harmonized' (Shoghi Effendi, *The World Order of Bahá'u'lláh*, p. 134).

93 Letter from Shoghi Effendi, quoted in Rabbaní, *The Priceless Pearl*, p. 46.

94 Sylvia Ioas, interview of Sachiro Fujita, 1965; also quoted in Redman, *Shoghi Effendi Through the Pilgrim's Eye*, vol. 1, p. 17.

Appendix 1: The Báb

1 A holy place for Shi'ah Muslims. It was where the martyrdom of Imám Ḥusayn took place and His Shrine is located. Bahá'u'lláh identified Himself with the Imám Ḥusayn (*Gleanings from the Writings of Bahá'u'lláh*, XXXIX, p. 89).

2 For a biography of Bahá'u'lláh, see Balyuzi, *Bahá'u'lláh, the King of Glory*; Momen, *Bahá'u'lláh: A Short Biography.*

3 The Crown Prince, Náṣiri'd-i-Dín Mírzá (1831–96) was 17 years old and had recently been made Governor of Azerbaijan. See Balyuzi. *The Báb*, p. 140. He ruled as Shah from 1848–96. He was assassinated while praying in a Shrine near where the Báb's sacred remains had once been concealed.

4 Mírzá Muḥammad-'Alíy-i-Zunúzí, surnamed Anis. See Shoghi Effendi, *God Passes By*, p. 52.

5 Balyuzi, *The* Báb, pp. 161–2. Mr Balyuzi (1908–80) was a relative of the Báb and was elevated to the spiritually high rank of Hand of the Cause of God by Shoghi Effendi.

6 Lord Curzon, *Persia and the Persian Question*, vol. 1, pp. 452–5, as cited in *The Dawn-Breakers,* pp. xlvii–xlviii.

7 'Abdu'l-Bahá, *Some Answered Questions*, no. 37, p. 165.

8 ibid. p. 167.

9 Such as Krishna, Buddha, Zoroaster, Abraham, Moses, Christ, Muhammad, the Báb and Bahá'u'lláh.

10 The term martyr refers to one who bears witness to the truth of their faith by

being willing not to recant but, if necessary, sacrifice their life in its path. It does not have the modern meaning associated with fanaticism, terrorism or holy war.

11 'Abdu'l-Bahá, *Some Answered Questions*, no. 40, p. 180.

12 Bahá'u'lláh, *Gleanings from the Writings of Bahá'u'lláh*, XXII, pp. 51–2. See also pp. 54–5: 'Were any of the all-embracing Manifestations of God to declare: "I am God," He, verily speaketh the truth, and no doubt attacheth thereto. For it hath been repeatedly demonstrated that through their Revelation, their attributes and names, the Revelation of God, His names and His attributes, are made manifest in the world . . . And were they all to proclaim, "I am the Seal of the Prophets," they, verily, utter but the truth, beyond the faintest shadow of doubt. For they are all but one person, one soul, one spirit, one being, one revelation. They are all the manifestation of the "Beginning" and the "End," the "First" and the "Last," the "Seen" and the "Hidden" – all of which pertain to Him Who is the Innermost Spirit of Spirits and Eternal Essence of Essences. And were they to say, "We are the Servants of God," this also is a manifest and indisputable fact. For they have been made manifest in the uttermost state of servitude, a servitude the like of which no man can possibly attain.'

13 Shoghi Effendi, *God Passes By*, p. 58.

14 *The Dawn-Breakers*, p. 315.

15 Bahá'u'lláh, *Prayers and Meditations*, p. 84.

16 Shoghi Effendi, *God Passes By*, p. 57. See also 'Abdu'l-Bahá, *Some Answered Questions*, no. 8, pp. 30–31.

17 ibid. pp. 56–7.

18 M. Mochenin, a student at St Petersburg University and later Dragoman of the Russian Consulate-General in Tabriz, appears to have seen the Báb addressing people in Chihriq, but he does not describe Him. He says there were so many people that the place the Báb was speaking could not contain all the people and most 'remained in the road and listened, engrossed, to the new Qur'án' (Momen, *The Bábí and Bahá'í Religions*, 1844–1944, p. 75).

19 Dr Cormick had been seconded as a physician to the Crown Prince, Náṣiri'd-i-Din Mírzá, and accompanied the royal party when the Prince was appointed Governor of Azerbaijan, the capital of which was Tabriz. See Flannery, 'Dr. William Cormick', p. 8.

20 For the text of his report, see Momen, *The Bábí and Bahá'í Religions, 1844–1944*, pp. 74–5.

21 A question has been raised as to whether Dr Cormick gave his account to Rev. J. H. Shedd; see Flannery, 'Dr. William Cormick', p. 19.

22 His wife, Tamar Daoudian, was the daughter of a general in the Persian army; see McNamara, 'The man who met the Báb'. For more information, see Flannery, 'Dr William Cormick'.

23 Shoghi Effendi, *God Passes By*, p. 52.

24 Momen, *The Bábí and Bahá'í Religions, 1844–1944*, p. 75.

25 Sheil, *Glimpses of Life and Manners in Persia*, p. 178. Lady Sheil was also from an Irish background and so had that in common with Dr Cormick. They would have known each other from the time six years earlier when Dr Cormick began his Persian medical career in Tehran at a time when Lady Sheil's husband was a British diplomat there.

26 The first one to believe in the Báb as a Manifestation of God was His wife.
27 See Balyuzi, *The Báb*, pp. 17–22.
28 *The Dawn-Breakers*, p. 53.
29 A descendant of the Prophet Muḥammad.
30 *The Dawn-Breakers*, pp. 61–3 passim.
31 ibid. p. 65.
32 ibid. p. 66.
33 The Prime Minister of Persia, Ḥájí Mírzá Áqásí, who ordered the imprisonment of the Báb in Maku, was born there.
34 *The Dawn-Breakers*, p. 249.
35 Shoghi Effendi, *God Passes By*, p. 19.
36 Description by Siyyid Ḥusayn in *The Dawn-Breakers*, pp. 246–8.
37 ibid.
38 ibid.
39 Shoghi Effendi, *God Passes By*, p. 37.
40 Ṭáhirih and Qurratu'l-'Ayn are both titles of Fatimah Baraghani (1814–52).
41 See the accounts in *The Dawn-Breakers*.
42 Quoted in Momen, *The Bábí and Bahá'í Religions, 1844–1944*, p. 73.
43 ibid. p. 74, quoting Adams, *Persia by a Persian*, p. 456. Also available at: http://bahai-library.com/adams_bab_babism.
44 Dunbar, *Forces of Our Time: The Dynamics of Light and Darkness*, p. 4.
45 Quoted in Momen, *The Bábí and Bahá'í Religions, 1844–1944*, p. 69.
46 ibid; see also p. 4. For *The Times*' and other reports on persecutions, see pp. 132–6.
47 ibid. p. 4. The report appeared in the *Eclectic Magazine* (published in New York and Philadelphia) and in the *Port Phillip Herald* (published in Melbourne).
48 ibid.
49 ibid. p. 5.
50 ibid. p. 11; citing *Gazzetta Uffiziale di Venezia*, 12 September 1850.

Appendix 2: The Spiritual Significance of the Shrine

1 For the full text of the Tablet, see Annex 4, and Bahá'u'lláh, *Gleanings from the Writings of Bahá'u'lláh*, XI, pp. 14–17.
2 Shoghi Effendi, *Citadel of Faith*, p. 85; also quoted in Rabbani, *The Priceless Pearl*, p. 247.
3 Rabbani, *The Priceless Pearl*, p. 247.
4 Written in 1951.
5 The superstructure, a project of Shoghi Effendi following the guidance of 'Abdu'l-Bahá, was completed in 1953.
6 Shoghi Effendi, *Citadel of Faith*, p. 95.
7 Concourse on high: a Bahá'í term for the gathering of God's prophets, and His holy and chosen souls.
8 Shoghi Effendi, *Citadel of Faith*, p. 96.
9 ibid.
10 Quoted in the Universal House of Justice, *Synopsis and Codification of the Kitáb-i-Aqdas*, p. 61.
11 See Chapman, *Leroy Ioas*, p. 163.

12 Except on certain formal occasions.
13 Local Bahá'í administrative institutions.
14 From a letter written by Shoghi Effendi, available at: https://bahai.bwc.org/pilgrimage/Intro/quote_1.asp.
15 ibid.
16 See https://bahai.bwc.org/pilgrimage/. Bahá'ís may visit the Bahá'í World Centre only upon receiving an invitation from the Universal House of Justice. This is usually arranged via a request from the Bahá'í for a visit (normally three days) or a pilgrimage (nine days). The immediate families of Bahá'ís serving as staff members at the Bahá'í World Centre may visit when time permits.
17 Bahá'u'lláh, *Gleanings from the Writings of Bahá'u'lláh*, XI, p. 16.
18 For the full texts see Annex 5.
19 White, *Notes Postmarked The Mountain of God.*
20 Bahá'u'lláh, *Epistle to the Son of the Wolf*, p. 33.

Appendix 3: The Holy Land and Mount Carmel

1 Bahá'u'lláh.
2 Shoghi Effendi, *God Passes By*, p. 183.
3 Qiblih: Term meaning point of adoration, to which believers turn when saying their daily obligatory prayer.
4 Shoghi Effendi, *Citadel of Faith*, p. 96.
5 The name Mount Carmel is often used by others to refer to the entire 39-kilometre-long mountain range stretching back to the south-east.
6 A culture that existed from 13,000 to 11,000 BC in the Levant in the Eastern Mediterranean.
7 UNESCO: 'Sites of human evolution at Mount Carmel: The Nahal Me'arot/ Wadi el-Mughara Caves'; see also Sharon Udasin, 'Four Mount Carmel caves nominated to join UNESCO', in *The Jerusalem Post*, 29 June 2012.
8 See www/bahaipr.org/terraces/carmel; also Wikipedia, at http://en.wikipedia.org/wiki/Mount_Carmel#cite_note-J_Enc-2.
9 I Kings 18.
10 Ruhe, *Door of Hope*, pp. 187–9.
11 A monotheistic faith found in Israel and surrounding countries.
12 Isa. 2:2–5 (King James Version). See for example Taherzadeh, *The Revelation of Bahá'u'lláh*, vol. 4, p. 361.
13 Translation by Dr Vahid Rafati, quoted in Izadinia, *The Major Opus.*
14 For the full text see Annex 4.
15 Bahá'u'lláh, *Epistle to the Son of the Wolf*, p. 145.
16 'Abdu'l-Bahá, quoted in 'Mount Carmel, the Vineyard of God', in *Star of the West*, vol. 14, no. 5 (August 1923), pp. 148–9.
17 'Abdu'l-Bahá, in Zikrullah Khadem: 'Carmel: The Mountain of God and the Tablet of Carmel', pp. 279–80.
18 ibid. p. 280, from Mú'ayyad, *Khâṭirát-i-Ḥabíb*, pp. 19, 21, 22, 53. 'Abdu'l-Bahá is reported to have made these statements in 1907.
19 Grundy, *Ten Days in the Light of 'Akká*, p. 8. 'Abdu'l-Bahá stayed in a building near the cave of Elijah, and it is not certain if Ms Grundy's reference is to another place.

20 Shoghi Effendi, *God Passes By*, p. 277.
21 Shoghi Effendi, *Citadel of Faith*, p. 96.
22 Shoghi Effendi, *God Passes By*, p. 194.
23 A future Bahá'í Temple, lit. dawning-place of the mention of God.
24 Letter from Shoghi Effendi to the National Spiritual Assembly of the Bahá'ís of the United States and Canada, 21 December 1939, in Shoghi Effendi, *Messages to America*, pp. 32–3.
25 Zikrullah Khadem: 'Carmel: The Mountain of God and the Tablet of Carmel', p. 291.
26 ibid. p. 297. Mr Khadem writes: 'While walking in the mountains, waving his hand, he [Shoghi Effendi] said that it means "The Laws of God will flow from Thee, O Mount Carmel, to the world and its inhabitants."' See also Taherzadeh, *The Revelation of Bahá'u'lláh*, vol. 4, p. 361.
27 ibid. pp. 297–8.
28 Quoted ibid. pp. 282–3, translated by the Universal House of Justice.

Appendix 4: The Tablet of Carmel

1 Bahá'u'lláh, *Gleanings from the Wiritings of Bahá'u'lláh*, XI, pp. 14–17.

Appendix 5: Tablets of Visitation

1 From *Bahá'í Prayers*, pp. 230–35.

INDEX

Ábádih'í, Layla 211, 212
Abbás-'Alí Kazeruni, Ghulam Ḥusayn 199
Abbas Effendi *see* 'Abdu'l-Bahá
'Abbás-Qulí 74-5, 76, 79, 108-9, 112, 124, 125, 128, 132, 207, 212, 219
Abbas Street, Haifa 127, 225
'Abdu'l-Aẓím, Shrine 10-12
'Abdu'l-Azíz, Sultan 157
'Abdu'l-Bahá 186-7, 228
  and Bahá'u'lláh 18-19, 80, 186-7, 189
  and Commission of Inquiry 54-8, 98, 204-5
  imprisonment 13, 25, 52-3, 55, 62-3, 66, 70- 72-4
  in Acre 25, 26, 44, 46, 52, 56-7, 61, 66, 69, 72, 77, 88, 90, 93, 100, 101, 164, 190, 203, 204, 205, 224, 225
  in Haifa 13, 27, 42, 44, 45, 50, 53, 77-82, 88, 90, 98-101, 102, 111, 113-14
  journey to the West 88-91, 202, 214, 227
  life and character 17, 23, 41-2, 56, 72-4, 79-81, 86, 90-91, 103, 104-9, 111, 113-14, 134, 164, 200-01, 202, 221, 225, 228
    eulogies of 128-31
  passing and funeral 123-32, 221-3, 225
  responsibilities as Head of the Bahá'í Faith 20, 25, 80, 83, 186-7, 215
  and Shoghi Effendi 24-5, 83-4, 103, 121, 133, 158, 214, 215, 221, 228
  Shrine (of 'Abdu'l-Bahá) 131-4, 154
  and Shrine of the Báb 23, 35, 41, 50, 65-6, 74-5, 77-83, 91, 97-8, 102-10, 116-19, 124-5, 126-34, 162, 216, 226
  talks and reported words 64, 69-71, 87-8, 91-2, 94, 100-01, 102, 109-10 115, 118, 138-9, 163-4, 192-3, 197, 199, 202, 214, 216, 221, 226
  and Templers 14, 42, 112-13, 225
  in World War I 93-101, 217
  Writings 29, 54-8, 64-5, 72-4, 81-2, 120-21, 140, 158, 163-4, 195, 199, 202, 207, 210, 212, 215
    A Traveler's Narrative 184, 185, 187
    Memorials of the Faithful 193, 196, 211
    Tablet of Visitation 172
    Tablets of the Divine Plan 94-5, 209, 216
    Will and Testament 133-4, 209
  see also Báb, Pilgrim House, sarcophagus, Shrine of the Báb
'Abdu'l-Ḥusayn Mírzá (Farmanfarma) 194-5
'Abdu'l-Hamid II, Sultan 20, 25, 46, 51, 52-3, 58, 72, 96, 203
'Abdu'l-Karím, Ustád 43, 62, 65, 211, 213
'Abdu'l-Karím-i-Qazvíní, Mírzá (Mírzá Aḥmad) 6, 186
'Abdullah Arab 78, 79
'Abdu'lláh Páshá, House of 53, 88, 197
'Abdu'l-Razzaq Tabrízí, Áqá 30
Abraham 67, 157, 163, 229
Abu'l-Faḍl, Mírzá 63, 65
Abu'l-Ḥasan-i-Ardikání (Amín-i-Iláhi, Ḥájí Amín) 62-3, 65, 206, 223
Abu-Sinan village 93, 226
Abú-Ṭálib-i-Karimoff, Mullá 43, 201
Abyad, Elyas 18
Acre (Akka, St Jean d'Acre)
  and 'Abdu'l-Bahá *see* 'Abdu'l-Bahá
  and Bahá'u'lláh *see* Bahá'u'lláh
  city of 13, 14, 25, 26, 30, 41, 65, 84, 86, 104, 153, 188, 200, 206
  future of 70, 91-2, 132, 163, 208, 227
  Governor of 46, 53, 55, 202
  pilgrims to 16, 29, 31, 34, 44, 52, 55, 63, 88, 97, 138, 196, 201
and remains of the Báb *see* Báb
  in World War I 93, 99, 101
Adams, Rev. Dr Isaac 148
Adhirbáyján *see* Azerbaijan
Adonis 160
Adrianople (Edirne) 10, 13, 92, 157, 204, 216
Afnán, Mírzá Muḥammad-Báqir 62, 206
Afnán, Mírzá Muḥsín 40, 111
Afnán, Rúhí 106-8, 219
Afroukhteh, Youness *see* Yúnis Khán
Aḥmad Al-Aḥsá'í, Shaykh 185
Aḥmad Míláni, Ḥájí 5, 9, 185
Ahab 159
Ahaziah 159
Ahmadiyya community 161
Alexandria, Egypt 13, 64, 214
'Alí-Akbar-i-Shahmírzádí (Ḥájí Ákhund) 10-12, 15, 63, 187
'Alí-Ashraf Láhijání, Mírzá ('Andalíb) 86, 213
'Alí-Ashraf, Ustád Áqá 43, 62, 65, 213
'Alí-'Askar, Ḥájí 30, 184, 193
Ali Ferruh Bey 51
'Alí Khán 146-7
Ali-Kuli Khan 40, 51, 203, 207
'Alíy-i- Basṭámí, Mullá 196
Alkan, Necati 204, 205
al-Khaṭíb, Shaykh Yúnus 129
al-Khaṭíb, Yúsuf 128
Alláh-Yár, Ḥájí 5

Allenby Street, Haifa 189
Allenby, General Sir Edmund 99-100. 125-6, 218
American University (Syrian Protestant College), Beirut 34, 217
Amín Effendi 202
Amínu'l-Bayán *see* Sháh Muḥammad-i-Manshádí
'Andalíb 86 *see* 'Alí-Ashraf Láhijání
Anís (Mírzá Muḥammad-'Alí-i-Zunúzí) 3-5, 136, 183, 185
Apostles of Bahá'u'lláh 34, 64, 194, 196, 206, 209
Áqá Ján-i-Khamsih 4
Áqásí, Ḥájí Mírzá, Amír-Niẓám (Prime Minister) 136, 230
Áqáy-i-Kalím, Mírzá (Mírzá Músá) 5, 6, 10, 186, 190, 203
Arabic language 24, 39, 69, 158, 166, 196, 199, 206, 224
Arabs 26, 39, 51, 68, 77, 103, 204, 227, 122, 126, 127, 160, 201, 205, 217, 222
Arak, Iran 32, 194
archaeology 158-9
Ardibil, Iran 184
'Arif Bey 205
Ark
- of the Covenant 29, 192, 203
- of God 20, 165-6, 169

Armenians 4, 58, 143-4, 183, 218
Asadu'lláh-i-Iṣfáhání, Mírzá 15-16, 26, 29-36, 67, 88, 188, 191-5 passim, 197
Asadu'lláh Khán, Mírzá (Vizier of Isfahan), 31, 194
Ashraf Garden 43
Assyrian Church 226
'Aṭá'u'lláh Núrbakhsh, Mírzá 31, 33, 195
Atlit, near Haifa 59
Australia 149, 185, 186, 189, 191, 220, 234
Avárih, 'Abdu'l-Ḥusayn 187
Azerbaijan 43, 136, 201, 206, 228, 229

Baal 67, 159-60
Bab Memorial Stairway 116
Báb, the (Siyyid Muḥammad-'Alí)
- and Bahá'u'lláh xi, 9, 18-19, 139, 140, 151-2, 162, 170-71, 189, 214
- Declaration 87, 135, 144-5, 214, 218
- execution 3-4, 88, 136, 148, 183-4
- imprisonment 117, 136, 146-7, 171
- life, teachings and Writings 16, 30, 48 56, 57, 67, 135-49, 229
- Messenger of God xi, 135, 138-9, 153-4, 164, 230
- sacred remains 64, 81-2, 184, 186, 192-3
  - concealment in Acre 34-6, 50-51, 76, 195
  - concealment in Haifa 39-40, 51-3, 76-7, 191, 192, 194, 199, 203
  - concealment in Iran 5-12, 15-16, 25-6, 124, 185, 195
  - interment in Shrine 76-82, 124, 194, 131, 212
  - recovery after execution 3-5
  - transfer to the Holy Land 18-19, 23, 25, 29-36, 83, 124, 193, 197
- Shrine *see* Shrine of the Báb

Bábís 3, 5, 8-9, 11, 12, 15, 51-3, 56-7, 62, 68, 136, 150, 183, 184, 185
Badí'u'lláh 27, 52, 190, 203
Bagdadi, Muḥammad Muṣṭafá 34-6, 196
Bagdadi, Zeenat 37, 196, 197
Bagdadi, Zia 34-5, 196, 199, 202
Baghdad 9, 32-3, 84, 92, 157, 188, 192, 193, 195, 196, 197, 198
Bahaduran regiment 4
Bahá'í Faith xi, 3, 8-9, 19, 20, 29, 44, 88, 94, 98, 136, 161, 186-7, 191, 217
Bahá'í pilgrimage today xi, 142, 154-6, 189, 205, 214, 231
Bahá'í World Centre 151, 162, 231
Bahá'u'lláh (Mírzá Ḥusayn-'Alí) x, 3, 5-6, 9-10, 13-20, 23, 27-8, 33-4, 44, 54, 46, 62-3, 65, 83-4, 94, 108, 111, 115, 136, 156, 160-71, 196, 207, 228
- and 'Abdu'l-Bahá 18-19, 80, 186-7, 189
- and the Báb xi, 9, 18-19, 139, 140, 151-2, 162, 170-71, 189, 214
- Covenant of 83, 152, 203, 228
- in Acre 15, 17, 30, 157, 162, 201, 203, 216
- in Haifa 13, 17-18, 162, 164
- Shrine of xii, 40, 55, 71, 79, 90, 91, 98, 101, 106, 117-19, 151-2, 154, 157, 199, 204, 228
- Writings 16, 30, 31-2, 54, 130, 156, 1162-3, 187, 192
  - Tablet of Carmel 19-20, 151, 154, 162, 164-6, 168-9
  - Tablet of Hirtik (Hardegg) 14
  - Tablet of Visitation 170-71
  - Will and Testament 20, 23, 186-7

Bahereh Khánum *see* Rowhani
Bahíyyih Khánum (Greatest Holy Leaf), 37, 76, 79, 89, 91, 113, 123-4, 131, 133, 162, 165, 190, 197, 211, 223
Bahjí, Mansion and Shrine 20, 27, 53, 112, 113, 123, 132, 151, 203, 223
Bakhtaran 32 *see also* Kermanshah
Baku, 43, 201
Bakulin, Feodor 184
Bálá, Ustád Áqá 43, 62, 65, 200-01, 213
Balfour, Lord 99
Balyuzi, H. M. 96-7, 137, 193, 202, 217-18, 223, 228
Báqir, Ḥájí 32, 115, 194
Baraghani, Fatimah (Qurratu'l-Ayn, Ṭáhirih) 148, 196, 230
Barney, Laura 138
Bassilious, Bishop 129
Bedouins 54
Beirut 29, 33-6, 64, 79, 97, 192, 193, 196, 197, 200, 217, 222
Ben Gurion Avenue (Koloniestrasse), Haifa 14, 225
Berthold, Count of Limoges 160
Bethlehem in Galilee 43
Bible 92, 94, 143, 159-60, 161
Bihjat, Mihraban 203
Blake, Andrew xiii, 208, 209, 227
Blomfield, Lady 80, 99, 121, 133, 185, 192
Bombay, India 39, 85, 198, 199, 220
Bosch, John and Louise 123, 126, 221-6
Bouzaglo, Salomon 130, 226
Boy Scouts, Haifa 127, 128
Britain, British

Army 93, 97-100, 103, 184, 216, 224
authorities 45, 52, 99, 100-01, 125, 149-50, 204, 220, 224, 230
Empire 38-9, 137, 224
Intelligence Service 98
see also England
Brittingham, Isabella D. 86, 214
Browne, Edward Granville 100, 156, 224
Bubeck, Gerhard 113, 191, 220
Bubeck, Gertrud 191
Buddha 138, 229
Bukhara 64
Burma, Bahá'ís of 38-9, 77, 198, 211, 214
Bushihr 135, 149
Bushrui, Badi 88
Bustání, Wadí' 129

Cairo, Egypt 64, 68, 118, 217
Carmel, Mount 5, 13-14, 17-20, 23-6, 45, 52-4, 59-60, 65-71, 74, 76-84, 98-9, 107, 109, 115-16, 127-8, 139, 157-67, 185, 204, 205, 209, 218, 226, 231
future of 69-71, 91-2, 109-10
see also Tablet of Carmel
Carmel Avenue, Haifa 225
Carmelites 19, 160, 161, 164, 165
Carriage Square, Haifa (Sahna'tul-Hanatir, Paris Square, Taxi Square) 40, 199
Cave of Elijah 19, 66, 67, 70, 83, 84, 153, 160, 163-4, 166, 211, 232
Cedric 214
Ceichanover, Aaron 208
Chase, Thornton 67-9
Chashmih-'Alí, village 11
Chicago 51-2, 67, 196, 204, 212, 215
Chihriq 136, 229
China 120, 214, 221
Christ *see* Jesus Christ
Christians, Christianity 4, 13, 14, 19, 26, 41, 49, 87, 94, 96, 122, 126-7, 129, 143-4, 157, 160-61, 222
Churchill, Winston 125, 223
Ciffrin, Dr Assaf 116, 220
Commission of Inquiry 54-8, 72, 98, 204, 205, 217
Committee of Union and Progress 90, 96, 215
Concourse on high 84, 153, 154, 166, 168, 230
Cormick, Dr William 142-3, 229-30
Coy, Genevieve 105-7, 111, 219
Crusades, Crusaders 59, 160-61, 188
Curtis, William E. 204
Curzon, Lord 137-8

Ḍíyá'u'lláh (Ziya'u'llah) 190
Dadash-'Alí 78, 79
Damascus, Syria 34, 52, 95, 193
Dames de Nazareth, school 127
Daoudian, Tamar 229
Deiss, Maria (Vonberg) 27-8, 191
Deiss, Wilhelm 18, 27-8, 189, 191
Druzes 93, 96, 127, 160, 231

Edhem Pasha 205
Edinburgh, Scotland 115
Edirne *see* Adrianople

Egypt, Egyptians 13, 41, 54, 57, 79, 88, 90-91, 104, 125, 127, 134, 159, 200, 205, 214, 217, 224
during World War I 93, 97-101, 216
Elburz mountains, Iran 18
Elijah, prophet 19, 66, 67, 70, 83, 84, 139, 153, 158, 159-60, 163-4, 166
England, English 97, 100, 122, 131, 133, 134, 143, 214, 221, 224
see also Britain
English language 38, 69, 106, 144, 207, 215
Escobino 205
Europe, Europeans 6, 63, 88, 93, 103, 127, 130, 137, 143, 149-50, 161, 215

Faḍil-i-Mázindarání 183, 184, 187, 207, 221
Faizi, M.-A. 183, 186, 191
Fareed, Amin 197
Fatimih Khánum, 37
Fezzan (Fizan) desert, Libya 56, 73, 205
France 64, 94 97, 214
French language 130
Fujita, Sachiro 111, 118, 123
Furútan, 'Alí-Akbar xv, 189

Gail, Marzieh 65
Galilee 43, 54, 84, 94, 153, 164, 166, 217
Gallipoli 13, 94
Geddes, Sir Patrick 115-16
German Colony, Haifa 17-18, 98, 224
German Consul 48, 101, 190, 218
Germany, Germans 48, 62, 93, 98, 99, 101, 113, 123, 134, 214, 218, 223
see also Templers
Getsinger, Edward 206, 207
Getsinger, Lua 64, 214, 126, 228
Ghulám-Riḍá, Ḥájí 63
Giachery, Ugo 190, 199, 211
Government Village, Haifa 40
Greatest Holy Leaf *see* Bahíyyih Khánum
Great War 93, 94-100, 103, 115, 117, 218, 224
Greek Catholic Church 129
Green Acre, Maine 112, 219
Grey, Cora 106-8
Grundy, Julia M. 164, 232
Guardian *see* Shoghi Effendi

Hábib, Dr (Christian Arab physician) 122, 222
Hagefen Street, Haifa 18, 127, 225
Haifa
and 'Abdu'l-Bahá *see* 'Abdu'l-Bahá
and Bahá'u'lláh *see* Bahá'u'lláh
city of xi, 13-14, 41, 59, 93, 104, 117, 158, 200, 204, 207, 224, 225
funeral of 'Abdu'l-Bahá 123-32, 225
future of 70-71, 91-2. 109, 163, 208, 227
interment of the Báb in the Shrine 76-82, 194
officials 45-6, 57, 115-16, 122, 126-31
Mufti 122, 127, 128, 129
pilgrims to 52, 63, 65, 69, 86, 91, 93, 97, 104, 111, 185, 211, 214, 217
remains of the Báb hidden 39-40, 51-3, 76-7, 191, 192, 194, 199, 203

and World War I 93, 98-101, 218, 224
see also Templers, Pilgrim House, Shrine of the Báb
Ḥájí Akhund *see* 'Alí-Akbar-i-Shahmírzádí
Ḥájí Amín *see* Abu'l-Ḥasan-i-Ardikání
Hakim, Lotfullah 106, 108-9, 132-3, 219
Hamadan, Iran 32
Hannen, Joseph 197
Haparsim (Persian) Street, Haifa 88, 111, 126, 127, 225
Hardegg, Georg David 14, 161, 225
Ḥasan Adíb Taliqání, Mírzá 185, 186, 188
Ḥasan-'Alí, Mírzá (uncle of the Báb)
Ḥasan Áqá Tafríshí 6, 186, 187
Ḥasan-i-Khurásání, Ḥájí Mírzá 39
Ḥasan-i-Vazir 12, 15
Ḥasan-i-Zunúzí, Shaykh 146
Hatzionut Avenue *see* Mountain Road
Hauff, Johanna 123, 125, 126, 223, 226
Ḥaydar-'Alí, Ḥájí Mírzá 79, 93, 104-5, 193, 194, 195, 198, 216, 219
Ḥaẓíratu'l-Quds 40, 45, 64-5, 199, 203, 206-7, 210, 211
Hearst, Phoebe 48-9, 90, 202
Hearst, William Randolph 202
Hoagg, Emogene 105-7, 219
Hoffmann, Christoph 161
Holy Land 13, 14, 17, 19, 23, 25-6, 29-32, 36-7. 40, 41, 43, 56, 62, 67, 70, 72, 75, 76, 83, 88, 90, 91, 94, 97-103, 109, 124, 125, 130, 157-87, 187, 188, 192-3, 196, 199, 202, 204, 211, 213, 214
Hotel Pross, Haifa 67
House of 'Abdu'lláh Páshá 53, 88, 197, 205
House of 'Abdu'l-Bahá, Haifa 88, 98, 126, 127
Ḥuqúqu'lláh 62-3, 202, 203
Ḥusayn 'Abdu'l-Karím *gush borideh* 78, 211, 212
Ḥusayn-'Alí, Mírzá *see* Bahá'u'lláh
Ḥusayn-'Alíy-i-Iṣfahání, Mírzá (Núr) 16, 25-6
Ḥusayn-i-Bushrú'í (Mullá Ḥusayn) 135, 144-6, 183, 196
Ḥusayn-i-Mílání 5, 9, 184
Ḥusayn-i-Vakil 33, 193, 195
Ḥusayn Áshchí 78
Ḥusayn Iqbál 18
Ḥusayn Rúhí 30, 193

Iamblicus 159
Ibn-i-Aṣdaq, Mírzá 'Alí-Muḥammad 188
Ibrahim Khalíl, Siyyid 186
Ibrahim Pasha 200
Imám Ḥusayn 193, 228
Imám-Zádih Ḥasan, Shrine 6, 8
Imám-Zádih Ma'ṣúm, Shrine (Ibn Babuyyih) 6, 8, 10, 187
Imám-Zádih Zayd, Shrine 15
India, Indians 120, 121, 125, 134, 137, 214, 220
Indian Army 99-100, 103, 218
International Bahá'í Archives 141-2
Ioas, Leroy 153-4
Iraq 9, 30, 32, 33, 72, 135, 192
Ireland, Irish 143, 229
Isfahan, Iran 30-32, 136, 193, 194, 209
Iṣfaháni, Mírzá Jalál 126, 217
Ishqabad *see* Mashriqu'l-Adhkár
Ishráq Khávarí 192, 199
Islam 23, 49, 61, 63, 98, 128, 153, 157, 158, 161, 188, 194
Shí'ah 30, 135, 146, 148, 195, 228
Sunni 25, 136, 146, 191
Ismá'íl, Siyyid 38, 193
Ismá'íl Úbudíyyát, 'Ustád 30, 76-7, 79, 193-4, 210, 211
Israel 70, 131, 157, 159, 163, 203, 208, 231
Istanbul (Constantinople) 9, 10, 14, 25, 46, 54-5, 57-8, 203, 204, 205
Italian Steamship Company 205
Italy 134, 205
Izadinia, Faruq 188
Izadinia, Fuad xiii, 186, 192, 193, 194, 197, 198, 202, 206, 209, 211, 220, 223, 224, 225

Ja'far Shírází Raḥmání, Mírzá
Jaffa 14, 161, 217
Jahrum 85, 213
Jamal Pasha 95-101, 203, 216-17, 218
Jamál-i-Burújirdí 10-12, 187
Ján Big, Áqá 183-4
Japan, Japanese 103, 111, 118, 120, 134, 214
Jerusalem 14, 95, 98, 100, 126, 153, 161, 165, 217, 218, 220, 224
Jesus Christ 14, 17, 19, 71, 87, 130, 138, 140-41, 153, 163, 166, 196, 229
Jews 14, 29, 63, 87, 96, 126-7, 130-31, 139, 141, 159-60, 192, 203, 226-7
Jezebel, Queen 159
Jodhpur Lancers 99-100, 218
Jordan 54
Jordan Valley 99, 166
Judaism 157, 159

Kahrubá'í, Ḥusayn 117-18
Kaiser (Wilhelm II) 218, 225
Karand (Kerend-e-Gharb or Eslemebad-e-Gharb), Iran 33
Karbila (Karbala), Iraq 30, 135, 183, 186
Karmelstrasse (Carmel Street), Haifa 14, 225
Kashan, Iran 31, 193
Kashgar, China 221
Kázim-i-Rashtí, Siyyid 183
Kelsey, Curtis 117-18, 123, 131
Kelsey, Valeria 118, 220
Kermanshah (Bakhtaran), Iran 32, 193, 194
Khadem, Zikrullah 165-6, 1889, 207, 216
Khadijah, wife of Prophet Muhammad 49
Khadíjih-Bagum, wife of the Báb 135
Khan, Ali-Kuli 40, 51, 203, 207
Khan, Florence Breed 65-6, 207
Khaniqayn (Khanaqin), Iran 33
Khayru'lláh, Ibráhím 44, 64, 201
Khurasan 15
Khusraw 123
King, Brigadier General A. D'A. 100
King of Martyrs 217
Kiryat-Ha-Mimshala (Government Village), Haifa 40
Kitchener, Lord 218, 224

Klingeman (Struve), Clara 113-14, 127, 224-5
Knights Templar 188, 206
Krishna 229
Krug, Florian and Grace 122-3, 222
Kúh-i-Núr (Mountin of Light) 166
Kúh-i-Qaf, Caucasus 115
Kurdistan, Kurds 103, 127, 146

Labaree, Rev. Benjamin 142
Lamington, Lord 99, 125, 223
Lange, Friedrich 127, 224-5
Lange, Peter 113, 224-5
Latimer, George 103-4
Letters of the Living 185, 196
Libya 56

Mahdi 135, 136, 148
Mahmood Mosque 161
Majdi'd-Dín (Majdu'd-Dín) 52-3, 78, 96, 203
Maku 117, 136, 146-7, 230
Mandalay, Burma (Myanmar) 38, 198, 199
Manifestation of God 38, 63, 138-9, 154, 229, 230
Man<u>sh</u>ádí, Muḥammad-Taqí 204
Manú<u>ch</u>ihr <u>Kh</u>án 31
martyrs, martyrdom 35, 63, 81, 82, 153, 184, 186, 189, 198, 212-13, 223, 228, 229 *see also* Báb
Mashhad 183
Ma<u>sh</u>riqu'l-A<u>dh</u>kár (Bahá'í Temple, House of Worship) 71, 109, 165, 220, 232
  Ishqabad 87, 91, 211, 213, 215, 221
  Wilmette 66, 190, 212
Masjid Ma<u>sh</u>á'u'lláh 11
Matran (Assyrian Church) 226
Maxwell, Mary 227 *see also* Ruḥíyyih <u>Kh</u>ánum
Mazra'ih 131, 201
Mecca 30, 54, 161
Medina 54
Mehrabkhani, R. 183
Melchizedek 67
Messiah 14
Mihdí, Áqá 210
Mi<u>dh</u>í <u>Kh</u>án 4, 184
Miḥdí, Mírzá, son of Bahá'u'lláh 162
Milan village 5, 185
Míláni, Ḥusayn 5, 9, 184
Milani, Inayatollah 185
Milani, Samandar 185
Mírzá Aḥmad *see* 'Abdu'l-Karím-Qazvíní
Mírzá Hádí *see* <u>Sh</u>írází
Mírzá Jalál *see* Iṣfaháni
Mi<u>sh</u>kín-Qalam 38-9, 198
Mochenin, M. 229
Modavvar, Elias 27, 191
Mohammad Said Adham 222, 226
Momen, Moojan 204
Monahan, James 45, 52-3, 204
Montefiore, Simon Sebag 95
Moore, Ruby (Hebe) 214
Morad Keramin Lane, Haifa 18
Mosaic law 13
Moses 157, 163, 192, 203, 229
Mount Carmel *see* Carmel
Mount of Olives 95
Mountain Road (Hatzionut Avenue, formerly UNO Avenue, Zionism Avenue), Haifa 75, 128, 189, 202, 207, 225
Mu'ayyad, Habíb 86, 96, 189, 216, 222, 226
Muhammad (Prophet) 49, 138, 142, 191, 196, 229, 230
Muḥammad-'Alí, half-brother of 'Abdu'l-Bahá 27, 52, 54-5, 190, 203
Muḥammad-'Alí, Siyyid *see* Báb
Muḥammad-'Alí Yazdi, Ustád 48, 68, 78, 79, 210
Muḥammad-'Alí-i-Zunúzí, Mírzá (Anís) 3-5, 136, 183, 185
Muḥammad-Báqir Afnán, Mírzá 62, 206
Muḥammad-Ḥusayn, Áqá 185, 193, 195
Muḥammad-Ibráhím, Áqá 210
Muḥammad-i-<u>Sh</u>ibl, <u>Sh</u>ay<u>kh</u> 196
Muḥammad-Karím 'Aṭṭar, Áqá 26
Muḥammad Murád, Mufti of Haifa 122, 127, 128, 129
Muḥammad Muṣṭafá, Mírzá (Bagdadi) 34-6, 196
Muḥammad-Taqí, Afnán-i-Yazdi (Vakílu'd-Dawlih), Ḥájí Mírzá 79, 87, 207, 211
Muḥammad-Taqí Man<u>sh</u>ádí 204
Muḥammad-Táqí Míláni, Ḥájí 5
Muhammarih 184
Mu<u>kh</u>liṣ, 'Abdu'lláh 129
Mullá Ḥusayn (Ḥusayn-i-Bushrú'í) 135, 144-6, 183, 196
Munavvar <u>Kh</u>ánum 121-3, 221
Munírih <u>Kh</u>ánum, wife of 'Abdu'l-Bahá 24, 79, 123, 131, 188, 190, 191, 222, 223
Munir (Moneer) Zayn, Mírzá 78, 79, 198, 209, 210, 212
Muqarrábí, <u>Sh</u>ay<u>kh</u> 36
Murchie, Guy 185
Murg<u>h</u> Maḥallih (Abode of the Birds) 18, 115
Músá, Mírzá (Áqáy-i-Kalím) 5, 6, 10, 186, 190, 203
Muslims 3, 30, 41, 87, 94, 122, 127-9, 161, 228
Musmus Pass 99
Muṣṭafá Rúmí, Siyyid 38-9, 198, 199
Musterhaus 200
Myanmar *see* Burma
Mysore Lancers 99, 218

Nabatian culture 44, 231
Nabíl-i-Zarandí 6, 186
Nahariya 206
Najafabad, Iran 32, 194, 209
Najaf-Ábádí, Raḥmatu'lláh 49, 68, 75, 76, 77-80, 82, 131-2, 207, 208, 210, 211, 227
Najaf-'Alí, Áqá 78, 79, 210
Na<u>kh</u>javání, 'Alí 37, 126, 195, 196, 197, 198, 199, 201, 208, 209, 225, 227
Náṣiri'd-i-Dín (Crown Prince of Iran, later Shah) 228, 229
Nassár, Ibráhím 129
Natanz, Iran 31
Natufian culture 159
Navváb, wife of Bahá'u'lláh 23, 162
Naw-Rúz 77, 81, 166, 207, 210, 211, 212
Nayriz, Bahá'ís of 82, 212-13
Nazareth 43

Nazim Pasha, Governor of Syria 52
Nazireh Khanum 208
'Nearer My God to Thee' 134, 228
New York City 90, 117, 214, 222
Núr *see* Ḥusayn-'Alíy-i-Iṣfahání
Núrbakhsh, 'Atá'u'lláh 31, 33, 195
Núru'd-Dín Zayn, Mírzá 35, 104, 197

Oliphant House, Haifa 18
Ottoman Empire, Ottomans 9, 10 13, 18, 20, 25, 35, 41, 51-6, 62, 72, 90, 146, 157-8, 192, 107, 200, 203, 204-5, 216, 225
  in World War I 93, 95, 97, 99

Pacific islands 120
Paine, Mabel and Sylvia 106-7
Palestine 70, 99-100, 113, 115-16, 125, 126-7, 130, 157, 188, 200, 217, 223, 224, 226
Paris Square, Haifa (Taxi Square) 40, 199
Parthenon, Athens 141
Paulus, Christoph 161
Persian Street (Haparsim), Haifa 88, 111, 126, 127, 225
Pfander family 189, 191
Pilgrim House, Oriental (Eastern) 43, 85-8, 97, 134, 213, 214
Pilgrim House, Western 86, 111-13
Port Said, Egypt 88, 191, 200
Prayer for the Dead 80, 126
Pro-Carmel organization 115-16
Pro-Jerusalem Society 220
Prophets, Israelite 70, 157, 159-60, 163-4
Pythagoras 159

Qa'im 135
Qá'im-Maqám 45-6
Qanbar-'Alí, Áqá 210
Qazvin, Iran 63, 196
Qiblih 84, 153, 158, 164, 166, 231
Qom, Iran 30, 74, 76, 193, 194, 207
Qur'án 127, 193, 195, 210, 229

Rabbani, Ahang 188
Rabbani, Rúḥangiz 133
Rabbani, Rúḥíyyih *see* Rúḥiyyih Khánum
Rafati, Vahid 193, 194, 203, 204
Raḥmání, Abu'l-Faḍl 213-14
Raḥmání, Hádí 213
Raḥmání, Mírzá Ja'far Shírází 85-6, 213-14
Raḥmatu'lláh *see* Najaf-Ábádí, Raḥmatu'lláh
Randall, Ruth 112, 221
Randall, William Henry (Harry) 103, 112, 219
Rangoon, Burman (Myanmar) 38-9, 193, 198, 199, 211
Rasim Pasha 205
Remey, Charles Mason 88, 125, 131, 132, 192, 195, 197, 201, 214, 223, 227
Rey (Rayy) 6-7, 186
Riḍáy-i-Qannad, Áqá 48, 202
Riḍván Garden 43, 93
Riza'iyyih 4, 136, 148
Romans, Roman Empire 159, 160, 217
Rosenberg, Ethel Jenner 133, 222-3
Rowhani, 'Abdu'l-Raouf 214
Rowhani, Bahereh 214
Royal Engineers 99-100
Ruḥíyyih Khánum, Amatu'l-Bahá (Ruḥíyyih Rabbani, Mary Maxwell) 133, 151, 227
Rúḥá Khánum 66-7, 122, 222
Ruhe, David 160, 185, 186
Rúḥí (Rouhi) Effendi *see* Afnán
Rúḥí, Ḥusayn 30, 193
running throne (*takht-i-raván*) 29-31, 34, 192
Russia, Russians 4, 85, 146, 149-50, 184, 213, 221, 229

Ṣalih Effendi 46, 202
Ṣádiq-i-Muqaddas, Mullá 15
Ṣádiq Páshá 47
Ṣálih Effendi 46, 202
Sakinatu'lláh (Abode of God) 192-3, 203 *see also* Shekinah
Samarqand 64
Sám Khán, Colonel 4, 144, 183
Samuel, Edwin 226-7
Samuel, Sir Herbert 125-6, 127, 131, 223-4, 226-7
Sanderson, Edith 216
Sar-Chashmih, Tehran 6
sarcophagus 38-40, 44, 51, 77-82, 132, 152, 154, 192-3, 198-9, 201, 203, 210, 211, 223
Sar Qabr Aqa, Tehran 188
Schmelzle, Gisela 191
Schumacher, Gottlieb and Jacob 220
Schushtari, Mohammed 68
Scott, Edwin 79, 211
Sháh Muḥammad-i-Manshádí, Ḥájí (Amínu'l-Bayán) 15, 63, 188, 206
Shah of Persia 8, 31, 136, 184, 228
Shahshanan, Isfahan 31
Shaykhu'r-Ra'ís 207
Shedd, Rev. J. H. 148, 229
Sheil, Lady 144, 229-30
Shekhinah 29 *see also* Sakinatu'lláh
Sherwood Rangers 99
Shimiran, Iran 18, 115, 186
Shiraz, Iran 30, 38, 80, 92, 135, 144, 149, 194
Shírází, Mírzá Hádí 87
Shoghi Effendi, Guardian of the Bahá'í Faith 34, 62, 63-4, 79, 87, 88, 89, 91, 97, 102-3, 110, 131-4, 190, 191, 194, 196, 198, 201, 203, 204, 2008-9, 211, 217, 218, 221-2
  Writings 19, 24-5, 80, 83, 101, 109, 110, 121, 134, 139, 140-41, 146-9, 151-4, 157-8, 164-6, 203, 211, 212, 213, 215, 217, 221, 227, 228
Shrine of the Báb
  and 'Abdu'l-Bahá 23, 35, 41, 50, 65-6, 74-5, 77-83, 91, 97-8, 102-10, 116-19, 124-5, 126-34, 162, 216, 226
  and Bahá'u'lláh 17-20, 158, 162-3, 166, 189
  construction 42-4, 47-9, 50, 51, 53, 56-7, 59-62, 94, 116-17, 206, 209, 213, 214
  doors 62-5, 190
  gardens xi, 18, 26, 28, 49, 66, 68, 69, 71, 74, 75,

89, 90, 92, 102, 105, 106, 115, 155, 162, 208, 209, 210
illumination 117-19
interment of the remains of the Báb 76-83, 210, 211
opposition to 23, 26, 45-6, 47-9, 52-7, 78, 204, 205
pilgrimage to 65-9, 85-7, 102-9, 153-6, 222
purchase of land 26-8, 47-9, 189, 191, 209, 226
and Shoghi Effendi 102-3, 110, 165, 166-7, 217
significance of xi, 19-20, 69-71, 82-3, 151-6, 162, 165, 166-7, 190
and Templers 27-8, 42-3, 51, 200
terraces 115-16, 162, 189
see also Tablets of Visitation
Síyáh-Chál 9
Sohrab, Ahmad 206, 212, 215
Stevens, Ethel Stefana (Lady Drower) 209
Storrs, Sir Ronald 199, 126, 127, 131, 218, 220, 224
Struve, Gertrud 127
Struve, Theodore Jonathan 127
Struven, Howard 87-8, 214
Sudan 224
Suez Canal 101, 216
Sufis 4
Sukru Pasha 205
Sulaymán Khán 3-11, 30, 183, 185, 186
Symes, Lieutenant-Colonel Stewart 127, 131, 134, 224
Syria 52, 53, 95, 205, 217
Syrian Protestant College (American University), Beirut 34, 217

Ṭáhirih (Qurratu'l-'Ayn, Fatimah Baraghani) 148, 196, 230
Ṭúbá Khánum 111
Tablet of Carmel 19-20, 151, 154, 162, 164-6, 168-9
Tablets of Visitation 6, 64, 97, 105, 107, 170-02, 207, 211, 213, 227
Tablets of the Divine Plan 94-5, 209, 216
Tabriz 3-6, 30, 136, 142, 183, 184, 185, 186, 193, 212, 229
Tacitus 159
Taherzadeh, Adib 19, 185, 186, 189, 193
Ṭáhirih 148, 196, 230
Tammúz 160
Táqí Khán, Mírzá, Amír-Niẓám (Prime Minister) 3, 6, 183, 186
Tar, Iran 31
Tarbíyát Bahá'í School 219
Tarq, Iran 31
Taxi Square, Haifa 40, 199
Tehran 3, 5, 6, 10, 15-16, 18, 30, 63, 115, 136, 150, 183, 184, 186, 193-4, 196, 212, 230
Templars (Crusader Knights) 188, 206
Templers 13-14, 18, 26-7, 46, 112-14, 127, 158, 189, 191, 200, 206, 209, 213, 218, 220, 221, 224-5
architecture 42-3, 51, 59-60, 200, 205, 213
children 112-14
Terraces, Haifa xi, 61, 62, 66, 69, 71, 115-19, 162, 185, 189, 209, 218
Theosophical Society, London 125
Thotmes III, King of Egypt 159
Tiberias, Galilee 53, 217
Tiflis, Armenia 218
The Times
India 125
London 149, 205
Titanic 214
Torah 163
True, Corinne 66, 207
Ṭúbá Khánum 111
Tudor-Pole, Wellesley 98, 133, 217
Turkey, Turks, 10, 58, 63, 72, 216 *see also* Ottomans
Turkish language 24, 43, 56, 97, 205
Turkmenistan 63, 85

UNESCO World Heritage xi, 158
Universal House of Justice, The 86, 162, 165-6, 189, 190, 231
UNO Avenue *see* Mountain Road
Urumiyyih (Riza'iyyih) 4, 136, 148

Vahdat, Bizhan 220
Vahdat, Khosro 186
Vákil Rúhí 193, 195
Vakílu'd-Dawlih *see* Muḥammad-Taqí, Ḥájí Mírzá (Afnán-i-Yazdi)
Vespasian, Emperor 159, 160
Wadi Nisnas, Haifa 200
Weinstrasse, (Vine Street, now Hagefen), Haifa 127, 225
water cistern 65, 85
Wennagel, Josef 43
Western Pilgrim House 86, 111-12
White, Roger 155-6
Wilhelm, Roy 69, 117-18, 208, 230
Will and Testament of 'Abdu'l-Bahá 133-4, 209
Wilmette, Illinois 66, 196, 212
Woodcock, May 79, 210, 212
World War I (Great War) 93, 94-100, 102, 115, 117, 218, 224
Wortz, Cornelia 113
Württemberg, Germany 13, 200
Yaḥyá Ṭábúr Áqásí 203
Yaḥyá Unsí Iṣfahání 74
Yazd, Iran 211, 223
Yazdi, Ali 95, 97-8, 217
Yazdi, Aziz 190
Yazdi, Muḥammad-'Alí 48, 68, 78, 79, 210
Yildiz Palace, Istanbul 58
Young Turk revolution 72
Yúnis Khán (Youness Afroukhteh) 42, 47-8, 50, 53, 88, 190, 201

Ẓillu's-Sulṭán 31
Zagros mountains, Iran 33
Zanjan 6
Zayn, Núru'd-Din 35, 104, 197
Zaynu'l-Muqarrabín (Mullá Zaynu'l-'Abidín) 32, 194, 209
Zion 161, 165, 169
Zionism Avenue *see* Mountain Road
Zoroaster, Zoroastrians 87, 121 (Parsi), 157, 219
Zunuzi, Áqá Siyyid 'Alí 183

ABOUT THE AUTHOR

Michael V. Day is a journalist who was the editor of the *Bahá'í World News Service* at the Bahá'í World Centre in Haifa, Israel from 2003 to 2006, where he lived and worked within a few hundred metres of the Shrine of the Báb. Born and raised in New Zealand he was briefly a lawyer before becoming a newspaper reporter, leader writer and editor. He first visited the Shrine of the Báb while on pilgrimage in 1980. After moving to Australia in 1988 with his wife, Chris, and sons Thomas and George, he was a journalist with Murdoch University in Perth before joining the staff of *The West Australian* newspaper where he was an education and feature writer. He was then appointed the newspaper's Asia Desk Chief, specializing in covering Indonesia. He is a currently a part-time staff member of the Office of External Affairs of the Australian Bahá'í Community. He is continuing to write on Bahá'í topics, especially aspects of the Faith's history. Michael and Chris live in Brisbane, Queensland, Australia.